The Closing Chapter

'O teach us to number our days: that we may apply our hearts unto wisdom'.

Psalm 90:12
The Book of Common Prayer (1815 edition)

The
Closing Chapter

by the Rt Hon
LORD DENNING

London
BUTTERWORTHS
1983

England	Butterworth & Co (Publishers) Ltd, 88 Kingsway, LONDON WC2B 6AB
Australia	Butterworths Pty Ltd, SYDNEY, MELBOURNE, BRISBANE, ADELAIDE and PERTH
Canada	Butterworth & Co (Canada) Ltd, TORONTO
	Butterworth & Co (Western Canada) Ltd, VANCOUVER
New Zealand	Butterworths of New Zealand Ltd, WELLINGTON
Singapore	Butterworth & Co (Asia) Pte Ltd, SINGAPORE
South Africa	Butterworth Publishers (Pty) Ltd, DURBAN
U.S.A.	Mason Publishing Co, ST PAUL, Minnesota
	Butterworth Legal Publishers, SEATTLE, Washington; BOSTON, Massachusetts; and AUSTIN, Texas
	D & S Publishers, CLEARWATER, Florida

© The Rt Hon Lord Denning 1983

British Library Cataloguing in Publication Data

Denning, Alfred Denning, *Baron*
   The closing chapter.
   1. Denning, Alfred Denning, *Baron.* Commentaries on
   the laws of England   2. Law–England
   I. Title
   340'.0924   KD660

ISBN hardcover 0 406 17611 6
    softcover 0 406 17612 4

Typeset by Cotswold Typesetting Ltd, Gloucester
Printed by Billings Bookplan, Worcester

Preface

On 29 September 1982 I retired from the office of Master of the Rolls. I had held it for over 20 years. It was a great wrench for me. But it was time to go. I walked with a stick, limping slowly, for short distances. I could not hear as well as I used to do. The newspapers were speaking of me as an old man of 83 years of age.

Thousands of people wished me well on my retirement. I was often asked, 'What are you going to do?' I replied, 'I would like to write one more book.' 'What is it to be about?' I made answer, '*The Closing Chapter*.' This was because the last few years had seen some important issues with which I had been concerned. I thought it might be worth while to describe them.

This I have tried to do. In the first part of the book I have told of the events leading up to my retirement and after it. It is, in a way, a continuation of my part of *The Family Story*. In the second part of the book I have told of some of the matters that came under discussion during the last period of my time. These are, in a way, a sequel to *The Discipline of Law* and *The Due Process of Law*, bringing them up to date.

I have had principally in mind the students of the law. Both those who are just starting and those who are already in practice. They should know more about the controversies of our day: and then lead the way to a solution of them. So I have told of the problems of statutory interpretation, of the granting of injunctions and the conduct of arbitrations.

I have had next in mind the general reader. Most of the

leading stories in the newspapers find their way, sooner or later, into the courts of law. They have legal repercussions on which the 'reasonable man' should take a stand. So I have told of the three dockers and the five dockers, of the general steel strike, of the 25 per cent cut in London Transport fares and the Sikh boy's turban.

I have sought to make everything as up to date as can be. So I have told of the latest decisions right up to the end of the summer term of 1983. I have done this in several places – even after having written the Epilogue.

Time after time I have suggested that the present law is mistaken and is in need of reform. It should be amended so as to secure, as near as may be, the doing of justice. It was a great lawyer, Edmund Plowden, in the time of the first Elizabeth, who commended the amendment of the law with the words, 'Blessed be the amending hand'.

The bust of Edmund Plowden still stands in a place of honour in the Middle Temple. It is in the lovely hall in the making of which he played so large a part.

His advice was endorsed by the best of exemplars, Sir Edward Coke. He ended the last of his four *Institutes* with a plea for amendment. He compared the jurisdiction of the courts to a building which had many defects. His final words to posterity were:

'. . . I shall heartily desire the wise hearted and expert builders (justice being *architectonica virtus*) to amend both the method or uniformity, and the structure it selfe, wherein they shall finde either want of windowes, or sufficient lights, or other deficiency in the architecture whatsoever. And we will conclude with the aphorisme of the great lawyer[1] and sage of the law (which we have heard him often say) *Blessed be the amending hand*.'

As always, I have tried to make my meaning clear. That is necessary if you are to influence others. As St Paul said:[2]

[1] Edmund Plowden.
[2] 1 *Corinthians* 14:8–9 (Authorised version).

'For if the trumpet give an uncertain sound, who shall prepare himself to the battle? So likewise ye, except ye utter by the tongue words easy to be understood, how shall it be known what is spoken? for ye shall speak into the air.'

Denning

September 1983

Contents

Book Two   Discipline up to Date

Table of Cases

Acknowledgments

Grateful acknowledgment is made to the following for their kind permission to reproduce extracts from their newspapers and magazines:

The Times and *The Sunday Times*, extracts © Times Newspapers Ltd
The Financial Times
The Standard
The Observer
The Guardian
Private Eye

Book One

Retirement

Section One

My Last Months as Master

1 A calamitous fortnight

1 The book is produced

i *When are you going to retire?*

On 23 January 1982 I became 83 years of age. Often I was asked, 'When are you going to retire?' I deliberately kept my options open. I always replied, 'I shall go on as long as I can do the job.' Next question, 'Who will be the judge of that?' 'I will be, myself.'

In my heart of hearts, I knew that I could not go on much longer. One of my friends in a high place dropped a hint: 'You are at the peak of your fame now. Do not go on too long.' Joan said so lovingly as well. I told her, 'I would like to go on till the book is published.' That would be in May. I had in my mind that I would retire at the end of the summer term.

I knew that the old enemy, Time, was turning against me:

> The enemy increaseth every day,
> We, at the height, are ready to decline.
> There is a tide in the affairs of men,
> Which taken at the flood, leads on to fortune;
> Omitted, all the voyage of their life
> Is bound in shallows, and in miseries.[1]

ii *The writing of the book*

During the long vacation of 1981 I worked hard at the book. It was to be called *What Next in the Law*. I wrote it in a

---

[1] Shakespeare, *Julius Caesar*, Act IV, sc. 3.

5

notebook in my own hand with crossings and recrossings, and insertions and re-insertions, on every page. It was put into typescript with much patience, accuracy and skill. I had to finish my part of it by the end of September. Once term started on 1 October, all my time till Christmas was filled with hearing cases and writing reserved judgments. In the Christmas vacation we went through the proofs. We delivered them to the publishers.

iii *The launching of the book*

On Thursday 20 May 1982 the new book was launched. The boardroom of Butterworths in Kingsway was full to overflowing. The book was on display. Congratulations abounded.

The next day, Friday, after sitting in court, I went to Butterworths' bookshop in Bell Yard. There was a long queue of students. I had a word with each and signed their books.

Little did I realise what trouble was ahead of me. It was an Achilles' heel.

iv *The Achilles' heel*

You will often have heard tell of the Achilles' heel: but you may not know the story of it. It is from Greek mythology. When Achilles was a baby, his mother sought to make him invulnerable. So she plunged him into the river Styx – every bit of his body – except his heel by which she held him. He became a great warrior and slew Hector, the champion of Troy. But he carried his boldness too far. He solicited the hand of a lady in the Temple of Athens. As he did so Paris wounded him in the heel and he died.

That story is centuries old. Our medical men call one of the tendons of the foot the Tendon of Achilles. It is the tendon by which the muscles of the calf of the leg are attached to the heel. Two short passages in a chapter on juries in my book turned out to be my Achilles' heel.

2 Offence is given

i *One offending passage*

One passage gave offence to those who had come here from overseas. I suggested that some of them might not be suitable to serve on juries: and that there should be a new way of selecting jurors. The passage in question was seized upon by many commentators. Review copies had been distributed to the press beforehand. So the commentators were able to step in as soon as the book was launched. On Saturday 22 May 1982 *The Times* had a heading:

DENNING JURY REFORMS ANGER BLACK LAWYERS

Controversy erupted yesterday over Lord Denning's latest book, *What Next in the Law*, with a call from the Society of Black Lawyers for the Master of the Rolls to retire. . . .

Mr Sibghat Kadri, the society's chairman, said the **remarks** were insulting and degrading and 'couched in terms virulent enough to destroy any remaining credibility he may have as an unbiased and impartial interpreter of the law'.

The society would be calling on the Lord Chancellor to ask Lord Denning 'politely but firmly' to retire. The Standing Conference of Pakistani Organisations, of which Mr Kadri is president, is to call a meeting to start a campaign to that end.

Later that Saturday morning Mr Ludovic Kennedy came to 'The Lawn' to interview me for the BBC. He also seized on the passage and asked, 'Do you stand by it?' I hesitated for a moment. Then I said, 'I do.'

ii *It is misinterpreted*

I then realised for the first time that the passage was a mistake. It was being interpreted as if I was actuated by racial prejudice. Nothing was further from my intention or my thoughts. Joan and I have been all over the world to the countries of the Commonwealth. We have friends of all races and colours. I was the last person, I hope, who would be accused of racial prejudice. Yet here in this book I had so expressed myself as to be accused of it.

7

iii *Another offending passage*

The other passage which gave offence was of a similar nature. I suggested that some accused persons were using the 'peremptory challenge' so as to pack the jury-box with jurors who were sympathetic to their side. I took as an instance a trial at Bristol about some riots which had taken place there. I suggested that the accused used their peremptory challenges so as to secure as many coloured people on the jury as possible. I am very sorry that I made that suggestion. I did it on the basis of a letter I had received. But I have since been shown the transcript. It shows that the challenges were used quite properly. They were used at the invitation of the judge so as to secure a representative jury.

So I had made a mistake of fact. It was to cost me dear. No comment is fair if it is based on a mistake of fact.

iv The Observer *on the telephone*

On the Saturday evening the telephone rang. I lifted the receiver. The caller said:

I am David Leigh of *The Observer*. I understand that black jurors are going to sue you. Do you wish to comment on it?

I replied:

I don't think I want to comment on anything like that.

That call was ominous. Was I, a serving judge, to be sued? I was sorely worried. I had a sleepless night.

v *'Black jurors to sue'*

On Sunday morning I went to Church as usual at 8 o'clock. Thence to the paper shop. I usually bought only *The Sunday Times*. But this time I bought *The Observer* as well. There was the big black headline:

BLACK JURORS TO SUE DENNING UNLESS. . . .
by David Leigh

Lord Denning, the Master of the Rolls, faces a libel action from two black jurors in the Bristol riot case, after claiming in a book published last week that they had failed to convict guilty people because they were 'their own'.

Lord Denning, 83, gave last year's Bristol riot trial as an example of a 'packed' jury overloaded with what he described as 'coloured people'. He then claimed that 'black, coloured and brown' people did not have the same standards of conduct as whites.

Last night Ms Gareth Pearce, of the London solicitors Birnberg & Co., said that letters had been sent to Lord Denning and to Butterworths, publishers of his book *What Next in the Law*, on behalf of two black jurors in the case.

After further comments, the article went on:

Lord Denning's account of what happened in Bristol contains a number of factual mistakes.

This was followed by a detailed description of what had happened, showing that the newspaper was fully informed by persons present at the trial.

3 Sorely troubled

i *Troubled day and night*

I was very troubled all day. *The Observer* had struck a wounding blow. I talked it over with Joan as with all my troubles. She tried to comfort me. It so happened that my son Robert and his wife Elizabeth and my two little grandsons came for the day. They are always my joy. I join in their games on the lawn. But that day I could not play with them. I was talking to Robert, seeking his advice. To and fro my mind went. It seemed to favour retirement. I felt that I could not continue as a serving judge with writs out against me. And in any case at my age of $83\frac{1}{2}$ I could only expect to have a little while to go.

I had another night of worry, sleepless, tossing to and fro in my bed. 'Thou fool', I kept saying to myself, recalling the parable of the rich man who had laid up treasure for himself:

But God said unto him, Thou fool, this night thy soul shall be required of thee: then whose shall those things be, which thou hast provided?[1]

[1] *St. Luke* 12:20 (Authorised version).

ii The Times *condemns me*

On Monday morning I caught my usual train at 8.25. I read *The Times*. It had a leading article headed 'A judgment too far' which included these paragraphs:

Lord Denning's ill-considered remarks on the unsuitability of many blacks for jury service have, understandably, caused considerable offence in the black community. Should he have to give judgment in a case in which race is a factor, he will be exposed to charges of prejudice and to suggestions that his decision might be affected by his personal feelings on racial matters. Such criticism would, it is hoped and expected, be unwarranted. But Lord Denning has only himself to blame for placing himself in a position where such attacks could be made.

It was the same on issues affecting industrial relations. The accusations which the political left and many trade unionists have made against Lord Denning have only partly been based on the judgments he has given against unions in a number of court cases. Much of the feeling against him has resulted from remarks he has made in lectures and in his books.

The Times had lived up to its name, *The Thunderer*.[1] It had charged me and found me guilty. It had sentenced me. It had made retirement inevitable. I had always advocated a free press. Now its consequences were being brought home to me.

iii *I write to the Lord Chancellor*

On getting to my room, I wrote a letter to the Lord Chancellor and sent it down by hand that very morning. I told him that I had had it in mind to retire at the end of the summer term. But that in the circumstances I offered to retire at once. He replied sympathetically in his own hand, suggesting that I should not retire at once, but at the end of the summer term. Later he added that it should be at the end of the long vacation, 29 September.

iv *I am very distressed*

The newspapers soon got to hear of it. *The Daily Mirror*

---

[1] This nickname was given to *The Times* in about 1840 because of the style of writing of Edward Sterling, one of its staff.

spoke to Joan. She said:

He is very distressed. He has done more for the black people in this
country than any other judge. He is very upset. He realises that he has
made a mistake.

v *The black lawyers are understanding*

Mr Rudy Narayan is one of the leaders of the coloured
people in England. He is a member of the Bar of Lincoln's
Inn. On Wednesday 26 May he wrote to *The Times* as
Secretary of the Society of Black Lawyers. His letter said:

Lord Denning remains one of the greatest judicial minds of this century;
he was my sponsor on call to the Bar. . . .

The remarks are clearly wrong and it is good to read Lady Denning's
quoted remarks. Lord and Lady Denning have thousands of friends in
Africa, Asia and the Caribbean who will be surprised at his remarks and
his own and Lady Denning's distress is plain to see.

A great judge has erred greatly in the intellectual loneliness of
advanced years; while his remarks should be rejected and rebutted he is
yet, in a personal way, entitled to draw on that reservoir of community
regard which he has in many quarters and to seek understanding, if not
forgiveness.

4 The way it ended

i *I consult lawyers*

Alongside all this there loomed the threatened actions
against me. What was to be done about them? I telephoned
my good friend Mr (now Sir) Max Williams who was then
the Vice-President of the Law Society. I sought his advice.
He gave it unstintingly. He put everything else aside. For the
whole of that week he was up early and stayed late – all on
my affairs. He chose counsel of the very best. Andrew
Leggatt of Queen's Counsel who was the Chairman of the
Bar, and David Eady, a junior who was expert in libel
matters.

In the end agreement was reached. No writs were ever
issued against me or the publishers. No damages were
sought. The book was to be withdrawn and the offending
passages removed. I made a public apology in terms that
were agreed.

ii *'Farewell to all my greatness!'*

So there it is. All over in a fortnight. The book launched on Thursday 20 May. Retirement announced on Friday 28 May. Apology on Tuesday 1 June.

Sadly I recalled the fate of those whose career has ended in disgrace or failure. It is a long list: Thomas Wolsey, Francis Bacon, Warren Hastings, Cecil Rhodes, and many others. Never so well put as in the soliloquy of Thomas Wolsey as recorded by Shakespeare:

> Farewell, a long farewell, to all my greatness!
> This is the state of man; today he puts forth
> The tender leaves of hope, tomorrow blossoms,
> And bears his blushing honours thick upon him:
> The third day, comes a frost, a killing frost;
> And, – when he thinks, good easy man, full surely
> His greatness is a ripening, – nips his root,
> And then he falls, as I do. I have ventur'd,
> Like little wanton boys that swim on bladders,
> This many summers in a sea of glory;
> But far beyond my depth: my high-blown pride
> At length broke under me; and now has left me,
> Weary, and old with service, to the mercy
> Of a rude stream, that must for ever hide me.[1]

iii *Comment by* Private Eye

A little later *Private Eye* came out with a cartoon showing two facetious barristers reading the headline:

DENNING TO RETIRE

and one of them saying to the other:

I expect the House of Lords will overrule his decision.

iv *'Who will take his place?'*

As always happens, everyone at once speculated, 'Who will take his place?' Hugo Young wrote in *The Sunday Times* of 30 May 1982:

When Lord Chancellor Hailsham considers the field of successors, it is

---

[1] *King Henry VIII*, Act III, sc. 2.

12

safe to say he will choose no one like Denning. There is no such beast on the bench of judges. . . .

When all the raucous headlines have been forgotten, and the last regrettable calamity has passed insignificantly into the dustbin, Denning's great works will endure for ever. To anyone who believes the law should liberate, not enslave, he is a beacon. He discovered that young, as a poor student, in the 1920s. He is just about the only octogenarian who has never forgotten it.

2 The summer term

1 Much as usual

i *A shadow over it*

The publishers acted quickly. They withdrew the book and removed the two offending passages. These did not affect the tenor of the book. It was reissued in July and was well received.

The trouble over the book cast a shadow over the term: but no one mentioned it or talked about it to me. We passed through the Whitsun vacation and the summer term as if it had never occurred.

ii *Busy as ever*

We went, as we often did, to talk to magistrates in the counties. This time to North Wales and Chester. We stayed in the Judges' Lodgings at Mold. We were entertained by the Lord Lieutenant, the High Sheriff, the Judges and the Bar. We made trips to Snowdonia and the Bodnant Gardens. But behind it – to me – was the distress caused by the book. We came back to the London season. I was sitting in court all day and preparing judgments at weekends. But every other moment was filled. Dinners on most evenings. Often an after-dinner speech. Tennis at Wimbledon in the Royal Box. The garden-party at Buckingham Palace where we were invited to the Royal Tent. Speech-days at schools. Call day at Lincoln's Inn. The summer dinner of the Law Society. The church fête at home. We did everything as we had done in the previous 20 years.

2 The Speaker's dinner

The most memorable of all was a dinner given by the Speaker, Mr George Thomas, MP (now Viscount Tonypandy). It was in Speaker's House on 5 July. He gave it in my honour on my retirement. The Prime Minister Mrs Margaret Thatcher herself came. So did the Archbishop of Canterbury Dr Runcie, the Lord Chancellor Lord Hailsham of Saint Marylebone and the Chancellor of the Exchequer Sir Geoffrey Howe. The Lord Chief Justice Lord Lane and the Home Secretary Mr William Whitelaw. The Attorney-General Sir Michael Havers. The Lord Mayor of London Sir Christopher Leaver. All with their ladies.

i *Speaker's House*

Speaker's House is in the Palace of Westminster. From its windows you have the finest outlook in all the world. The river Thames flows alongside, busy with ships and barges. Across the water there are the impressive buildings of Saint Thomas's Hospital and of the Greater London Authority. Down river you have the view which Wordsworth described in 1807 from Westminster Bridge at dawn, with the dome of Saint Paul's Cathedral in the far distance.

ii *Mr Speaker*

The Speaker of the House of Commons is the guardian of the liberties of England. Constitutionally, he is just a member of the Commons, elected by them to preside over their deliberations. But his authority is immense. His prestige unequalled. He represents the Commons on all state occasions. Only once in our long history has he been unseated: and that was when Oliver Cromwell dissolved the

'Rump' of the Long Parliament. It had abused its power grossly. When the Speaker refused to quit his seat, Cromwell had him removed. Cromwell lifted the mace from the table. 'What shall we do with this bauble?' he said. 'Take it away.'

When constitutional government was restored, the mace was restored. It is the symbol of the authority of the House.

iii *A glittering occasion*

When the present Palace of Westminster was built, due recognition was given to the Speaker. His house – Speaker's House – is noble, dignified and impressive. Approached by a massive staircase, the state rooms are grand and gorgeous. Here in the dining-room was the dinner in my honour. As it happened, the BBC had a team there that very evening. They portrayed the dinner as an incident in the life of Parliament. So some of you may have seen it on television.

The long table sparkled with silver. The chandeliers shone with softening light. The ladies' dresses glittered with diamonds and jewels. On the walls the portraits of previous Speakers looked down.

The Speaker made a most delightful speech in proposing my health with a special tribute to my wife 'the lovely lady by his side' without whom I could do nothing. It gave us the greatest pleasure.

3 The last day of the summer term

1 My 'last' day

i *Dressed as usual*

It was Friday 30 July 1982. Not quite my last day. I had yet to prepare and deliver four judgments that we had reserved. But it was treated by all as my last day.

I walked from the flat through New Square to the Courts. Dressed as usual. Bowler hat, black coat and striped trousers. Limping, stick in hand. Photographers went ahead of me, running backwards. The policeman guided me across Carey Street. 'Good morning' to him. More photographs.

Inside my room, I changed as usual into my winged collar and bands. I put on my court coat and waistcoat, tattered wig and silk gown.

ii *The final ceremony*

At two o'clock, there was the final ceremony. Not in my own court. It was too small. But in the court of the Lord Chief Justice. It is the largest and holds hundreds. The Lord Chancellor presided. He wore his gorgeous apparel. Silk gown adorned with gold, and full-bottomed wig. The rest of us in our everyday robes. The Lord Chief Justice on his right. Me on his left. The President Sir John Arnold, the Vice-Chancellor Sir Robert Megarry, the Lords Justices and 40 judges crowding in on the Bench. Facing us across the well of the court there was a sea of wigs. The aisles and public galleries were filled to the brim. Outside there were scores and scores unable to get in.

2 Farewell speeches

The speeches touched on many different aspects of my career. The Lord Chancellor began and was followed by the Attorney-General. They said many kind things about me, as did Mr Simon Brown, the Treasury Devil – who added a humorous reference to my style of judgment:

My Lord, we shall continue also, as will generations to come, to read your Lordship's judgments in the reports; and how refreshingly easy it is to read them compared to so many others. We shall recall that short sentences are best and that verbs are optional! [*Laughter.*]

3 The leaders of the profession

i *T-shirts in the United States of America*

Mr Ashe Lincoln QC, the senior silk, recalled his service in the Royal Navy with my brother, Admiral Sir Norman Denning, saying that:

few realised that the very existence of the country really depended upon the magnificent work which he did for the Intelligence Service of the Royal Navy.

He then brought in the T-shirts, saying:

So long as the common law exists, the name of Lord Denning will be revered and remembered not only in this country but throughout the world. I remember in the United States of America how greatly he is respected and how when I visited law colleges and law schools in that country I found that the students had embroidered their T-shirts with the words 'Root for Denning'. [*Laughter.*] It occurred to me that it might be a useful garment to wear before the Court of Appeal. [*Laughter.*]

ii *And elsewhere*

Mr Ashe Lincoln QC mentioned the United States of America. Yet I am the proud possessor of T-shirts from universities all the world over. On them there is reproduced a photograph of me in my full-bottomed wig – or a cartoon – with 'Lord Denning MR' underneath. Then an appropriate caption such as:

Toronto: 'LEAVE TO APPEAL REFUSED'
Manitoba: 'EQUITY'
Alberta: 'IT WAS BLUEBELL TIME IN KENT'[1]
Malaysia: 'BRADDELL MEMORIAL LECTURE'[2]

The University of British Columbia put in a team for their race with T-shirts inscribed:

DENNING'S DEMONS
9TH ANNUAL TRIKE RACE
UBC LAW

iii *A circuiteer*

Mr Platts-Mills QC spoke for my old circuit, the Western Circuit, and recalled the old days when the circuit van, drawn by horses, started from Brick Court:

Your Lordship was indeed a circuiteer. Your Lordship's name and example are still used with the torrent of pupils who want to know where to go: 'Go north, young man; go even west'.

Your Lordship opened sessions in other counties than your own. This is the mark of a circuiteer. Your Lordship as well rode shotgun on the mythical coach that carried the great laundry hamper that was said to hold the file and all the papers and the Clerk of Assize's gear and robes and food.

iv *Something of comfort for everybody*

Mr Joseph Jackson QC spoke for the Family Division and the Family Law Bar Association emphasising, he said, 'the great contribution that you have made to family law':

You helped wives to achieve some justice in respect of the matrimonial home. The deserted wives' equity it was called in those days, although it was destroyed by an Exocet fired from on high in due course. You gave the judgment of the Court of Appeal in *Wachtel* which ever since, you will be pleased to know, has been the Bible in our division, although, like the Bible, it had something of comfort in it for everybody.

---

[1] My opening words in *Hinz v Berry* [1970] 2 QB 40, 42.
[2] Edward Braddell was a foremost lawyer in Malaysia.

v *Vigilance*

Mr (now Sir) Max Williams, who had recently become President of the Law Society, quoted the words of Mr J. P. Curran of the Middle Temple spoken in 1790:

It is the common fate of the indolent to see their rights become a prey to the active. The condition upon which God hath given liberty to man is eternal vigilance.

Mr Max Williams went on:

My Lords, if I were to summarise the greatness of Lord Denning in one word, it would be 'vigilance' – vigilance in upholding his standards and beliefs.

4 My reply

i '*A debtor to his profession*'

I was much moved by this eloquence. In my reply I used several of my favourite quotations. In particular I repeated the familiar words of Lord Bacon:

Hold every man a debtor to his profession; from the which as men of course, do seek to receive countenance and profit; so ought they of duty to endeavour themselves by way of amends to be a help and ornament thereunto.[1]

ii *The great white elephant*

In going on with my speech, I pointed to a delicate model which I had before me. It was a silver chariot drawn by seven elephants. One of them was in white alabaster. The model had been given by a lady – Meher Master, a member of Lincoln's Inn and a leader of the Parsee community in India. I read extracts from her letter:

Here are seven elephants drawing a dainty silver carriage. The square piece on the rear of the carriage has the single word 'Justice' inscribed on it. All the elephants are engaged in the task of pulling the carriage of Justice along the narrow white path, the straight and narrow road. . . .

[1] *The Elements of the Common Law*, preface.

The great white elephant has no tusks for he does not need tusks to do his work in Nature. This elephant's mind and thought force power is so highly developed in Nature that he can do the work of spreading Justice and maintaining the Divine Law and Order among all souls. . . . This elephant represents you, Lord Denning [*Laughter*], as the greatest force for truth and Justice tempered with mercy, alive today.

This was her last wish:

I wish you would place this figure in some room in the Law Courts building where all your Judges can see it, for it would serve as a constant reminder to them that Justice must ever be done, and the time may come in the future when the great white elephant may no longer be in their midst. [*Laughter*.]

I continued:

The time has come. Henceforward I shall be no longer in your midst. At 83 it is time for me to retire.

iii '*I have finished my course*'

This is how I ended:

I am most grateful for the wonderful support given to me by all my colleagues on the Bench, by all of you at the Bar, by all the solicitors, and friends everywhere. I wish I could say as a great man once did when his departure was at hand: 'I have fought a good fight, I have finished my course, I have kept the faith.'[1]

---

[1] 2 *Timothy* 4:7 (Authorised version).

4 The long vacation

1 On holiday

i *On the Hoe*

There were still two months to go. My retirement date was 29 September 1982. On Saturday 31 July Joan and I went off straightway for a few days at Plymouth. Long years ago I was the Recorder there. I never sat because I was appointed a judge of the High Court. Yet I am remembered there. Year after year the Lord Mayor has invited us to a lovely house on the Hoe. It was owned by Lady Astor – the first woman member of Parliament – and she had given it to the city. It has the most beautiful outlook in all England. It looks over the Sound towards Drake's Island and across to Mount Edgcumbe. We used to sit in the drawing-room watching the ships of war go in and out. They were so close that you could pick out the sailors lining the rail. The good butler and his wife saw to our every need.

ii *Back from the Falklands*

During this stay in August 1982 there was a thrill. Two of the frigates came home from the Falklands. One with a hole right through her hull by an Exocet. Fortunately above the water-line. With our luncheon guests we joined in the welcome. We had a large Union Jack flying from the window. We cheered and cheered. My own nephew, Norman's son James, had been in the campaign with the

Royal Navy. Once more the words of Shakespeare which I quoted in *The Family Story* came to mind:

> This England never did (nor never shall)
> Lie at the proud foot of a conqueror,
> But when it first did help to wound itself.
> Now these her princes are come home again,
> Come the three corners of the world in arms,
> And we shall shock them: Nought shall make us rue,
> If England to itself do rest but true.[1]

I thought to myself: In peace, as in war, we must rest but true.

2 Back at home

i *The television people*

Back home during August and September I was working at the four reserved judgments. They were difficult and important. Each of them took me a week or so. But the time was split up with visits from the television people. The BBC were preparing a documentary, *Judgment on Denning;* Granada another, *A law unto himself;* and TVS another, *A full life.* They came with a team of a dozen or more. They set up their equipment in the library. They took pictures of me there. They took pictures of Joan and me in the garden.

ii *The cricket match*

But the highlight was the cricket match. I was the President of the Lincoln's Inn Cricket Club and also the Whitchurch Cricket Club. We gave them lunch at 'The Lawn'. They played on our lovely ground, quite near, with the background of the barn and the church. Lincoln's Inn won. I presented them with a shield to be played for each year. I recalled the cricketing story of the schoolboy's definition of the game of cricket. It is a play on 'in' and 'out'.

[1] *King John*, Act V, sc. 7.

You have two sides – one out in the field – one in. Each man on the side that's in goes out: and when he's out, he comes in and the next man goes in until he's out. When they are all out, the side that's been out comes in and the side that's been in goes out and tries to get those coming in out. Then when they're all out including the 'not outs' that's the end of the game.

iii *My last appearance*

I finished my four reserved judgments just in time. We delivered them in the last week of the vacation. On 29 September 1982 we gave judgment in the very last. Farmers were claiming damages from the suppliers of cabbage seed. They had planted it and there came up – not cabbages – but a lot of loose green leaves. I started off:[1]

Many of you know Lewis Carroll's *Through the Looking Glass*. In it there are these words (ch IV):

> 'The time has come,' the Walrus said,
> 'to talk of many things:
> Of shoes – and ships – and sealing-wax –
> Of cabbages – and kings –.'

Today it is not 'of cabbages and kings' – but of cabbages and what-nots.

At the end we gave judgment for the farmers. The suppliers asked for leave to appeal to the Lords. I said, 'No, we do not grant leave.' Those were my last words in the court. I walked out and along the corridor to my room. I took off my robes and put on my ordinary clothes. I said goodbye to my clerk and secretary who had served me well. I left the building. I had entered it first 60 years before as a pupil. I have never been in it since.

---

[1] *George Mitchell (Chesterhall) Ltd v Finney Lock Seeds Ltd* [1982] 3 WLR 1036, 1040.

Section Two

Autumn Leaves

After my retirement I was kept busy. Invitations poured in: 'Now that you have retired, perhaps you will have time to speak to us.' Many I refused. But some I accepted. Throughout the autumn I spoke at gatherings of one kind and another. In case you may be interested, I will describe some of these occasions for you. I have called them 'Autumn leaves' because they are leaves fallen from many trees and gathered by me in the autumn of my days.

1 A judge of silk

1 The silk mill at Whitchurch

i *Recorded in Domesday*

At the top end of our garden there is a mill. We – by 'we' I mean the people of Whitchurch – have had a mill there for nearly 1,000 years. It is recorded in the Domesday survey. It was built by our forefathers who are described by Edmund Blunden:

> These were men of pith and thew
> Whom the city never call'd;
> Scarce could read or hold a quill,
> Built the barn, the forge, the mill.[1]

ii *Silk for the 'silks'*

For the last 100 years we have made the silk for the gowns of the 'silks', that is, the Queen's Counsel who plead in the courts of law. We also make the silk for the facings of university gowns. They are gorgeous – of many colours. We make exquisite shirts and scarves of real silk for the ladies – nothing artificial about them. Even silk socks for the men so that you can dream (according to W. S. Gilbert) that you are

in your shirt and your socks (the black silk with gold clocks), crossing Salisbury Plain on a bicycle.[2]

[1] *Forefathers.*
[2] *Iolanthe.*

iii *The water-wheel*

Nowadays the mill is worked by electric power. But when I was a boy it was worked by water-power. Our forefathers built up the banks of the river so as to get a head of water. The water fell on to the paddles and turned them round. But for the last 40 years the wheel had been silent. The wooden paddles had rotted. It was about to be scrapped. Then good friends in the county got together and restored it. I was invited to start it up again. It was on Saturday 2 October 1982. Good folk came from roundabout. I told them:

Until recently I was a starter-up of controversy. Now I am the starter-up of a water-wheel.
Until recently I was a judge of men. Now I am a judge of silk.

iv '*More water glideth*'

I turned the handle. A moment's pause. The great wheel began to turn. Slowly at first. Then faster. The water fell on-to the paddles. It drove the wheel round and round. Then came the sound I remembered as a boy. Clang – clang. Swish – swish. The water-wheel was at work again. A cheer went up. All pressed forward to see. Then they started on the sandwiches and lemonade. Shakespeare knew all about it:

> What, man! more water glideth by the mill
> Than wots the miller of.[1]

Our good Ted Moss who runs the mill knows it too.

2 Silk in story

i *HMS* Mulberry

Everyone knows that the silk fibres are made by silkworms. These worms feed on the leaves of the mulberry tree. You may think we have many of these trees in England. The children still sing, 'Here we go round the mulberry bush.'

But there are very few mulberry trees in England. There is

---

[1] *Titus Andronicus*, Act II, sc. 1.

only one in Whitchurch so far as I know. At any rate our silk fibre all comes by sea from China. The hot climate suits the mulberry trees and the silkworms.

I have often wondered why in 1944 we talked of the 'Mulberry' Harbour. That was, you may remember, the prefabricated harbour which was towed across to Normandy for the landings. It was called 'Mulberry' because – in the list of names to be used for warships – it was the next in line for use – 'HMS *Mulberry*'.

ii *The English Justinian*

To make a silk fabric, the silk yarn or thread is coiled on bobbins and fed into the looms and woven together, lengthways (the 'warp') and sideways (the 'woof'). This process gave rise to the most effective piece of alliteration in the English language. It is in Thomas Gray's poem *The Bard*. He describes the curse of the Welsh bard upon Edward I. That King was called the 'English Justinian' because of his judicial reforms. Amongst other things, he set up our justices of the peace. But there is a tradition that he invaded Wales and massacred the bards. This is the curse which Thomas Gray put into the mouth of one of the Welsh bards who survived:

> Weave the warp and weave the woof,
> The winding-sheet of Edward's race:
> Give ample room and verge enough
> The characters of hell to trace. . . .
> Now, brothers, bending o'er the accursed loom,
> Stamp we our vengeance deep, and ratify his doom.
>
> Edward, lo! to sudden fate
> (Weave we the woof; The thread is spun;)
> Half of thy heart we consecrate,
> (The web is wove; The work is done.)[1]

iii *The mills of God*

Often in our court-rooms we use the metaphor of the mill and the millstones. 'It is all grist to the mill', we say, meaning

---

[1] *The Bard.*

that, like the corn, it is all turned to good account. Then when a defendant is in dire peril we speak of him being 'crushed between the upper and nether millstones'. The upper millstone goes round very fast. It is called the 'runner stone'. The nether or lower millstone is firmly fixed and very hard. Job knew all about it. Talking of hardness of heart he said:

His heart is as firm as a stone; yea, as hard as a piece of the nether millstone.[1]

Then when we watch the machinery of the law slowly catching up with the defaulter we quote Longfellow's verse translated from the German von Logau:

> Though the mills of God grind slowly, yet they grind
>   exceeding small;
> Though with patience He stands waiting, with
>   exactness grinds He all.[2]

And when we study the coat of arms of Lincoln's Inn, we see several little squiggles. They are in heraldry supposed to represent mill-rinds. But what are mill-rinds? They are little bits of iron which support the upper or 'runner' millstone.

iv Visitors

I have told you this about our mill in case you should come to our little town. Go and see the silk mill. Watch the water-wheel turning round. Walk down by our lawn. We shall be pleased to see you.

---

[1] *Job* 41:24 (Authorised version).
[2] Friedrich von Logau *Sinngedichte* (1653) III, ii 24 (translated by H. W. Longfellow).

2 The cathedral at Winchester

1 Legal Sunday

i *The lesson*

Next came the service on 17 October 1982 in our cathedral at Winchester. It takes place every year. It is held especially for the judges and magistrates of the county and the legal profession. When I was Master of the Rolls I used to go in my full robes together with the Lord Lieutenant escorted by javelin men. In this October I went in morning dress. I was invited to read the lesson. On previous occasions I had been asked to read the Sermon on the Mount. This time it was a passage from *Exodus*, chapter 18:13–27. It was new to me. Perhaps it may be to you. It contains good advice on judicial administration.

ii *Moses takes the hard cases*

It tells that when Moses sat to judge the people of Israel, there was such a backlog of work that he could not get through it in the day:

And it came to pass on the morrow, that Moses sat to judge the people: and the people stood by Moses from the morning unto the evening.

There was such a delay that Moses' father-in-law took it up with him:

The thing that thou doest is not good. Thou wilt surely wear away, both thou, and this people that is with thee: for this thing is too heavy for thee; thou art not able to perform it thyself alone.

The remedy was to appoint more judges and to set up a hierarchy of courts:

Thou shalt provide out of all the people able men, such as fear God, men of truth, hating covetousness; and place such over them, to be rulers of thousands, and rulers of hundreds, rulers of fifties, and rulers of tens: And let them judge the people at all seasons: and it shall be, that every great matter they shall bring unto thee, but every small matter they shall judge: so shall it be easier for thyself, and they shall bear the burden with thee.

Moses did as he was commanded with beneficial results:

And they judged the people at all seasons: the hard cases they brought unto Moses, but every small matter they judged themselves.

When I was Master of the Rolls, my clerk so arranged the lists that the hard cases were brought to me: but, unlike Moses, they did not stop at me. They went on sometimes to the House of Lords – occasionally, perhaps, to be reversed.

2 Recalling Saint Swithun

i *Rain for 40 days*

The patron saint of the cathedral is Saint Swithun. He is commemorated on 15 July in every year. On the Saturday nearest to it the Friends of the Cathedral hold their annual festival. Everyone knows that if it rains on Saint Swithun's Day, it will rain on every day for 40 days afterwards. At the festival service in 1965 I gave an address which tells something of him and of the cathedral.

ii *Scrambled eggs*

Today we recall Saint Swithun. It is nearly 1,000 years since the remains of Saint Swithun were carried into the precincts of this cathedral. The day was the fifteenth of July. It rained on that day and for forty days after. Hence the legend which you all know. Let us forget the legend and remember the man. He was the Bishop of Winchester, but yet so humble that he went throughout the diocese on foot to be with the people. He was a builder. He built and repaired many churches. And he built a stone bridge, the first of its kind in these parts, across the River Itchen at the

33

eastern gate of this city. He used to sit by it, speeding the workmen. He was a teacher. He it was who taught the King's sons and set the boy Alfred on his way to become the great warrior, scholar and law-giver. Swithun did such great things for the people that, in that superstitious age, he was credited with supernatural powers. When a woman going to market dropped a basketful of eggs on the bridge, he mended them with shells entire. After his burial here, many of the sick who visited his shrine were healed by faith. So many that the monks wearied of returning thanks.

3 A massive pile

i *Smashed windows*

On this day we remember not only Saint Swithun. We think of the part this cathedral and its forerunners on this site have played in our history. It has resounded with acclaims at the coronation of a score of kings, Saxon, Dane and Norman. It has been the place where great bishops have found their strength through faith in God. William of Wykeham, the Founder of the College here and of New College at Oxford, William of Waynflete who founded my own college. This massive pile was built by many hands in divers ages. Just look at the work of the Normans – the simple round arches and the plain round pillars. The Normans impressed even these forms with a superhuman majesty. Then the nave – long-drawn, silver-grey, perpendicular: the window at the end. You will remember that on Cheriton Down, one March day in 1644, the Roundheads smote the Cavaliers and came grimly down to this cathedral and smashed the windows and monuments. The gathered bits of glass, broken as they are, make splendid this tall greenish-blueish West Window.

ii *A narrow passage*

Nearby, as you know, is the narrow passage to the Close. At one time the people used to go through the cathedral as a thoroughfare. Bishop Curle made the passage for them instead. You can see the inscriptions in Latin still: 'Worshippers go that way' (to the cathedral); 'Travellers go this'.

iii *Foundations sinking*

This great edifice, rich in history, must be kept intact. When I was a boy there was a great fear that it might fall. The foundations were sinking. It was saved by the work and skill of those who loved it, Dean Furneaux and William Walker the diver. It is not in danger now but it needs constant work. See that pillar which has split. It must be mended. So with all this holy fabric. . . .

iv *The Dean and Chapter*

The Dean and Chapter in days past have had much influence on contemporary affairs. You may recall the Bloody Assize when Judge Jeffreys came. He tried the noble Lady Alice Lisle, who had done nothing wrong save give shelter to some fugitives. He bullied the Hampshire jury into finding her guilty and sentenced her to be burned alive. The clergy of the cathedral protested and besought him to be merciful. The utmost that they could achieve was that instead of being burned alive, she should be beheaded. She was put to death in the Market Place and underwent her fate with serene courage. In a last message she wrote, 'I forgive all persons who have done me wrong and I desire that God will do so likewise'. . . .

3 Dinner at the Inner Temple

1 A memorable occasion

i *All the Lords Justices*

Then followed a memorable occasion. On Tuesday 2 November 1982 the Lords Justices gave a dinner for Joan and me at the Inner Temple. It was arranged by John Stephenson who was then the most senior Lord Justice – and the most accomplished of judges. It was given for us by all those who had sat with me in the Court of Appeal during the 20 years. They numbered 36. Each brought his lady. It was held in the beautiful Parliament Chamber. The meal was chosen especially to please us. Lord Diplock (now the senior Law Lord) made a delightful speech in our honour.

ii *I prepare a speech*

Then came my reply. I had prepared it carefully. But I have often found that if I prepare a speech carefully, it does not go down so well. It is not spontaneous. That happened here. But some parts may interest you.

iii *A Wise Old Bird*

I told them of Theo Mathew's advice on retirement as given in his *Forensic Fables*:

There was Once a Wise Old Bird who Retired from the Bench the Very Moment he had Done his Fifteen Years. The Wise Old Bird's Friends Assured him he would be Bored to Tears. They also Hinted Darkly that,

Deprived of his Customary Employment, he would Probably Pass Away in the Near Future. Were they Right in their Gloomy Prognostications? Did he Miss the Dear Old Courts of Justice? Not a Bit of it. The Wise Old Bird took a Nice Little Place in the Country, and Thought Out an Admirable Routine. He Rose Late, Breakfasted Comfortably, Read *The Times* (Skipping the Law Reports) and had a Look at the Pigs. Then he Lunched and Read a Novel. At Four-Thirty the Wise Old Bird Took a Cup of Tea and had Another Look at the Pigs. At Seven-Thirty he Dined, Finishing up with Two Glasses of Vintage Port, an Old Brandy, and a Cigar. Before Retiring to Rest he Consumed a Stiff Whisky and Soda, and had Another if he Felt he Wanted it. . . . The Wise Old Bird Firmly Declined to be Bothered with Quarter Sessions, Petty Sessions, or Any Nonsense of that Kind. He thus Survived to Celebrate his Ninety-Eighth Birthday and had the Extreme Satisfaction of Outliving All his Contemporaries. Moral. – *Retire*.

2 Too sad a note

i *The curtain drops*

I concluded by using a picture drawn by Thackeray, but adapted to suit my case:

> The play is done; the curtain drops,
> Slow falling to the prompter's bell:
> A moment yet the actor stops,
> And looks around, to say farewell.
> The approving audience give him cheer,
> He bows to them and says his say;
> Yet down his cheek there falls a tear –
> For him 'tis the ending of his day.[1]

It was the ending of my day. It was too sad a note on which to finish.

ii *Joan steals the show*

But then there were calls for Joan to speak. The dinner was in her honour as well. She stole the show by a true story.

I do want to thank you all. . . .
    I have never made an after-dinner speech in my life. Tom does all the

---

[1] Adapted from W. M. Thackeray *The End of the Play*.

speaking. But once he did show me a judgment he was going to give. I told him I thought he was coming out the wrong way. He said, 'Oh, do you?' and wrote a judgment the other way. The other two judges did not agree but afterwards the Lords overruled them. So he won in the Lords.

There were roars of laughter and applause.

4 A luncheon at the Savoy

1 A play for 30 years

i *Who done it?*

Later that same month there was a unique celebration. It was on Thursday 25 November 1982. You will all have heard of Agatha Christie. She was a writer of thrillers. She specialised in murders. She wrote one play which has gone on for 30 years. It is called *The Mousetrap*. It has a commonplace theme. An elderly woman magistrate is murdered in a guest-house. The audience are invited to guess 'Who done it?' or, in American slang 'Who dunnit?'

ii *Three blind mice*

There are three murders to the story. Throughout the play the nursery rhyme recurs time and again:

> Three blind mice, see how they run.
> They all ran after the farmer's wife,
> Who cut off their tails with a carving knife.
> Did you ever see such a sight in your life
> As three blind mice?

iii *Why call it* The Mousetrap?

To mark its thirtieth year Sir Peter Saunders, the producer, invited me to speak at a celebration luncheon at the Savoy Hotel. Joan came too. It was a brilliant occasion with 1,000 guests from the theatre, the films, the newspapers, the professions and all. In my speech I made a guess why it was called *The Mousetrap*. Was it not because of Emerson's famous saying:

If a man write a better book, preach a better sermon, or make a better mousetrap than his neighbour, tho' he build his house in the woods, the world will make a beaten path to his door.

This *Mousetrap* is a better thriller than any other. It has gone on for 30 years because each generation in England takes its children to see it and every tourist from overseas is sure of entertainment.

5 The cathedral at Norwich

1 Another Legal Sunday

i *Second to none*

Event followed event. Next was a visit to Norwich. The High Sheriff of Norfolk wished to start a Legal Service in the cathedral at Norwich, similar to the one we have at Winchester. It was arranged for Sunday 5 December 1982. He invited me to give an address. We stayed at the oldest inn in England, *The Maid's Head*, at Norwich. It is just opposite the cathedral. The cathedral was full. I went up into the pulpit and said:

Mr Dean: I have long wanted to come to this great cathedral of Norwich – with its spire second only in height to our own at Salisbury – and its nave second only in length to our own at Winchester – but together this outdoes in glory each of them.

My Lord Mayor: I have long wanted to come to your ancient city. I would recall that Sir Edward Coke – the great Chief Justice in the time of the first Elizabeth – went to the grammar school here. It stood in the cathedral close. He loved this city. He called it 'this famous and free city of Norwich'.

Mr High Sheriff: I am glad you have arranged this service – the first – for the judges and men of law of this county of Norfolk and neighbourhood: so that all may pray that they may have the spirit of discernment, the spirit of uprightness and the spirit of love.

ii *The candle is not put out*

I would have liked to have come in my robes as Master of the Rolls – but being now retired, I have come in the gown and hood of a Doctor of

Laws of the University of Oxford.

Oxford – where one of the greatest sons of Norfolk – Bishop Hugh Latimer – a yeoman's son – was burned at the stake in 1555. He used these well-known words:

> 'Be of good cheer, Master Ridley, and play the man. We shall this day light such a candle by God's grace in England, as (I trust) shall never be put out.'

That was over 400 years ago. This service today shows that the candle has not been put out.

iii 'Dissolve me into ecstasies'

Here in this great cathedral we can catch something of the feeling which inspired John Milton (I recited the lovely words, pointing upwards and along to the roof, the pillars, windows, organ and quire):

> But let my due feet never fail
> To walk the studious cloister's pale,
> And love the high embowed roof,
> With antique pillars massy proof,
> And storied windows richly dight,
> Casting a dim religious light.
> There let the pealing organ blow,
> To the full-voiced quire below,
> In service high, and anthems clear
> As may, with sweetness, through mine ear,
> Dissolve me into ecstasies,
> And bring all Heaven before mine eyes.[1]

iv How I finished

And at the end I said:

If you have followed me so far, you may well say that this is no sermon. I know. I cannot preach a sermon. But I would say this. I would not be here unless I believed in God. My belief in God is in part due to my upbringing – to what I have been taught – and in part to what I have found out in going through life. That is the case with all knowledge. No man knows anything except what he has been taught and what he has found out for himself.

The fundamental point in my experience is that there is a spirit in man – quite separate from his body and from his intellect – which, when it reaches its highest and best, is but the reflection of the spirit of God. Now

[1] *Il Penseroso* 1.158.

42

I know nothing of theology. Nor can I say that I have seen the sudden light of conversion as some have, but I do know that in the great experiences of life – and in the small ones too – such strength as I have is of God, and the weakness is mine.

Need I relate the experiences? Take the hard things. When faced with a task on which great issues depend; when high hopes lie shattered; when anxieties gnaw deep; or when overwhelmed by grief: where can I turn for help but to God?

Or take the joyful things. A hard task attempted and done; the happiness of family life; or the beauty of nature: where can I turn in thankfulness but to God?

All experiences convince me, not only that God is ever present: but also that it is by contact with the spirit of God that the spirit of man reaches its highest and its best.

6 Abortion in the Lords

1 Speaking in debate

During this autumn I also attended the House of Lords and spoke in debates. One I would mention was on a Bill to amend the Abortion Acts. It was on Monday 6 December 1982. I take it from Hansard. It is a little disjointed, but that is because it was spoken, not written.

i *Illegal abortion*

I have been much concerned in abortion from the legal point of view. As a trial judge, I have tried cases of illegal abortion. I have sentenced men to some years, and one woman backstairs abortionist to nine months when the mother concerned had either died or been rendered very ill. . . . I should like to say that I will support the Second Reading of the Bill. . . .

ii *The unborn child*

. . . it is not only the Christian doctrine but it is the doctrine of our law and our common law that the unborn child has a life of its own and a right of its own which is recognised by the law at least from the time of quickening, and the common law has always recognised that. Our great jurist, Sir William Blackstone, put it in this way:

> Life is the immediate gift of God, a right inherent by nature in every individual, and it begins in contemplation at law as soon as the infant is able to stir in its mother's womb.

Such a child was protected by the law almost to the same extent as a newborn baby. If anyone terminated the pregnancy and thus destroyed the life of the child he or she was guilty of a felony punishable by life imprisonment.

In 1939 in *Bourne's* case that was modified to this extent by the common law. It was a defence if the termination was necessary to save the life of the mother. If the probable consequences of not terminating was to make the mother a physical or mental wreck then it was justifiable, but that was the only circumstance in which in the common law it was justifiable to terminate the pregnancy. So the common law laid great stress on the existence in the unborn child of a life of its own and a right of its own.

iii *Responsibility on the medical profession*

Now for the 1967 Act. As I read it, it does not alter that fundamental principle, but what it does do is to define the circumstances in which pregnancy can be terminated. . . .

. . . the whole design of the Act was to put a great social responsibility on the medical profession in regard to the termination of pregnancy. It is a great social responsibility. I do not believe that it can be effectively enforced by the law. If the doctor gives his opinion honestly and in good faith, no jury will challenge it, no law will challenge it. That is why there have been no prosecutions under the Act. The responsibility is firmly placed by the law on the medical profession. It is the profession's responsibility. But here comes the crux: weighing the balance and telling of the risk. . . . The doctors have to weigh that nice balance. Surely they ought to be given some guidance to show that the 'greater' balance has to be to save injury to the mother. . . .

iv *Obtainable on demand*

(The Act) has been interpreted by some medical practitioners so loosely that abortion has become virtually obtainable on demand. Whenever a woman has an unwanted pregnancy there are doctors who will say that a risk is involved to her mental health. . . . It is because there is not enough guidance given to the medical profession. . . .

7 A look at the Law Lords

During the autumn I also did some broadcasts. One of these was a review of a book recently written by Dr Alan Paterson, called *The Law Lords*. In the course of it I expressed appreciation of his work, but I give you a few extracts of what I said about the Law Lords themselves.

1 How they have behaved

i *They have been introspective*

When we speak of the Law Lords nowadays, we mean those distinguished and sometimes elderly gentlemen who sit in the House of Lords in its judicial capacity. They are all learned in the law. Five of them sit together, hearing appeals from lower courts. They can and do sometimes overrule the Court of Appeal. They are chosen for their high qualities of intellect and learning. There is no appeal from them to any higher body. They cannot be overruled. Nor can their decisions be impeached. Hence the belief has grown up that they are infallible – that they never make mistakes. For many years their predecessors acted in that belief. Yet in the last few years they have become more self-conscious. More introspective, I might say. They have begun to realise that they may sometimes make mistakes themselves. Or, if not themselves, that their predecessors may have done. So they have on occasion been prepared – in their polite language – to 'depart' from the previous decisions of their predecessors.

In straightforward language they may openly confess that they were wrong in a previous case.

ii *Do they listen to counsel?*

Are the Law Lords influenced by the arguments of counsel? In England the tradition coming down for centuries has been that arguments are to be by word of mouth. The discussion is known as the Socratic method. The advocate on the one side frames his argument in the form of questions so as to arrive at the conclusion he desires. Thus, if he wishes to arrive by calculation at the number 10 he will say:

> 'You will agree with me that two and two make four?'

Answer: 'Of course, Yes.'

Then, after a few irrelevances he will say:

> 'Accepting, as you do, that two and two make five, then if you double it, that makes ten?'

Answer: 'I suppose so, Yes.'

It is then for the advocate on the other side to point out the error.

But the tradition of oral argument is being broken down in modern times. It has already broken down in the United States. It is in danger of being broken down here. In the United States the lawyers there prepare printed 'briefs' of great length setting out all the facts and the arguments and the cases – which the judges are expected to read beforehand. Then, when the appeal is heard, the lawyers are restricted to half-an-hour on each side. The judges take several weeks before they write their opinions. By that time they have forgotten the oral argument. They rely solely on the written briefs.

2 How they should behave

i *Should they read papers beforehand?*

There is a danger – more than a danger – of this happening in England. There is a growing body of opinion that all Appeal

Judges should read all the papers beforehand. In the past, some of the most eminent Law Lords never read them in advance. Nowadays all are supposed to do so. Often in the House of Lords the presiding judge will say:

Mr Smith, I would have you know that their Lordships have read all the papers in this case. So will you please confine yourself to this point.

That, no doubt, saves a lot of time in court. It is the object of the exercise. But I myself think it better to keep to the traditional system of oral argument.

ii *Should there be one judgment only?*

Next, should each of the Law Lords write a separate opinion of his own? Or should there be only one judgment in which all agree? Up to Lord Reid's death in 1975 the great majority of the Law Lords were in favour of separate judgments, each writing his own. Lord Reid said that he found that when the Law Lords gave only one judgment there was a tendency for the lower courts to approach that judgment as if it were an Act of Parliament. He said that, in one case, it led to an absolute 'disaster'. But since 1975 the pendulum has been swinging strongly against separate judgments. It has gathered momentum in the last two or three years. Time after time, in cases of the first importance, there has only been one judgment. Time after time the lower courts have felt bound by that one judgment and by all the sayings in that judgment. They are called obiter dicta. They are really sayings just by the way, as if an aside. Yet they are treated as binding. I do not think that is right.

iii *Justice v certainty*

Should the Law Lords seek to do justice? Or should they prefer certainty? In the 1950s, under the influence of Lord Simonds, the law was static. But under Lord Reid it became moderately progressive. Nowadays the Law Lords have varying views. Some are for certainty rather than justice. Some are for progress rather than standing still. I have made my own view clear time out of mind. I would always strive to do justice. Certainty I regard, often, as a will-o'-the-wisp.

3 Speeches no longer

The judgments of the Law Lords are still called 'speeches'. This is because the Lords used always to sit in the Legislative Chamber of the House of Lords. The Law Lords, in giving their opinions, gave them as if they were in a debate. In coming to a decision, the motion was put to the House just as after a debate. For instance: That the decision of the Court of Appeal be affirmed. Those in favour say 'Aye'. Those against say 'Nay'. The 'Ayes' have it, sometimes. But at other times the decision is reversed.

Nowadays the judgments are never 'speeches'. The House sits in a Committee Room, not in the Legislative Chamber. That is to hear the arguments. But when they give their judgments, they sit in the Chamber itself. Instead of being speeches, they are essays. They are never delivered by word of mouth. They are only handed out to the parties. They are sometimes so complicated that they cannot be readily understood on a first reading. They have to be studied and analysed word by word. All this inevitably leads to long sentences. Every statement of principle has to be qualified by exceptions of some kind or other. Then practitioners and academics pore over them to approve – to comment – or to criticise. Always of course 'with respect'.

That is the catchword with which the Law Lords on occasion reverse the court below. They differ 'with respect', sometimes 'with great respect', occasionally 'with the utmost possible respect'. It is just a polite way of saying that they wholeheartedly disagree.

8 The family at Christmas

When we came to Christmas 1982, all the children and grandchildren came to us over the holiday: some on Christmas Eve, and some on Boxing Day. But for Christmas Day itself we went to the younger generation at Beaconsfield. I had occasion to write an article for *The Mail on Sunday*. It was slightly edited by the paper, but this is what I wrote. It tells how we have spent Christmas in younger days and now.

1 All gather together

i *The microcosm of society*

Christmas Day is family day. It is the day on which sons and daughters – of all ages – gather together with their parents. They come from near. They come from far. To be at home with the family. Yes – at home – with the family and with the children. The future of the country depends on the upbringing of the children. Their upbringing depends on their home-life. Their home-life depends on their family ties. These ties are bonded by Christmas. The family is the microcosm of society. As bricks go to make a house, so do families go to make a people.

ii *Why is it called Christmas?*

Why is it called Christmas? Simply because it is 'Christ's

Mass' – that is, 'Christ's Feast Day'. Why is it so? Simply because on that day Jesus Christ was born. There is one sentence in the Bible which tells us of the first Christmas Day. It says quite simply of a mother in Bethlehem in Palestine:

She brought forth her first-born son and wrapped him in swaddling clothes and laid him in a manger, because there was no room for them in the inn.

The birth of that child was the beginning of an epoch. It is now 1,982 years ago. Anno Domini (In the year of our Lord) 1982.

The story is recalled in homes, in schools and in churches. It is told in words. It is sung in carols. It is acted by children. It is portrayed in paintings.

Yet its significance is only too often forgotten. Some have never known it. But there is this to remember. Although many forget the origin of Christmas, nearly everyone knows the spirit of Christmas. No matter how much they believe or disbelieve, they celebrate Christmas. Everyone you meet says, 'A merry Christmas to you'. All the world over people repeat the Christmas message from the Bible:

On earth peace, goodwill towards men.

iii *Once in Bethlehem*

How far is the spirit of Christmas to be found today? Does it exist even in Bethlehem? Many tourists go there. Some come back inspired. Others disappointed. We went once during the Christmas vacation. I confess I was among those disappointed. It was so different from what I had pictured. There was no stable. There was no manger. Only a huge church with a narrow entrance. So low that you had to crouch to get into it. One by one. Thousands of tourists were milling about awaiting a service.

We went outside beyond the town of Bethlehem. There were no 'shepherds watching their flocks by night'. No fields. No 'pastures green'. Only a bleak and stony landscape.

Not a sheep in sight. Not a blade of grass. But there was some lovely singing. We joined in. There were no 'wise men from the East'. Only Palestinians in their loose garments. There was no 'star which went before them'. But it was a clear night. It showed our way by road the few miles to Jerusalem.

iv *And in Jerusalem*

We went at midnight to our English church there, Saint George's. It was a moving service after the pattern of our midnight service at home. Full of people gathered in worship, with hymns and prayers. We visited the Church of the Sepulchre. There again I was disillusioned. There was to me no trace of holiness or sanctity. The approach was through a dark tunnel to a low cave lit by red lamps. But in the countryside you could see again the Bible scenes. You could go down the road winding from Jerusalem to Jericho. You could fall among thieves. You could go up the mount where the sermon was preached. You could walk by the sea where the fishermen cast their nets. All these were much as they were 2,000 years ago.

2 Keeping Christmas

i *The spirit of Christmas*

To me the spirit of Christmas is not to be found in Bethlehem, nor in any building or place. It is to be found only in the hearts of man and wife: and in a home made by them together for their family.

What is the spirit of Christmas? It lies in friendship for all around you. In giving them happiness so far as in you lies. In greeting them with a cheerful smile. Even in decorating the home. Yes – still more in providing good fare for all: so that they may eat, drink and be merry. In the giving of presents and receiving them. In remembering those at a distance. In sending them good wishes. In helping those in need. In bearing goodwill to all and bad will to none. In short, to do your part towards making the earth a better place.

ii *How we kept Christmas*

Let me tell how we kept Christmas in our family when we were younger. We kept it as our parents and grandparents had done: and as many of you keep it now.

Preparations start well ahead. Mother makes the Christmas pudding. We all help stir. Christmas cards come in. A trickle. A stream. A flood. Mother answers them. We get the Christmas tree from the wood. We decorate it with tinsel, spangles and fairy lights. Everyone helps. We get the holly from the hedgerows. We put it up all over the house. We hang the mistletoe over the door for kissing. Everyone gets presents for everyone else: and does them up in fancy paper. The small children hang up their stockings. Father fills them with good things. We go to church. We come back to Christmas dinner. We have it as our fathers before us. Turkey, Christmas pudding, mincepies, the lot. We pull the crackers. We wear the paper caps of many colours. We listen to The Queen's broadcast. We have our presents. We undo them. Everyone says, 'This is just what I wanted.' We have games. Everyone takes part. We play charades. Half go out and dress up. Half stay in and guess. Hunt the thimble. Musical chairs. Blind man's buff. And the rest. Till bedtime.

Boxing Day. In the morning there is exercise for everyone. Some for a long walk. Some to see the meet of the hunt. In the afternoon we take the children to the pantomime. Back home tired but happy.

iii *Now we are old*

Now we are old. The youngsters are all grown up and married. They have their own families. They are too numerous now to stay in our house overnight. Each family comes to us for the day – on Christmas Eve, on Christmas Day or on Boxing Day. They have Christmas in their own homes. They visit one another. They visit us. They keep

Christmas much as we did. We join them. We are happy watching them. They are keeping up the Christmas spirit. It goes on from one generation to another.

iv 'Goodwill towards men'

Is it worthwhile keeping Christmas Day? Do you mean keeping it as a holiday? Yes, well worth it. As a break in the dark winter? Yes, too. As an occasion for merriment? Yes, of course. As a season for goodwill? Yes, certainly. But its real worth transcends all these. It maintains family ties: and in maintaining them, it strengthens them. These ties are vital for the well-being of our society. In a well-knit family each member upholds the other. The strong support the weak. The good reprove the bad. The prodigal son is welcomed back. They may have differences between one another. But if attacked from outside, they join together. They are like the house that is built upon a rock. They stand firm for all that is right and good. So let us keep up our Christmas-tide. This Christmas and all Christmases to come. In the hope that there may at length be

On earth peace, goodwill towards men.

Section Three

Afterthoughts

1 Plain English

On 9 December 1982 we went to make the Plain English Awards at the Waldorf Hotel. The sponsors were the Plain English Campaign and the National Consumer Council. I presented six genuine awards for good English: and six booby prizes for bad English.

In *The Discipline of Law* I told you something of the value of plain English. Now I enlarge upon it.

1 Brings in Humpty Dumpty

i *The key to success*

To my mind command of language is the key to success, not only in the law, but in the other professions in which words count. It is a sine qua non for statesmen and politicians. Hardly less so for authors and journalists. Lecturers and teachers should have it. So should ministers of religion. Civil servants should be specially versed in it.

ii *A perfect instrument*

Yet we have to our hand a perfect instrument. In his Preface to *The Oxford Book of English Prose*, Sir Arthur Quiller-Couch wrote:

Our fathers have, in the process of centuries, provided this realm, its colonies and wide dependencies, with a speech malleable and pliant as Attic, dignified as Latin, masculine, yet free of Teutonic guttural, capable of being precise as French, dulcet as Italian, sonorous as Spanish, and captaining all these excellencies to its service.

iii *It has become blunted*

This fine instrument has, however, become blunted in use. The reason is because many a person, whether speaker or writer, is thinking too much of *himself:* whereas he ought to be thinking much more of *his hearers or readers.* He uses a word in the meaning which *he himself* puts on it: whereas he should be using it in the meaning which *his hearers or readers* put upon it. He is convinced that his meaning is correct: but he does not realise that it may be incorrect. In so doing he is himself abusing our language.

iv *Humpty Dumpty sat on a wall*

This is the truth which underlies the allegory so delightfully drawn by Lewis Carroll in *Through the Looking-Glass:*

'There's glory for you!' said Humpty Dumpty.
'I don't know what you mean by "glory",' Alice said.
'I meant, "there's a nice knock-down argument for you!"'
'But "glory" doesn't mean "a nice knock-down argument",' Alice objected.
'When *I* use a word,' Humpty Dumpty said in a rather scornful tone, 'it means just what I choose it to mean – neither more nor less.'
'The question is,' said Alice, 'whether you *can* make words mean different things.'
'The question is,' said Humpty Dumpty, 'which is to be master – that's all.'

v *Had a great fall*

So in the allegory Humpty Dumpty makes the word mean just what *he* chooses it to mean. When he does that, he is riding for a fall. He does fall and is broken in pieces. We all know the nursery rhyme:

> Humpty Dumpty sat on a wall,
> Humpty Dumpty had a great fall;
> All the king's horses,
> And all the king's men,
> Couldn't put Humpty together again.

vi *Lord Atkin sees him fall*

One of our greatest judges, Lord Atkin, used that allegory with effect in his celebrated judgment in *Liversidge v Anderson*.[1] The question there was as to the meaning of Regulation 18B. It gave the Home Secretary the power to detain a person 'if he has reasonable cause to believe him to be of hostile origin or association'. Could the courts inquire into the validity of the Home Secretary's decision? The majority of the House of Lords said the courts could not do so. Lord Atkin dissented. He said:

I know of only one authority which might justify the suggested method of construction.

He then gave Humpty Dumpty as that one authority – and gave his own opinion in these words:

After all this long discussion, the question is whether the words 'If a man has' can mean 'If a man thinks he has'. I am of opinion that they cannot.

2 Gives the central principle

i *The central principle*

The central principle is that when you speak or write, you should be thinking all the time of others; that is, of course, the people who are listening to you – in the court-room or the Parliament Chamber or the council-room: or the people who are reading your essay or your opinion or your book. Make their task as easy as you can. There are many pitfalls which you must avoid.

ii *Don't use long words*

The first is, 'Don't use long words', unless you are sure your hearers or readers understand them. You may understand them yourself, but they may not. If your hearer says to himself, 'That is a word I've never heard before. What does it mean?', you have failed. If your reader says, 'I must look it

[1] [1942] AC 206, 245.

up in a dictionary', again you have failed. You have not conveyed your meaning to him.

A lot of speakers and writers do not appreciate that simple truth. They use long words so as to 'show off'. It gives them a feeling of superior knowledge or, at any rate, of a superior vocabulary. By so doing, they go wrong. Once a hearer says, 'He is a very able man but it was all above my head', then the speaker has failed. Even Macaulay was guilty when he said, 'In every human being there is a wish to *ameliorate* his condition'. It was a mistake to use the word 'ameliorate' which some of his readers would not know. He should have used the simple word 'better'.

iii *A one-sided contract*

In many professions there are technical expressions in use. They are called 'terms of art'. But again these should only be used when they are well-known in the profession. A little while ago I heard of a contract being a 'synallagmatic' contract. I had never heard of such a contract before. Nor had any other lawyer of my acquaintance. Nor had the textbook writers. At any rate, their books did not contain the word. I have since looked it up in the dictionary. I believe it only means a two-sided contract; but I am not quite sure about it. Perhaps it is a contract such as that of which I heard my predecessor, Lord Evershed, once say:

This contract is so one-sided that I am surprised to find it written on both sides of the paper.

iv *Humpty Dumpty pays it extra*

At this point I go back to the delightful Lewis Carroll:

After a minute Humpty Dumpty began again. . . . 'Impenetrability! That's what *I* say!'
'Would you tell me, please,' said Alice, 'what that means?'
'Now you talk like a reasonable child,' said Humpty Dumpty, looking very much pleased. 'I meant by "impenetrability" that we've had enough of that subject, and it would be just as well if you'd mention what you mean to do next, as I suppose you don't intend to stop here all the rest of your life.'

'That's a great deal to make one word mean,' Alice said in a thoughtful tone.

'When I make a word do a lot of work like that,' said Humpty Dumpty, 'I always pay it extra.'

'Oh!' said Alice. She was too much puzzled to make any other remark.

v *I just say 'Oh!'*

Like Alice, when I come across a long word which I do not understand I am afraid I often just say 'Oh!' and pass on. This is a mistake. I ought to look it up in the dictionary and so extend my vocabulary.

Particularly if the long word is in a statute you must find out what it means. You must first look to see if there is a definition clause. If it is defined, you have next to see what the definition clause means. It is sometimes long-winded and not much help. If there is no definition clause, then you have to give it the most sensible meaning you can think of.

3 A little more advice

i *Don't use over-long sentences*

If you use an over-long sentence in your speech, you will lose your hearer before you get to the end of it. He will not be concentrating as much as you are. If you write an over-long sentence in your opinion or judgment, the reader will get bemused. He will say to himself, 'I must read that sentence again so as to get the hang of it.' That destroys its effect altogether.

ii *You might lose yourself*

Charles Dickens (who was the master of the short sentence) occasionally used the long sentence to give effect. When Mr Micawber offered to show David Copperfield the way, he used this long one:

'Under the impression,' said Mr Micawber, 'that your peregrinations in this metropolis have not as yet been extensive, and that you might have some difficulty in penetrating the arcana of the Modern Babylon in the direction of the City Road – in short,' said Mr Micawber, in another burst of confidence, 'that you might lose yourself – I shall be happy to call this evening, and install you in the knowledge of the nearest way.'

iii *A booby prize*

Now I would revert to the Plain English Awards of which I told you. I will not say anything of those for good English, but I would like to tell you of one which was awarded a booby prize.

A village had asked for a bus shelter to be provided near the school. This was a sentence in the reply:

The stated requirement for a shelter at this location has been noted, but as you may be aware shelter erection at all locations within West Yorkshire has been constrained in recent times as a result of instructions issued by the West Yorkshire Metropolitan County Council in the light of the Government's cuts in public expenditure and, although it seems likely that the Capital Budget for shelter provision will be enhanced in the forthcoming Financial Year, it is axiomatic that residual requests in respect of prospective shelter sites identified as having priority, notably those named in earlier programmes of shelter erection, will take precedence in any future shelter programme.

iv *'Haigese' in the United States*

There is also a campaign in the United States in favour of plain English. Whereas I have advised you 'Don't use long words' and 'Don't use long sentences', their advice is 'Don't use multisyllabic jargon and verbal distortions.' Which advice do you prefer?

They have coined a new word to describe these contortions. They call them 'Haigese' because Mr Haig, the former Secretary of State, used them so much. This is the illustration they give:

One of Mr Haig's aides asked him for a pay increase. Mr Haig just could not say 'No.' Instead he replied:
'Because of the fluctuational predisposition of your position's productive capacity as juxtaposed to government standards, it would be momentarily injudicious to advocate an increment.'

The perplexed aide replied: 'I don't get it.'
Mr Haig replied: 'That's right.'

4 The moral of it all

i *Plain, simple words and sentences*

The moral of it all is that you should use plain, simple words
and sentences which all your hearers and readers will
understand. You should avoid the roundabout expression
and use instead the direct thrust. Sir Winston Churchill did
not begin his broadcast on 17 June 1940: 'The position in
regard to France is extremely serious.' He began: 'The news
from France is very bad.' He did not end it: 'We have
absolute confidence that eventually the situation will be
restored.' He ended: 'We are sure that in the end all will
come right.'

ii *Present them well*

Not only should you choose your words well. It is also
important that you should present them well. A good speech
can be ruined by a bad delivery. The spoken word is very
different from the written word. Prepare it beforehand. If
you have not done much speaking, you may write it out in
full. But do not read it. And do not learn it by heart. If you
do, you will be thinking of the mechanism of delivery:
whereas you should be thinking of the substance you wish to
convey. When you have gained experience, you will find it
best to make a note of each point that you are going to make.
Speak on it for two or three minutes. Then go on to the next
point. Always think of your hearers. Speak so that they can
understand all you say.

iii *Split them up*

When writing a book or an essay or opinion, you should
break up your pages into paragraphs: and your paragraphs
into sentences. A massive, unbroken page of print is ugly to

the eye and repulsive to the mind. A long unbroken paragraph is indigestible. Split it up into sentences. If you find that you must have a long sentence, break it up with suitable punctuation. Sometimes a dash. At other times a colon or semi-colon. Often a comma. It enables the reader to get the sense more readily.

Never stop at your first draft. Always go through it. See how it reads. Not only to see whether it is accurate but, what is more important, to see if it is clear to the reader. As I have told you, I did this for *What Next in the Law*. So here if you saw my notebook for this book, you would see that I have read and reread it, corrected and recorrected it, a dozen times, before letting it go out.

A good example is to be found from the Law Reports. At one time the judges used to deliver long judgments covering many pages without a break. I was, I think, the first to introduce a new system. I divided each judgment into separate parts: first the facts; second the law. I divided each of those parts into separate headings. I gave each heading a separate title. By so doing, the reader was able to go at once to the heading in which he was interested: and then to the passage material to him.

iv *Avoid unparliamentary language*

There is much variation in the language used in Parliament. In debates it is, or should be, plain and courteous. In statutes it is obscure and complex. In debates it is governed by rules evolved over the centuries. *Erskine May* says that:

Good temper and moderation are the characteristics of parliamentary language. Parliamentary language is never more desirable than when a Member is canvassing the opinions and conduct of his opponents in debate.[1]

He gives examples of expressions which are unparliamentary and call for prompt interference, such as charging a Member with uttering a deliberate falsehood or using abusive language likely to create disorder. *Erskine May* gives a list of

[1] *Parliamentary Practice* (20th edn) p 432.

46 expressions which have caused the Chair to intervene from time to time, either by compelling the withdrawal of the offending words, or, in default, by suspension. They include calling an honourable member a 'blackguard', 'cad', 'cheeky young pup', 'coward', 'dog', 'guttersnipe' or 'rat'; or describing his conduct as 'behaving like a jackass' or 'lousy'.[1]

You will do well to avoid the use of unparliamentary language.

---

[1] (19th edn) p 445. These expressions are, sadly, not included in the most recent, 20th, edition.

2 After Christmas – the water strike

Introduction

After Christmas I carried on despite my age. On 23 January 1983 I was 84. My one disability was the arthritis in my right hip. It had become so bad that I was very lame. I consulted Mr Sweetnam, one of the best surgeons in this field. He said that the time had come when I should have an operation to replace the arthritic hip with an artificial one. It was arranged for 1 March 1983 at King Edward VII's Hospital for Officers. I was last in that hospital in 1928 when I went as a young barrister (qualifying as an ex-officer) to have my tonsils removed. Sister Agnes (who founded it) was then alive. She used to hold the hand of each of us young ex-officers as we went under the anaesthetic.

1 My usual things

i *First come I*

Meanwhile, pending the operation, I did all my usual things. I went to Lincoln to address the Lincolnshire Law Society. I stayed in the Judges' Lodgings – between the Castle and the Cathedral – where I had stayed as a Judge of Assize 38 years before. I went to Cambridge to address the Cambridge Union Society. I stayed with my dear friend Bill Wade, the Master of Gonville and Caius College. By his book on *Administrative Law* he has had immense influence on the development of the subject. Speaking to the students I told

them of a rhyme suggested to me by Mr Justice Walton
(adapted from the well-known one about Benjamin Jowett
of Balliol):

> First come I; my name is Denning,
> What I don't know is not worth kenning.
> Twice a day I make new law,
> If there were time I'd make much more.[1]

The students enjoyed it hugely.

Joan and I went to Newquay for the centenary of the
Cornwall Law Society. We went across the Tamar as we had
done when I went to Bodmin as the Judge of Assize 37 years
before.

ii *A water strike*

But during this time there was a water strike. It brought me
into the news once again. The manual workers in the water
industry came out on strike. By all accounts in the
newspapers, they had previously agreed to arbitrate. But
they went back on it. They refused to enter into a binding
arbitration. They were on strike to enforce their claim.

These manual workers refused to repair broken or burst
water pipes. Many householders had to go without water or
had to get it in buckets some way off. There was much
distress and inconvenience and even danger to health.

2 I am asked a question

i *Can we repair the pipes ourselves?*

On Sunday 13 February 1983 Mr Patrick Evershed telephoned me around lunchtime. He said:

I am a cousin of your predecessor Lord Evershed. In our street in Pimlico
we have been without water for two days. Can we repair the pipes

[1] Beeching, *The Masque of Balliol:*
  First come I; my name is Jowett.
  There's no knowledge but I know it.
  I am Master of this college:
  What I don't know isn't knowledge.

ourselves or employ contractors to do it? If we do so, can we charge the expense to the water authority?

ii '*Yes – you can*'

At once on the Sunday afternoon I looked up the books in my library. It took me two hours. Then I telephoned Mr Evershed at about 3.30 pm and gave him my answer. It was on these lines:

The water authority are under a statutory duty to provide a supply of wholesome water in pipes to every part of their district in which there are houses or schools.

It is no answer for them to say that their own men are on strike. They should employ contractors to repair the pipes or get them repaired in some way or other.

If the water authority do not fulfil this duty, the householders are entitled to repair the pipes themselves or employ contractors for the purpose. On so doing they will be entitled to charge the water authority with the expense.

iii *What is the authority for it?*

The press soon got to know of my answer. Journalists telephoned repeatedly asking: What is your authority for saying this? I gave them it quite shortly, but I think it may interest you if I tell you the result of my two-hour research. I knew a good deal of the problem already. So it took me less time than it might do others. There are two lines of authority.

3 The first line of authority

In my researches I found that there was much learning on the defence of 'necessity'. One line favoured it. The other line was against it. I tell you now of the first line.

i *The Great Fire of London*

In the Great Fire of London in 1666 when the flames were raging through the city, it was quite lawful for the citizens to pull down the intervening houses so as to stop the fire from spreading. This pulling down would have been actionable as a trespass and perhaps punishable as malicious damage, but the 'necessity' to stop the fire gave a defence.

ii *Jettisoning cargo*

Again, when there is a storm at sea and the master jettisons some of the cargo – he throws it overboard so as to lighten the ship – he is guilty of no wrong. If the cargo-owner complains, the master has a defence of necessity, see *Mouse's* case.[1] In these cases the defence depends on the state of things when the act is done. If any reasonable person would think it reasonable to act in this way, that is sufficient. It was so decided in *Cope v Sharpe (No. 2)*.[2]

iii *The jail is on fire*

There is an amusing case where the defence of necessity was allowed. It is from the Year Book of 1499. A jail caught fire and a prisoner broke down the door in order to escape from the fire. Although the statute made prison-breaking a felony, he was held to have a defence of necessity: 'for he is not to be hanged because he would not stay to be burned.'

iv *A mother's life*

There is an important modern case where the defence of necessity was allowed. It is *R v Bourne*.[3] A young girl was raped and became pregnant in consequence. Dr Bourne operated so as to procure an abortion. He said that 'in his opinion the continuance of the pregnancy would probably cause serious injury to the girl, injury so serious as to justify the removal of the pregnancy at a time when the operation could be performed without any risk to the girl and under favourable conditions.' He was held to have the defence of necessity.

[1] (1608) 12 Co Rep 63.
[2] [1912] 1 KB 496.
[3] [1939] 1 KB 687, 688.

4 The second line of authority

But those cases in the first line are exceptional.

i *Squatters cannot raise the defence of 'necessity'*

In a case where squatters claimed that they were in dire need of housing and entered an empty house to sleep, the Court of Appeal refused to admit the defence of necessity. In *Southwark London Borough Council v Williams*[1] I said:

The doctrine so enunciated must, however, be carefully circumscribed. Else necessity would open the door to many an excuse. It was for this reason that it was not admitted in *R v Dudley and Stephens* (1884) 14 QBD 273, where the three shipwrecked sailors, in extreme despair, killed the cabin boy and ate him to save their own lives. They were held guilty of murder. The killing was not justified by necessity. Similarly, when a man, who is starving, enters a house and takes food in order to keep himself alive. Our English law does not admit the defence of necessity. It holds him guilty of larceny. Lord Hale said that 'if a person, being under necessity for want of victuals, or clothes, shall upon that account clandestinely, and animo furandi, steal another man's food, it is felony . . .': Hale *Pleas of Crown*, i. 54. The reason is because, if hunger were once allowed to be an excuse for stealing, it would open a way through which all kinds of disorder and lawlessness would pass. So here. If homelessness were once admitted as a defence to trespass, no one's house could be safe. Necessity would open a door which no man could shut. It would not only be those in extreme need who would enter. There would be others who would imagine that they were in need, or would invent a need, so as to gain entry. Each man would say his need was greater than the next man's. The plea would be an excuse for all sorts of wrongdoing. So the courts must, for the sake of law and order, take a firm stand. They must refuse to admit the plea of necessity to the hungry and the homeless: and trust that their distress will be relieved by the charitable and the good.

ii *The fire engine crashes the lights*

When the driver of a fire engine is answering an emergency call and comes to traffic lights which are at red, is he at liberty to cross them? In *Buckoke v Greater London Council*,[2] I answered it in this way:

During the argument I raised the question: Might not the driver of a fire

[1] [1971] Ch 734, 743.
[2] [1971] Ch 655, 668.

70

engine be able to raise the defence of necessity? I put this illustration: A driver of a fire escape with ladders approaches the traffic lights. He sees 200 yards down the road a blazing house with a man at an upstairs window in extreme peril. The road is clear in all directions. At that moment the lights turn red. Is the driver to wait for 60 seconds, or more, for the lights to turn green? If the driver waits for that time, the man's life will be lost. I suggested to both counsel that the driver might be excused in crossing the lights to save the man. He might have the defence of necessity. Both counsel denied it. They would not allow him any defence in law. The circumstances went to mitigation, they said, and did not take away his guilt. If counsel are correct – and I accept that they are – nevertheless such a man should not be prosecuted. He should be congratulated.

Is the defence of 'necessity' available?

i *'Yes – it is'*

After Mr Evershed's telephone call, I found in my library those two lines of authority. I had to make up my mind which line was to apply in the water strike. I decided in favour of the defence of necessity. I realised that prima facie it is a criminal offence to break up roads without the permission of the highway authorities or to interfere with water pipes without the consent of the water authorities, but I thought that the defence of necessity would avail Mr Evershed. It seems to me that, as a result of the cases, there are some criminal offences in which the defence of necessity is available: and that this was just one of them. The determining factor to my mind was the fact that water supply is an essential service. It is essential to the life of the community. The water authorities are put by Parliament under the responsibility of maintaining it. If that essential service is interrupted – and the authorities do not do their duty to restore the service – the householders affected are entitled to do whatever is reasonably necessary to avoid danger or injury – or, I would add, inconvenience – to themselves or their families. In short, they can restore the services themselves.

ii *Send in the bill*

Many of the newspapers asked the question: If the householders do the work themselves, or employ contractors to do it, can they send the bill in to the water authority? My answer was 'Yes.' There is a line of authority which says that if a person does not do his duty – and in consequence another justifiably does it for him – then he can charge the expense to the one who should have done it. In the old days it was put upon a requirement implied in law but in modern times it is because it is just and reasonable having regard to the relationship of the parties, see *Brook's Wharf v Goodman Bros.*[1]

iii *Are water rates payable?*

Another frequent question was: Are we bound to pay the water rates if we do not get the water? My answer was 'Yes.' You are bound to pay the water rates: but you are entitled to compensation from the water authority for the damage you have suffered and the inconvenience to which you have been put.

6 My advice is welcomed

i *By newspapers and television*

The newspapers and television took it up avidly. All day on Monday 14 February the telephone was ringing. We had the television people here at 'The Lawn'. I went to the studio in Southampton. Everywhere there was a warm welcome. To take a few headlines:

The Daily Telegraph
'Denning's water challenge "Repair pipes and send in bill"'

The Times had a neat little cartoon:
'It's the PLUMBER – and he's brought LORD DENNING with him'

[1] [1937] 1 KB 534.

The Guardian
'Plumber wanted but only the best need apply'
'Denning "ruling" may be right'

The Daily Mail
'Like a St. George of today, suddenly he's back in battle on the people's side'
'Denning takes on another dragon'

Daily Express
'Don't just sit there FIX IT! Denning's advice to water-hit Britons'

ii *But not by the water authorities*

There was coolness on the part of the authorities. The water authorities said:

Lord Denning is retired and should stay that way.

The Junior Environment Minister said in Parliament:

With all respect to the former Master of the Rolls I must warn householders they cannot go on digging up highways at will.

The water authorities added their warning. They said it was dangerous for householders to repair the pipes themselves. This came ill from them since it was their own failure to repair the pipes which had caused all the trouble.

iii *'Do it yourself'*

In many parts of the country householders took my advice. They made 'do it yourself (DIY)' repairs to the mains. But in London and other big towns the pipes are complex and need expert contractors. The householders tried to get contractors to do the repairs. But the contractors were afraid to undertake the work. They feared that trade unionists would 'black' any contractor who did repair the pipes. Such is the power of trade unions.

iv *The outcome*

At one time it was suggested that, if householders repaired the pipes, the strike would crumble. But it did not. The trade unions won. They refused binding arbitration. There was an inquiry on lines which suited them. As a result the workers got a big increase in their wages. They had succeeded in their claim. Victory for them. Defeat for the Government.

v *A Pyrrhic victory*

It is likely to turn out to be a Pyrrhic victory. Soon afterwards the Government announced that they were considering legislation to outlaw strikes by workers in essential industries. This is desirable – and indeed necessary – if our England is to be a place fit to live in.

7 Inundated with letters

All this arose after I retired from my office as Master of the Rolls. It looked to many as if I was available to give free legal advice on request. I was inundated with letters on subjects of all kinds. I had to decline most of them. But the commentary in *Private Eye* in February 1983 is so amusing that, with their permission I would repeat it for you:

YOUR LEGAL QUERIES ANSWERED
Dear Lord Denning,
    I've had no water in my home for 6 weeks.
    Am I within my rights to call in Private Contractors to ensure the supply to my home?
                            Yours faithfully,
                            Reginald Plunkett-Hythe,
                            Surbiton

Yes, you are. I have looked up in my law books and in 1311 it was decreed that each freeholder has the right to 'mend ye conduits and aqueducts and ye pipes wheresoever they may be, be they below the ground or above the ground. Wheresoever they may be, ye do no wrongdoing if ye do mend them.'
    That is the law as I understand it.

Dear Lord Denning,
    For the last two weeks policemen have been in my back garden

digging it up. As an ex-policeman I would like to ask, are they entitled to do this, or am I protected by the law of trespass?

D.N.

North London.

The law of the land quite clearly states 'No person nor persons, be they whomsoever they may be, shall commit Trestrail on the freehold of any citizen, be he high or low.' That is the law.

Dear Lord Denning,

We are commuters on the Southern Railway and we find ourselves increasingly irritated by the failure of British Rail to run the trains on time.

With some friends of ours we have just made our own train and we intend to run a service between Sevenoaks and Charing X.

Is this legal?

Doris and Maurice McWhirter,

Sevenoaks.

Yes it be so. I have consulted my books and discovered another statute from the days of King Ethelbarg in which he states that 'any journeyman, scrivener, franklin or merchantman, can in full righteousness of legalitee fashion unto himselfe a railway engine and drive it up and down the Southern Regione without lette or hindrance wheresoever he may choose to go, nor shall any Aslef varlet nor guildsman, ye Buckton and ye like, interfere with his progress, under paine of death.'

That is the law.

If you have a legal query you would like answered send it to Lord Denning, Dunjudgin', Whitchurch, Hants. (First left past the church.)

My answer is, of course, that I do not give legal advice. I tell everyone with a problem to consult a solicitor.

3 The Sikh boy's turban

Introduction

In the Race Relations Act 1976 Parliament tackled the problem of racial discrimination. It made it unlawful to discriminate on 'racial grounds' or against a 'racial group'. 'Racial' is defined so as to prohibit discrimination on the grounds of colour, race, nationality or 'ethnic or national origins'.

There is the rub. 'Ethnic' is a word of uncertain meaning. It has changed its meaning from time to time. I would expect that in using the words 'ethnic origins' Parliament had in mind particularly the Jews. There must be no discrimination against the Jews in England. Anti-semitism must not be allowed. It has produced great evils elsewhere. It must not be allowed here.

In a leading case just before my retirement we had to consider its application to the Sikhs. Our decision led to much discussion after my retirement. So I would tell you about it as part of my afterthoughts.

1 The facts

i *The headmaster's refusal*

On the last day but one of the summer term, 29 July 1982, we delivered judgment in *Mandla (Sewa Singh) v Dowell Lee*,[1]

[1] [1982] 3 WLR 932.

about a Sikh boy's turban. Could a Sikh schoolboy insist on wearing a turban at school? We said 'No.' These were the facts as I stated them in the Court of Appeal (page 934):

Sewa Singh Mandla, the first plaintiff, is a Sikh and rightly proud of it. He is a solicitor of the Supreme Court, practising in Birmingham. In 1978 he applied to send his son Gurinder, the second plaintiff, to a private school in Birmingham called the Park Grove School. The boy was then aged 13. The school was very suitable for him. It had a high reputation. It took boys of all races. There were 305 boys altogether. Over 200 were English, but there were many others. Five were Sikhs, 34 Hindus, 16 Persians, six negroes, seven Chinese and about 15 from European countries.

Mr Mandla took his son to see the headmaster. Both he and his son were wearing their turbans. The headmaster felt that it might give rise to difficulties if the boy wore his turban in school. He asked the father: 'Will you consent to his removing his turban and cutting his hair?' The father said: 'No. That is completely out of the question.' The headmaster said that he would think about it. Then on 24 July 1978, he wrote:

'Thank you for bringing your son to see me. As I promised, I have given much thought to the problem and I have reluctantly come to the conclusion that on balance it would be unwise to relax the school rules with regard to uniform. At the moment I do not see any way in which it would be possible to reconcile the two conflicting requirements. May I wish you well in your efforts to promote harmony and peace, and I hope you find a suitable school for your son without difficulty.'

Mr Mandla did find another school for his son where he is allowed to wear his turban. So all is now well with them. But Mr Mandla reported the headmaster to the Commission for Racial Equality. They took the matter up with the headmaster. On 19 September 1978, he wrote this letter:

'To make my position quite clear, the boy was not rejected because he was a Sikh since we do not make racial distinctions and we have several Sikhs in the school. It was the turban that was rejected, and I believe your Acts cover people, not clothes.'

ii *The Commission for Racial Equality*

The Commission, however, did not let the matter rest. They decided to assist Mr Mandla in legal proceedings against the headmaster. With their assistance in money and advice Mr Mandla issued proceedings against the headmaster of the school in the Birmingham County Court. He claimed damages limited to £500 and a declaration that the defendants had committed an act of unlawful discrimination. The judge heard the case for five days in February and June 1980, with many witnesses and much argument. The judge dismissed the claim.

The Commission for Racial Equality – in Mr Mandla's name – appealed to the Court of Appeal. The headmaster appeared before us in person. He had not the means to instruct counsel and solicitors. He put his case moderately and with restraint. He had himself done much research in the India Office Library and elsewhere. It must have taken him many hours and many days.

iii *The decision of the Court of Appeal*

We affirmed the decision of the judge. He came to his decision as a result of all the evidence before him. So did we. We held that the Sikhs were not a racial group. I said (page 938):

On all this evidence, it is plain to me that the Sikhs, as a group, cannot be distinguished from others in the Punjab by reference to any racial characteristic whatever. They are only to be distinguished by their religion and culture. That is not an ethnic difference at all.

2 The reaction of the Sikhs

i *The Sikhs are very upset*

The Sikhs were very upset by this ruling. They had been successful in many cases in wearing their turbans. When Parliament passed a law requiring that everyone on a motorcycle should wear a crash helmet, the Sikhs protested. They succeeded in getting an amending Act by which they could dispense with crash helmets and wear their turbans. Next, although it is the custom for all barristers and judges to wear wigs in court, the Sikhs do not follow that custom. They wear their turbans. No one objects. When all bus conductors in Wolverhampton were required to wear uniform caps, the

Sikhs declined. They were allowed to wear their turbans. Likewise, a Sikh policeman need not wear a helmet. He can wear a turban.

ii *They call it an 'outrageous ruling'*

On 31 July 1982 – the second day after our ruling – *The Times* came out with a headline:

DENNING'S TURBAN-BOY RULING ANGERS SIKHS

This was followed by an article which reported that the secretary of the supreme council of the Sikhs in Britain said that

the ruling was absolutely outrageous and that Lord Denning was living up to his reputation as a judge who was against ethnic minorities.

iii *They organise a national protest*

The Sikhs organised a national protest march. They assembled in thousands at Speaker's Corner in Hyde Park. They marched to 10 Downing Street and presented a petition. Dignified, bearded, turbaned Sikhs announced the plan. This is what the leaflet said:

CALL FOR NATIONAL PROTEST
MARCH
on Sunday 10th October, 1982

'AGAINST LORD DENNING'S RULING
AGAINST THE SIKHS'

ASSEMBLE AT HYDE PARK SPEAKERS
CORNER LONDON AT 12.30 p.m.
PRESS INTERVIEWS AND SPEECHES by
EMINENT PEOPLE FROM VARIOUS COMMUNITIES

Then PROCESSION Starts with the blessing of

SANT BABA PURAN SINGH JI
to 10, Downing Street,

Where a PETITION will be presented to
the PRIME MINISTER along with 75,000 or more
signatures against this ruling.

Day after day there were letters in the newspapers protesting against 'Lord Denning's ruling'. This was a mistake. It was not my ruling. It was the ruling of the Court of Appeal. The Court included two Lords Justices of the first quality, Lords Justices Oliver and Kerr.

3 The ruling was contrary to the intention of Parliament

It now appears that our ruling was contrary to the intention of Parliament. This was quite unknown to us in the Court of Appeal.

i *The proceedings in Parliament*

Many commentators were quick to point out that the 'Denning ruling' was contrary to the intention of Parliament. *The Times* in its article on 31 July 1982 said this:

Race relations experts yesterday pointed to the White Paper on racial discrimination, which preceded the 1976 Act, and specifically mentioned the wearing of turbans as an area which would be covered by the legislation.

On the following day, Sunday 1 August, *The Observer* had an article showing that they had examined the White Paper and all the proceedings in Parliament. They came out with this headline:

SIKH BOY: DENNING THWARTS COMMONS

and then said:

Lord Denning's judgment in the Court of Appeal last week that Britain's Sikh community is not a 'racial group' covered by the Race Relations Act is clearly contrary to Parliament's intention when the Act was passed in 1976.

In the White Paper which preceded legislation, the Labour Government expressly referred to its intention to protect people who were discriminated against for wearing turbans. Ministers confirmed that interpretation of the Bill while it was going through the Commons.

The marchers to Downing Street knew all about it too. They carried placards saying:

PARLIAMENT! HONOUR YOUR PLEDGE TO THE SIKHS

ii *The views of Members*

The Sikhs canvassed the views of many leading Members of Parliament and issued a press statement showing that all of them condemned the ruling. According to it, Mr Roy Hattersley, the Shadow Home Secretary, said:

Everyone who believes in a free society must despise the recent ruling by Lord Denning which effectively takes away from the Sikh Community the right to wear a turban. . . . No one can seriously doubt that the Sikhs are a separate race with a specifically identifiable culture and religion. I am confident that the next Labour Government will, therefore, incorporate those changes. . . .

Mr David Steel, the leader of the Liberal Party, said:

It is deeply regrettable that one of Lord Denning's final judgments should undermine the fundamental rights for the Sikhs to uphold a basic religious custom. I hope this bizarre judgment will be reversed on appeal, but if not we shall press for legislation at the earliest opportunity. . . .

The press statement added:

Although Honourable Minister Timothy Raison (Minister of State at the Home Office) has said that the judgment of Denning's is subject matter of an Appeal and is as such sub judice, yet Mr Timothy Raison has recently said that the records of the House of Commons debate make it clear that the 1976 Race Relations Act was intended to protect Sikhs from discrimination from wearing turbans.

4 The knowledge of the courts

i *The Court of Appeal did not know*

None of the parliamentary proceedings were known to the Court of Appeal. I have often said that the judges ought to be able to consult Hansard so as to see what the intention of Parliament was. But the House of Lords has repeatedly said that was wrong. So the Court of Appeal were told nothing of the White Paper or of the proceedings in the House of Commons. Nor was the trial judge told. If we had been told of them, or if the judge had been told of them, or if we had consulted them ourselves, it would certainly have influenced us. There would have been no occasion for the newspaper to say: 'SIKH BOY: DENNING THWARTS COMMONS'. It was never any part of our duty or business to thwart the Commons. Rather, it was our duty to carry out the intention of Parliament. If we had known of those proceedings, we might well have come to a different conclusion, and thereby saved any appeal to the House of Lords and any of the trouble that ensued as a result of our decision.

ii *Did the Lords know?*

The Commission for Racial Equality went to the House of Lords and asked for leave to appeal. They were given it. The House of Lords unanimously reversed our decision.[1] I cannot help asking myself: Did the House of Lords know about the White Paper and the proceedings in Parliament? Not *directly* of course. They would not be referred to them, nor would they consult them themselves. But would they have known *indirectly?* If they had read the newspapers they would have seen the flood of criticisms against the Court of Appeal's decision. They would have read that the Court of Appeal's ruling was contrary to the intention of Parliament. They would have read that it was the intention of Parliament that the Sikhs should be regarded as a 'racial group'. They would have seen that both Government and Opposition had intimated that they would introduce legislation to offset the decision of the Court of Appeal. I am tempted to suggest that if they do not read the newspapers, they must be sitting in an ivory tower. To my mind, that is not the right place for a judge to sit.

[1] [1983] 2 WLR 620.

iii *Do they read the newspapers?*

There is one sentence in the judgment of Lord Fraser of Tullybelton in the House of Lords which shows that their Lordships *do* read the newspapers. In analysing the meaning of the words 'ethnic group', he referred to the dictionary definitions and rejected all of them. He said:[1]

> . . . in seeking for the true meaning of 'ethnic' in the statute, we are not tied to the precise definition in any dictionary. The value of the 1972 definition is, in my view, that it shows that ethnic has come to be commonly used in a sense appreciably wider than the strictly racial or biological.

And then he made this illuminating comment:

> That appears to me to be consistent with the ordinary experience of those who read newspapers at the present day. In my opinion, the word 'ethnic' still retains a racial flavour but it is used nowadays in an extended sense to include other characteristics which may be commonly thought of as being associated with common racial origin.

Now, reading that paragraph, it seems to me that the House of Lords were being guided by what they thought was the 'ordinary experience of those who read newspapers at the present day.' I ask myself: How are the Lords themselves to find out what is the view taken by 'those who read newspapers'? They must be putting themselves into the same position as newspaper readers. In some branches of the law we look for the meaning of the ordinary 'reasonable man'. Here the Lords are looking for the meaning given by the 'ordinary newspaper reader'. I should have thought that, on reading the criticisms of our decision, most newspaper readers would have said: 'The Court of Appeal were quite wrong. The Lords ought to reverse their decision.'

Not that I doubt the wisdom of judges reading the newspapers. I think they ought to read them, so as to keep in touch with public opinion. The law ought to accord with the right public opinion of today, and not be against it. Otherwise, it will not be held in respect.

[1] [1983] 2 WLR 620, 625.

5 The reasoning of the Lords

i *They follow a decision about the Jews*

The House of Lords were referred to a decision of the Court of Appeal in New Zealand in *King-Ansell v Police*.[1] The National Socialist Party of New Zealand had issued a pamphlet which contained inflammatory propaganda against 'the Jews'. The publisher was charged with an offence of publishing matter likely to excite ill-will against a group 'on the ground of the ethnic origins of the group'. The New Zealand Court of Appeal held that the Jews were a group of 'ethnic origins'. The Court of Appeal in England were not referred to that case, but I am sure we would have held the same. Everybody would agree with it. Starting from that case, Lord Fraser of Tullybelton gave a definition in words which covered the Jews. He said:[2]

For a group to constitute an ethnic group in the sense of the Act of 1976, it must, in my opinion, regard itself, and be regarded by others, as a distinct community by virtue of certain characteristics. Some of these characteristics are essential; others are not essential but one or more of them will commonly be found and will help to distinguish the group from the surrounding community. The conditions which appear to me to be essential are these: (1) a long shared history, of which the group is conscious as distinguishing it from other groups, and the memory of which it keeps alive; (2) a cultural tradition of its own, including family and social customs and manners, often but not necessarily associated with religious observance. In addition to those two essential character- istics the following characteristics are, in my opinion, relevant; (3) either a common geographical origin, or descent from a small number of common ancestors; (4) a common language, not necessarily peculiar to the group; (5) a common literature peculiar to the group; (6) a common religion different from that of neighbouring groups or from the general community surrounding it; (7) being a minority or being an oppressed or a dominant group within a larger community, for example a conquered people (say, the inhabitants of England shortly after the Norman conquest) and their conquerors might both be ethnic groups.

ii *Does it cover the Sikhs?*

The Jews have all those characteristics – but have the Sikhs?

[1] [1979] 2 NZLR 531.
[2] [1983] 2 WLR 620, 625.

On the reasoning of the Court of Appeal it would seem that the Sikhs were different from the Jews because anyone can become a Sikh or not as he chooses, whereas a man cannot be a Jew by choice. He is born a Jew. Lord Justice Oliver put the view of the Court of appeal in these words (page 941):

. . . Mr Irvine (counsel for Mr Mandla) may be right in saying that 'ethnic', as a word on its own, embraces more than a merely racial concept – why otherwise, he asks, does the legislature use the word as an alternative to 'racial' or 'national'? – and I would accept that it embraces, perhaps, notions of cultural or linguistic community. Nevertheless, in its popular meaning, it does, in my judgment, involve essentially a racial concept – the concept of something with which the members of the group are born; some fixed or inherited characteristic. I do not believe that the man in the street would apply the word 'ethnic' to a characteristic which the propositus could assume or reject as a matter of choice. No one, for instance, in ordinary speech, would describe a member of the Church of England or the Conservative Party as a member of an ethnic group.

Now that is a fortiori the case, as it seems to me, when one uses the expression 'ethnic origins'. What is embraced in that expression, to my mind, is the notion of a group distinguished by some peculiarity of birth, perhaps as a result of intermarriage within a community, but lacking any element of free-will. It seems to me entirely inappropriate to describe a group into and out of which anyone may travel as a matter of free choice; and freedom of choice – to join or not to join, to remain or to leave – is inherent in the whole philosophy of Sikhism.

iii *It is widened so as to cover them*

The House of Lords widened the concept of 'ethnic group' in these later words of Lord Fraser of Tullybelton (page 625):

Provided a person who joins the group feels himself or herself to be a member of it, and is accepted by other members, then he is, for the purposes of the Act, a member.

By those words the House of Lords to my mind expanded the meaning of 'ethnic group' beyond that given to it by the Court of Appeal. Nevertheless, I would not complain of their decision. For we now know that Parliament in passing the Race Relations Act 1976, intended that the words 'ethnic origins' should include the Sikhs.

6 The reasoning on 'justifiable'

Although that was the main ground of decision, nevertheless there was another important point to be considered – namely, whether the conduct of the headmaster was in all the circumstances justifiable. The statute allows a defence to a person who can show that what he did was justifiable.

i *In the Court of Appeal*

In the Court of Appeal, Lord Justice Oliver thought it was. He said this (page 942):

. . . Mr Dowell Lee has put forward a number of considerations of varying cogency to justify his decision, including the not unreasonable one that, all other considerations apart, the school curriculum includes participation in sports such as swimming and rugby football which, almost of necessity, involve the removal of the turban. . . . For my part, I am far from persuaded that the judge was wrong in concluding that the condition was, in any event, a justifiable one.

ii *In the Lords*

In the House of Lords, Lord Fraser of Tullybelton was sympathetic to the view that the action of the headmaster was justifiable. He said (pages 628–629):

. . . Regarded purely from the point of view of the headmaster, it was no doubt perfectly justifiable. He explained that he had no intention of discriminating against Sikhs. . . . The reasons for having a school uniform were largely reasons of practical convenience – to minimise external differences between races and social classes, to discourage the 'competitive fashions' which he said tend to exist in a teenage community, and to present a Christian image of the school to outsiders, including prospective parents. . . .

Lord Fraser went on to say that the headmaster had said, as more serious justification, that he sought to run a Christian school, accepting pupils of all religions and races, and he objected to the turban on the ground that it was an outward manifestation of a non–Christian faith. Indeed, he regarded it as a challenge to that faith. Then Lord Fraser included this important statement:

I have much sympathy with the headmaster on this part of the case and I would have been glad to find that the rule was justifiable within the meaning of the statute, if I could have done so. But in my opinion that is impossible.

iii *A welcome decision*

So in the long run the House of Lords reversed both the judge and the Court of Appeal entirely. Their decision was welcomed by the Government because it relieved them from having to consider any legislation upon the point. It was in accord with the intention of Parliament when the Act was passed.

Book Two

Discipline up to Date

Statutory Interpretation again to the Fore

Introduction

Since my retirement the problem of statutory interpretation has come again to the fore. It has been debated in Parliament. It has been considered in the courts. The time is ripe for it to be reviewed. In *The Discipline of Law* I advocated a change. Instead of the old grammatical approach, I suggested there should be the modern purposive approach. That was over four years ago. Since that time the tide at first swept in favour of a purposive approach: but of late it has ebbed again in favour of a grammatical approach.

There is more in this than meets the eye. The Lord Chancellor, Lord Hailsham of Saint Marylebone, has recently suggested that at bottom the difference is of constitutional significance. This may well be true. It can be tested by asking this question: If Parliament has failed to provide for something unforeseen – so that there is a gap in the statute – can that gap be filled by the judges, or must there be an amending Act? Does our constitution authorise the judges to legislate by themselves filling in the gap?

Since I wrote *The Discipline of Law* there have been some cases of the first importance which highlight the problem. I would like to tell you of them – so as to show you the conflicting views.

1 The present obscurity

i *Is a lawyer necessary?*

I start with this principle: Every statute passed by Parliament should be expressed in such words that all those affected by them should understand them. It should not be necessary for anyone to run off to a lawyer. But that principle is broken upon every page of the statute book. No man should trust to his own unaided interpretation of a statute. He is almost sure to be wrong. He should go to his lawyer. Even then his lawyer will often say: 'This is too difficult for me. We must take counsel's opinion.' Then counsel will say: 'I cannot be sure. It depends on what the judge will say.' The judge will do his best. He has to give an answer one way or the other. But it will not stop with the judge. He may be reversed by the Court of Appeal. They may be reversed by the House of Lords – by three to two. Such is the uncertainty of statutory interpretation. It takes an excursion to the House of Lords to get a final answer. Ninety per cent of the cases that come before the courts are on the interpretation of one statute or another.

The need for lawyers is well shown by the story told by John Maynard Keynes. He went to the great conference on Money at Bretton Woods, accompanied only by his secretary. His American friends asked him: 'Where is your lawyer?' 'I haven't got one,' said Keynes. 'Who then does your thinking for you?'

ii *Blame the draftsmen*

Time after time when a judge finds it difficult to interpret a statute he blames the draftsman of it. Two instances will suffice. The first is the robust saying of Lord Justice Scrutton in *Roe v Russell*.[1] I was in the court and heard him say it:

I regret that I cannot order the costs to be paid by the draftsmen of the Rent Restriction Acts, and the members of the Legislature who passed them, and are responsible for the obscurity of the Acts.

[1] [1928] 2 KB 117, 130.

94

The other is the elegant sentence of Lord Justice Russell in *Camrose (Viscount) v Basingstoke Corpn*[1] on a section of the Land Compensation Act. He was sitting beside me. He said:

> The drafting of this section appears to me calculated to postpone as long as possible comprehension of its purport.

iii *Blame the judges*

But in truth the judges ought not to blame the draftsmen overmuch. They ought to blame themselves or their predecessors in their judicial seats. The reason why draftsmen have become so difficult is because the judges have for years expected too much of them. The judges require certainty above all else. They think that a statute should provide for every contingency down to the very last detail. In former times if there was an omission by oversight – or due to lack of foresight – the judges used to say: 'There is a lacuna in the statute. We can do nothing about it.' What is a lacuna? You might think that it was an animal of some kind which had eaten a hole in the statute. But it is only the Latin for a gap. Nowadays the judges are more plain-spoken. If there is an oversight – or lack of foresight – the judge will say: 'There is a gap. We cannot fill it.'

iv *The duty of the draftsman*

Faced with this attitude of the judges, what is the duty of the draftsman? It was well stated by Sir Ernest Gowers in his *Plain Words*.[2] It is his duty

> to try to imagine every possible combination of circumstances to which his words might apply and every conceivable misinterpretation that might be put on them, and to take precautions accordingly. . . . All the time he must keep his eye on the rules of legal interpretation and the case-law on the meaning of particular words [and on the previous statutes on the same subject-matter], and choose his phraseology to fit them. . . . No one can expect pretty writing from anyone thus burdened.

[1] [1966] 1 WLR 1100, 1110.
[2] (1948) HMSO 63–108.

v '*A monstrous legislative morass*'

Such being the duty of the draftsman, the end of it is that he produces a mass of verbiage which is often unintelligible. I remember well the case of *Davy v Leeds Corpn*[1] where Leeds Corporation were clearing a large area of slums near the centre of the city. What compensation was payable to the owners of the houses? We gave judgment straightway. I spoke plainly (at page 1222):

I must say that rarely have I come across such a mass of obscurity, even in a statute. I cannot conceive how any ordinary person can be expected to understand it.

I was delighted with the picturesque metaphor with which Lord Justice Harman followed me:

To reach a conclusion on this matter involved the court in wading through a monstrous legislative morass, staggering from stone to stone and ignoring the marsh gas exhaling from the forest of schedules lining the way on each side. I regarded it at one time, I must confess, as a slough of despond through which the court would never drag its feet, but I have, by leaping from tussock to tussock as best I might, eventually, pale and exhausted, reached the other side where I find myself, I am glad to say, at the same point as that arrived at with more agility by my Lord.

There are hundreds of statutes in which the judges have to wade through such a 'monstrous legislative morass'.

vi *Another booby prize*

I would like to tell you of another booby prize which was awarded in the Plain English competition. It was awarded to the parliamentary draftsmen who drafted the Criminal Justice Act 1982. It was enacted as recently as 28 October 1982. It contained a section which was intended to increase fines for summary offences. That section contained one sentence of ten lines without a comma:

An enactment in which section 31(6) and (7) of the Criminal Law Act 1977 (pre-1949 enactments) produced the same fine or maximum fine for different convictions shall be treated for the purposes of this section as if

[1] [1964] 1 WLR 1218.

there were omitted from it so much of it as before 29th July 1977 had the effect that a person guilty of an offence under it was liable on summary conviction to a fine or maximum fine less than the highest fine or maximum fine to which he would have been liable if his conviction had satisfied the conditions required for the imposition of the highest fine or maximum fine.

It needs a day's work to understand it.

vii *Lord Renton's Committee*

The situation became so bad that in 1973 a Committee was appointed under Sir David Renton (now Lord Renton) who reported in May 1975. It is entitled *The Preparation of Legislation.*[1] It contains most valuable proposals but some have never been implemented. They ought to be. One of the most important proposals is that statutes should be construed so as to promote the 'general legislative purpose'. Since that time the House of Lords have said they are willing to adopt a 'purposive approach'. But what does this mean? It means at least this: the judges ought not to go by the letter of the statute. They ought to go by the spirit of it.

2 Sticking to the letter

i *The old way*

In the middle of the 19th century the judges spoke of a 'golden rule' by which statutes were to be interpreted according to the grammatical and ordinary sense of the words. Even if it gave rise to unjust results which Parliament never intended, the grammatical meaning must prevail. Although speaking of the grammatical meaning, they took the literal meaning. They stuck to the letter.

That is the way in which the Pharisees interpreted the Fourth Commandment about the Sabbath Day. It ordained that on it 'Thou shalt do no manner of work.' It so happened that, on the Sabbath Day, as the disciples went through the cornfields, they began, as they went, to pluck the ears of

[1] Cmnd 6053.

corn. The Pharisees said to Our Lord: 'Behold, why do they on the Sabbath Day that which is not lawful?' He replied: 'The Sabbath was made for man, and not man for the Sabbath.' And St Paul put the principle, saying: 'The letter killeth, the spirit giveth life.'

When I was a boy, we were not allowed to play cricket or tennis or any other game on a Sunday. Nor was anyone else in Whitchurch. Were our parents all Pharisees? Not in the least. It just shows how a bad interpretation of a Commandment continues from one generation to another.

On rare occasions it may serve the ends of justice to stick to the letter: as when Portia argued that 'a pound of flesh' gave 'no jot of blood.' She was justified in thus sticking to the letter because she was interpreting a forfeiture clause, and the courts always lean against a forfeiture.

ii *Look to the spirit*

During the last 50 years the 'golden rule' has been abandoned. The judges always say that they look for the 'intention' of the Legislature. That is the same thing as looking for its 'purpose'. They do it in this way: they go by the words of the section. If they are clear and cover the situation in hand, there is no need to go further. But, if they are unclear or ambiguous or doubtful, the judges do not stop at the words of the section. They call for help in every direction open to them. They look at the statute as a whole. They look at the social conditions which gave rise to it. They look at the mischief which it was passed to remedy. They look at the 'factual matrix'. They use every legitimate aid. By this means they clear up many things which would be unclear or ambiguous or doubtful.

3 When there is a gap

The one point at which the judges always get stuck is when there is a gap. The words are clear enough. The meaning of them is clear enough. But they do not cover the matter in hand. Something has taken place which the draftsmen have not foreseen. Nor have the Members of Parliament. So they have not provided for it. Or else, by some mistake, they have overlooked something, or not provided for it. There is a gap. Can it be filled by the judges?

i *In 1946 the House of Lords said 'No'*

In 1946 the House of Lords held emphatically that the judges could not fill the gap. Lord Simonds said in *IRC v Ayrshire Employers Mutual Insurance Association Ltd:*[1]

The section (under discussion) is clearly a remedial section. . . . It is at least clear what is the gap which is intended to be filled, and hardly less clear how it is intended to fill that gap. Yet I can come to no other conclusion than that the language of the section fails to achieve its *apparent purpose* and I must decline to insert words or phrases which might succeed where the draftsman failed.

Note that the *purpose* of the section was apparent. There was a gap. It was clear how Parliament would have filled that gap. Yet the House refused to give it a purposive interpretation.

That was a taxing statute. But Lord Simonds repeated it afterwards in a general statute. It was in *Magor and St Mellons Rural District Council v Newport Corpn*[2] which I set out fully in *The Discipline of Law*. He said that for the judges to fill in a gap was 'a naked usurpation of the legislative function under the thin disguise of interpretation'.

ii *Lord Simonds is severely criticised*

Two years ago that attitude was severely criticised by Lord Diplock. It was in *Fothergill v Monarch Airlines*.[3] He quoted Lord Simonds and called it a 'narrowly semantic approach'. He said that it had left an 'unhappy legacy'. It had influenced the parliamentary draftsmen for the worse. It had led them to adopt the 'current English style of legislative draftsmanship'.

[1] [1946] 1 All ER 637, 641.
[2] [1952] AC 189.
[3] [1981] AC 251, 280.

They tried to 'provide in express detail what is to be done in each of all the foreseeable varieties of circumstances'. In short, they tried to think of every contingency and to fill the gap. An impossible task. No one can think of everything.

iii *Can we now fill the gap?*

In view of that criticism, I would ask the question: Nowadays, if the courts come across a gap in a statute, can they fill it? Can they remedy the omission by doing what good sense and justice require? This question lies at the heart of statutory interpretation today. In order to answer it, I now come to some recent cases. In one of them the House of Lords filled a gap and did justice. In the others the gap was not filled and injustice resulted.

4 The man who lost his shirt

Mr Fothergill went for a holiday on a package tour. He insured his luggage with an insurance company. He came home by air to Luton airport. He got his suitcase and found that it was badly damaged. He went to the reception desk and reported it. The lady filled in a form:

Nature of Damage: Side seam completely parted from case. Damage occurred on inbound flight.

Mr Fothergill did not at that time complain that any of the contents were missing. He went home to Colchester with his damaged suitcase. When he opened it, he found that his shirt was missing. He claimed on his insurance company, £12 for the damage to the suitcase and £16.50 for the loss of the shirt. His insurance company paid him for both.

But nobody told the airline about the loss of the shirt. No complaint was made to them for over three months. Then the insurance company, by virtue of their right of subrogation, made a claim. The airline admitted liability for the damage to the suitcase (because they had been notified of it within seven days) but they denied liability for the loss of the shirt (because they had received no complaint about it for three months). They said that, in case of pilferage, it was important that they should be notified of it promptly so that they could check it at once.

Mr Fothergill's insurance company took it up as a test case. They brought an action in Mr Fothergill's name against the airline. They relied on an Article in the Warsaw Convention. It laid down seven days as the time limit for a complaint:

In the case of *damage*, the person entitled to delivery must complain to the carrier forthwith after the discovery of the *damage*, and, at the latest, within seven days from the date of receipt of the baggage.

i *The meaning of 'damage'*

The great contest was as to the meaning of the word 'damage' in that Article. Mr Fothergill's insurance company said that it only applied to the damage to the suitcase, and not to the loss of the shirt. There was, they said, no time-bar for the loss of the shirt. So complaint could be made to the airline about it for the first time even after several months had passed.

Both the trial judge and the majority of the Court of Appeal (with me dissenting) accepted that view. They held that 'damage' meant physical damage and did not include partial loss of contents. So, despite the lateness of the claim, the airline were held liable for the missing shirt.

ii *It includes partial loss*

But the House of Lords reversed them. They accepted – or at any rate Lord Scarman did – that 'damage' in its ordinary sense meant damage and did not include loss. But the whole House went on to hold that in this Article 'damage' included 'partial loss of contents'. They filled in a gap in the Article by reading it as if it said 'in the case of damage or partial loss of contents'. They justified their attitude by reliance on a purposive interpretation. Lord Wilberforce took the considerations relevant to the word 'damage' in its literal sense, and said:[1]

If one then inquires whether these considerations are relevant to a case of partial loss of objects contained in baggage, the answer cannot be doubtful: they clearly are. . . . There seems to be no sense in making a distinction between damage to baggage . . . and loss of contents.

Lord Scarman said (at page 290):

If, therefore, the literal construction be legitimate, I would dismiss the appeal. But, in my judgment, it is not. It makes commercial sense to apply, if it be possible, the same time limits for giving notice of a complaint of partial loss of contents as for one of physical damage: and I am equally in no doubt that it is the duty of the English courts to apply, if possible, an interpretation which meets the commercial purpose of the Convention. In my judgment, such an interpretation is possible.

iii *Good sense prevails*

So the Lords did what good sense required. It would be unjust to allow a complaint of pilferage to be made months or even years afterwards.

5 Students from overseas

In later cases, however, the House of Lords have refused to fill in a gap. The first is one where students from overseas were claiming they were entitled as of right to have their university fees paid by the local authorities. It is *R v Barnet London Borough Council, ex parte Nilish Shah*.[2] I will take one of the students as an example. Hamid Akbarali lived with his parents in Pakistan. He went to school there. But in 1975, when he was 18, he wanted to become an engineer. The best place for training was England. His parents could pay for it. In order to get an entry to England he had to satisfy the authorities that he could meet the cost of the course and his own maintenance, and that he would leave at the end of the course. He did satisfy them. He was granted a student's visa. This gave him leave to enter for 12 months, and it was continued on the same basis each year. He went daily to a

[1] [1981] AC 251, 273.
[2] [1983] 2 WLR 16.

technical college here from January 1975 to September 1978. He lived at King's Road, Chelsea, in a rented flat. His parents paid for it. He returned twice to Pakistan – in 1977 and 1978 – on holiday visiting his parents. In October 1978 he started a course at Chelsea College in London, studying for a BSc degree. His parents paid his fees at the College and the cost of his maintenance. That was in accordance with the conditions of his student's visa.

i *He hears of a good thing*

Then he heard that he might be entitled to a mandatory grant from the local education authority, and thus save his parents the expense. That was because under the Education Act 1962 and the Regulations made in 1979, an authority was under a duty to pay an award to a person who is 'ordinarily resident' in the area throughout the three years before starting the course. The crucial question was whether he was 'ordinarily resident' in Chelsea during the three years 1975 to 1978. In their literal meaning the words 'ordinarily resident' mean that the person must be habitually and normally resident here, apart from temporary or occasional absences of long or short duration. That was true of Akbarali. He was habitually and normally resident in Chelsea, even though his home was in Pakistan and he went back there occasionally for holidays.

On the literal approach, therefore, Akbarali was entitled to a mandatory grant. He had brought himself within the literal meaning of the words.

ii *It is almost inconceivable*

The Court of Appeal refused to accept the literal meaning. They rejected Akbarali's claim. I said:[1]

In these circumstances I think we must abandon our traditional method of interpretation. The rebuffs in *Magor and St Mellons Rural District Council v Newport Corpn* [1952] AC 189 no longer hurt. We must ourselves fill in the gaps which Parliament has left. We must do our best

[1] [1982] QB 688, 720.

to legislate for a state of affairs for which Parliament has not legislated. We must say what is the meaning of the words 'ordinarily resident' in the context of the situation brought about by the Immigration Act 1971.

On this approach, it is my opinion that, whenever a boy comes from overseas on a student's visa, which is renewed every year, he is not to be regarded as 'ordinarily resident' here. He is allowed to enter on the terms that he or his parents or friends will pay all his fees and expenses whilst he is here, and that he will leave this country when his leave comes to an end. Such a boy is not 'ordinarily resident' here. No matter whether he goes home for holidays or not. No matter whether his parents are dead and he has no home to go to overseas. Suffice it that he has to leave at the end of his time, unless renewed.

In coming to this conclusion I was much influenced by the observations of Lord Justice Ormrod when this case had come before the Divisional Court:[1]

We are fortified in our construction of this regulation by the reflection that it is almost inconceivable that Parliament could have intended to bestow major awards for higher education, out of public funds, on persons permitted to enter this country on a temporary basis, solely for the purpose of engaging in courses of study at their own expense. Such an improbable result is not to be accepted if it can properly be avoided.

This meant filling in a gap. The Education Act 1962 and the 1979 Regulations had not dealt with the position of students coming from overseas on students' visas. It must have been overlooked. If they had dealt with it, they would have excluded them from any right to a mandatory grant. They would have inserted words for the purpose. It was inconceivable that they would have omitted to deal with it if they had thought of it.

iii *Yet the Lords do conceive*

Could this oversight be corrected by the judges? The Court of Appeal thought it could. But the House of Lords took a different view. There was only one speech. It was by Lord Scarman. The others agreed with it. They held that overseas students were 'ordinarily resident' for the three years in England: and that, on the wording of the statute, they were

[1] [1982] QB 688, 704.

entitled to a grant. Lord Scarman said that the Court of Appeal

were influenced by their own views of policy and by the immigration status of the students.[1]

He then said:

The way in which they used policy was, in my judgment, an impermissible approach to the interpretation of statutory language. Judges may not interpret statutes in the light of their own views as to policy. They may, of course, adopt a purposive interpretation if they can find in the statute read as a whole, or in material to which they are permitted by law to refer, as aids to interpretation, an expression of Parliament's purpose or policy. But that is not this case. The Education Act's only guidance is the requirement contained in the Regulations that, to be eligible for a mandatory award, a student must have been ordinarily resident in the United Kingdom for three years. There is no hint of any other restriction, provided, of course, he has the educational qualifications and his conduct is satisfactory.

In other words, the Court of Appeal ought not to have filled in the gap as they did.

iv *A professor's comment*

The House of Lords' decision was viewed with dismay by the Council for Local Education Authorities. For them it was said in *The Times*:

It is quite a bombshell. The financial implications are quite serious. Unless legislation is introduced as a matter of urgency it looks as though many who have been classified as overseas students will now be classed as home students, paying lower fees and entitled to mandatory grants.

The Times had a headline: 'Councils alarmed by grant ruling. It is also embarrassing for the Government.' Professor Zander wrote an article in *The Guardian* of 22 December 1982 describing it as:

A blinkered way to lay down the law
. . . This is to go back to the bad old traditional literal-minded approach
– with the judge looking for the solution to problems in the dictionary.

---

[1] [1983] 2 WLR 16, 30.

v *The Government overrule the Lords*

The Government acted promptly. In the House of Commons on 30 March 1983 Sir Keith Joseph, the Secretary of State for Education, intimated – very politely – that he was sorry that the House of Lords had overruled the Court of Appeal. He said:

The Government have decided to restore the position on mandatory awards to that which *successive Governments thought and intended it to be.*

He would have liked to have made the new regulations retrospective – but that would be contrary to principle – so the position was only restored as from 31 March 1983. It meant that many students from overseas got an uncovenanted bonus – in the shape of large grants tax free – owing to the decision of the House of Lords. The ordinary taxpayers and ratepayers had to bear the burden of some millions of pounds.

vi *Questions in the Commons*

When Sir Keith Joseph announced this decision, the Opposition spokesman, Mr Neil Kinnock, rose and asked a series of questions, which, no doubt, were very proper but were so many that *The Times* wrote lightheartedly about it. Their commentator tells us that one member

ironically inquired of the Speaker whether there had been any change in the rule that members on these occasions ask questions rather than make speeches.

'He's asked several questions already, and I think he is about to ask another,' replied the Speaker resignedly.

On swept Mr Kinnock.

The Tories became enraged. 'Finally,' said Mr Kinnock. The Tories cheered.

But Mr Kinnock showed no signs of finality. . . . 'Lastly.' It seemed there was for Mr Kinnock a large difference between 'finally' and 'lastly'.

At last he collapsed on to the Opposition front bench. One member made the masterly interjection: 'Answer the question!'

Sir Keith did so in the briefest of replies. So the regulations passed into law.

6 An appeal is out of time

i *A 'regrettable' decision*

The next case in the House of Lords was equally startling. It is *Griffiths v Secretary of State for the Environment.*[1] Mr Griffiths wanted to develop his land. The Secretary of State refused to grant planning permission. Mr Griffiths wished to appeal to the High Court. The statute gave him six weeks from the date on which 'action is taken' by the Secretary of State. The House of Lords, by a majority, held that 'the action' was taken at the moment when some officer in the department put the date-stamp on the decision-letter. That date was final, even though the letter was never posted, or was lost in the post, so that it never reached Mr Griffiths: and he had no notice of the decision.

ii *Lord Scarman dissents*

Lord Scarman dissented. He said that it was unjust that Mr Griffiths should have lost his right of appeal before he had any notice of 'the action'. Lord Scarman said:

I would not hold that Parliament intended anything so arbitrary.

Lord Elwyn-Jones said that the result was 'regrettable', but he did not formally dissent.

There was a simple way of doing justice. It was to fill in the gap by saying that the six weeks ran from the date on which Mr Griffiths received notice. But the majority refused to fill in the gap.

7 Twenty men are dismissed

A recent case is *Carrington v Therm-A-Stor Ltd*[2] in the Court of Appeal on 18 November 1982. In October 1979 a new factory opened at Peterborough. They took on 70 workmen. Six months later 60 out of those 70 had joined or applied to join the Transport and General Workers' Union. This number was so large that the union, naturally enough,

1 [1983] 2 WLR 172.
2 [1983] 1 WLR 138.

applied to the employers asking for recognition. The employers refused. They did not stop at a refusal. They told the chargehands to sack 20 of the men. The chargehands did so. Four of the men claimed for unfair dismissal.

i *Were they protected by the Act?*

Section 58 of the Employment Protection (Consolidation) Act 1978 made it unfair to dismiss an employee if the principal reason was that the employee 'was, or proposed to become, a member of an independent trade union'.

The employers argued that that section only applied to a dismissal of each man singly: and that it did not apply to the collective dismissal of 20 men together.

ii *Mr Justice Phillips fills the gap*

There was thus a gap in the statute. The Employment Appeal Tribunal, under the guidance of an excellent judge, Mr Justice Phillips, filled the gap. They held that the men had been unfairly dismissed. He said (at page 141) that

any other conclusion, it seems to us, would put an extraordinarily narrow construction upon section 58 and render it wholly inoperative in many instances where it must have been intended to apply.

iii *The Court of Appeal refuses to do so*

Yet the Court of Appeal reversed that decision. They declined to fill in the gap. The Master of the Rolls, Sir John Donaldson, said (at page 142):

If regard is had solely to the apparent mischief and the need for a remedy, it is only too easy for a judge to persuade himself that Parliament must have intended to provide the remedy which he himself would have decreed if he had had legislative power.

And Lord Justice May said (at page 143) that the dismissals could not be brought 'within the wording of section 58 even though that section was clearly aimed at a mischief very similar to that which befell the four employees'.

Both judges expressed their regret at their decision. They thus showed that they realised that it was unjust. And the Court of Appeal refused to give leave to appeal. So did the House of Lords. Why didn't they fill in the gap as Mr Justice Phillips had done?

8 A mother's right to work

i *'A legislative jungle'*

In a very recent case, *Lavery v Plessey Telecommunications Ltd*,[1] a mother claimed that she had a right to return to work after maternity leave. Her claim was morally justifiable but the obscurity of the Employment Protection (Consolidation) Act 1978 resulted in her losing it. In the Employment Appeal Tribunal Mr Justice Browne-Wilkinson said (at pages 379–380):

These statutory provisions are of inordinate complexity exceeding the worst excesses of a taxing statute; we find that especially regrettable bearing in mind that they are regulating the everyday rights of ordinary employers and employees. We feel no confidence that, even with the assistance of detailed arguments from skilled advocates, we have now correctly understood them: it is difficult to see how an ordinary employer or employee is expected to do so. . . .

Therefore, although we have considerable doubts whether we have traced the correct path through this legislative jungle, we regretfully reach the conclusion that . . . [her claim must fail].

The Court of Appeal agreed with all that Mr Justice Browne-Wilkinson had said.[2]

ii The Financial Times *comments*

This latest decision of the Court of Appeal prompted the legal correspondent of *The Financial Times* to comment on 31 March 1983:

The cold, logical and soulless approach defeats not only justice but also the intention of Parliament. Rigid legal thinking – a temporary aberration of the Middle Ages – seems to be making a come-back in spite of equity, Lord Mansfield and all the other efforts to humanise law.

1 [1982] ICR 373, EAT.
2 (1983) Times, 25 March.

9 A plea for clarity

In the section of this book dealing with trade unions, I venture to deplore the tortuous nature of section 17 of the Employment Act 1980. It was considered by the Court of Appeal and the House of Lords in the very recent case of *Merkur Island Shipping Corpn v Laughton*.[1] The comments of the judges are so pertinent that I would like to quote from them. In the Court of Appeal, the Master of the Rolls, Sir John Donaldson, said:[2]

In industrial relations it is of vital importance that the worker on the shop floor, the shop steward, the local union official, the district officer and the equivalent levels in management should know what is and what is not 'offside'. And they must be able to find this out for themselves by reading plain and simple words of guidance. The judges of this court are all skilled lawyers of very considerable experience, yet it has taken us hours to ascertain what is and what is not 'offside', even with the assistance of highly experienced counsel. This cannot be right.

. . . But I do not criticise the draftsman. His instructions may well have left him no option. My plea is that Parliament, when legislating in respect of circumstances which directly affect the 'man or woman in the street' or the 'man or woman on the shop floor' should give as high a priority to clarity and simplicity of expression as to refinements of policy. . . . When formulating policy, ministers, of whatever political persuasion, should at all times be asking themselves and asking parliamentary counsel: 'Is this concept too refined to be capable of expression in basic English? If so, is there some way in which we can modify the policy so that it can be so expressed?' Having to ask such questions would no doubt be frustrating for ministers and the legislature generally, but in my judgment this is part of the price which has to be paid if the rule of law is to be maintained.

And in the House of Lords Lord Diplock, speaking for the House, said:[3]

But what the law is, particularly in the field of industrial relations, ought to be plain. It should be expressed in terms that can be easily understood by those who have to apply it even at shop floor level. I echo everything that the Master of the Rolls has said in the last three paragraphs of his judgment in this case. Absence of clarity is destructive of the rule of law;

[1] [1983] 2 WLR 45; affd. [1983] 2 WLR 778, HL.
[2] [1983] 2 WLR 45, 66.
[3] [1983] 2 WLR 778, 790.

it is unfair to those who wish to preserve the rule of law; it encourages those who wish to undermine it. The statutory provisions . . . are drafted in a manner which . . . can in my view only be characterised as most regrettably lacking in the requisite degree of clarity.

10 A constitutional question

In a debate in the House of Lords on 15 December 1982 the Lord Chancellor suggested that statutory interpretation raised a constitutional question. He asked:

Are we not really in the presence of a political and constitutional problem which is endemic in our parliamentary institution to a greater extent than has wholly been realised?

. . . We should remember that much of what we are complaining of is actually due to the balances and checks which we have come to accept as part of our constitutional liberty.

i *Checks and balances*

As I see it, that balance is this: Parliament enacts statute law and the judges interpret it. Statute law is necessarily expressed in words. Parliament decides upon the words. The judges say what those words mean.

In one pan of the scales you put the proposition that every citizen is bound by the words which Parliament has used, and by the words only. That is the check upon Parliament. In the other pan you put the proposition that the judges are not to add to or subtract from the words. They are not to legislate. That is the check upon the judges.

The Lord Chancellor spoke of his experience of legislators:

How often when a minister has said, 'The courts will take a sensible view of this' have I heard the words from the back benches, 'Well, let us have it written into the statute'?

According to this point of view, our constitution requires legislation in such detail as to preclude any misunderstanding. In going into detail, the draftsmen are only fulfilling a constitutional requirement.

ii *Clarity should prevail*

To my mind there is this answer:

Legislation in detail has been found by experience to be self-defeating. It leads to statutory provisions which are so complicated as to be obscure and unintelligible. When this happens, it offends the fundamental principle that a statute should be so expressed as to be readily understood by those who are affected by it.

It is this principle – the principle of clarity – which should prevail. Accordingly, legislation in detail should be abandoned and replaced by legislation in principle. By this I mean that our statutes should expound principles in clear language and should leave the details, where necessary, to be worked out by some other means or in some other way. That was one of the recommendations of Lord Renton's Committee. It was in paragraph 10.13 of their Report, Cmnd 6053. Even so, there are bound to be gaps – due to oversight or lack of foresight or to draftsmanship. These gaps should be filled in by the judges according to their own good sense. They can and should be trusted thus far. They developed the common law in that way. They should be trusted, likewise, with the statute law.

iii *Lord Renton's peroration*

I find very apposite the eloquent plea for clarity which Lord Renton made at the end of his opening speech in the debate in the House of Lords:

If our Acts of Parliament cannot be understood even by clever experts it not only brings the law into contempt, it brings Parliament into contempt. It is a disservice to our democracy; it weakens the rights of the individual; it eases the way for wrongdoers and it places honest, humble people at the mercy of the state. In the name of reason and justice, *Let's get it straight!*

To my mind, the one way to get it straight is for Parliament to use plain, simple language expressing principles, and for the judges to fill in the gaps in a statute so as to do what good sense requires.

iv *Late news*

In his Hamlyn Lecture just delivered, Lord Hailsham of Saint Marylebone has said that statute law has assumed a vastly increased importance and that this

has greatly accentuated the need for fresh thinking about the draftsmanship and interpretation of statutes.[1]

The Times in a leader on 21 May 1983 says that 'his timing could hardly have been better'. It suggests a solution in these words:

What seems to be needed is some movement on both fronts: (a) a broader style of legislative drafting on the one hand, and (b) a somewhat more purposive approach to statutory interpretation by the courts. . . . It is probably inevitable that greater simplicity in legislative drafting will confer a greater discretion on the courts in interpreting statutes, but there is no alternative if the law is to remain accessible to the people.

That bears out all that I have been saying in this section.

v *The European Court gives a lead*

There is just to hand a judgment of the European Court at Luxembourg of 11 May 1983. It was on a reference by the Plymouth Magistrates' Court.

On 5 August 1981 a French fishing boat, the *Christine Marie*, was fishing in the English Channel inside British fishery limits. She had the ordinary fishing net but in addition she had a second piece of net attached to it.

Under the Community legislation, strictly construed, this second net was unlawful. The relevant Regulation said:

No device shall be used by means of which the mesh in any part of a fishing net is obstructed or otherwise effectively diminished.

But that Community legislation left a gap. It was this: the original net is liable to damage by wear and tear. In order to protect it, fishermen often use a device attached to the 'cod-end' of the net. The question was whether this device was lawful or unlawful. The European Commission

[1] *Hamlyn Revisited: The British Legal System Today* (1983) p 70.

113

had power to legislate but had not done so. The European Court held that the national courts could fill the gap. Their judgment said:

> In the absence of such legislation (by the Commission), it is for the competent courts *to fill the resulting lacuna* in a manner which is consistent with the aim of protecting fishing stocks and which also takes into account the fact that protection of fishing nets should be permitted.[1]

Under Community law, therefore, it is open to the judges of England to fill in a gap in Community legislation by doing what good sense requires. So it should be when there is a gap in English legislation.

---

[1] (1983) 147 JPN 520, 522.

Public and Private Law – A New Dichotomy

1 The coming of judicial review

1 A constitutional revolution

In recent years there has been a revolution in our constitution. It is in the relations between the public authorities and the citizen: and the emergence of a difference between public law and private law.

i *Dicey's* Law of the Constitution

In my young days we regarded Dicey's *Law of the Constitution* with almost as much reverence as the Bible. He wrote it in 1885 and declared that there is in England no difference between public and private law; and that we have no system of *droit administratif* as they have in France. He said:

> We mean, . . . when we speak of the 'rule of law' as a characteristic of our country, not only that with us no man is above the law, but (what is a different thing) that here every man, whatever be his rank or condition, is subject to the ordinary law of the realm and amenable to the jurisdiction of the ordinary tribunals.[1]

His views were repeated in Halsbury's *Laws of England*. Under the title 'Constitutional Law' – in all four editions – it is said and still said:

> Nevertheless the boundaries of constitutional law have never been satisfactorily defined, partly because there is no constitutional document possessing an extraordinary sanctity, partly because the constitutional rules are susceptible of change, and partly because there is no fundamental difference between public law and private law and it is not

[1] 4th edn, (1893) 183.

117

possible to assign exclusive provinces to each. Thus, generally speaking, the same courts of law have jurisdiction whether the case raises questions of public or private law.[1]

This is in conformity with the theory of John Austen who held that there is one sovereign who enacts the laws which all must obey. I always like the parallel drawn by Shakespeare with a hive of bees:

> Therefore doth heaven divide
> The state of man in divers functions,
> Setting endeavour in continual motion;
> To which is fixed, as an aim or butt,
> Obedience: for so work the honey-bees,
> Creatures that by a rule in nature teach
> The act of order to a peopled kingdom.
> They have a king and officers of sorts;
> Where some, like magistrates, correct at home,
> Others, like merchants, venture trade abroad,
> Others, like soldiers, armed in their stings,
> Make boot upon the summer's velvet buds,
> Which pillage they with merry march bring home
> To the tent-royal of their emperor;
> Who, busied in his majesty, surveys
> The singing masons building roofs of gold,
> The civil citizens kneading up the honey,
> The poor mechanic porters crowding in
> Their heavy burdens at his narrow gate,
> The sad-eyed justice, with his surly hum,
> Delivering o'er to executors pale
> The lazy yawning drone.[2]

ii *The law of the Roman empire*

This was in complete contrast to the law laid down by Justinian for the Roman empire and still prevailing in Europe today. In the very forefront of the *Institutes* of Justinian it is said that there is a fundamental difference between public law and private law:

Iuris praecepta sunt haec: honeste vivere, alterum non laedere, suum cuique tribuere. Huius studii duae sunt positiones, publicum et privatum. Publicum ius

[1] 4th edn, (1974) para. 801.
[2] *Henry V*, Act I, sc. 2.

est, quod ad statum rei Romanae spectat, privatum, quod ad singulorum utilitatem pertinet.

Put into English, this says:

The precepts of the law are these: to live honestly, not to injure your neighbour, to render each man his due. This study is divided into two parts, public and private. The public part is that which relates to the nature of public authority in Rome: the private part is that which appertains to the affairs of individual persons.

iii *The modern approach*

In the last few years we have thrown over Dicey and gone back to Justinian. In *O'Reilly v Mackman* I was able to say:[1]

In modern times we have come to recognise two separate fields of law: one of private law, the other of public law. Private law regulates the affairs of subjects as between themselves. Public law regulates the affairs of subjects vis-à-vis public authorities.

iv *The reason for the change*

The reason for the change-over into two fields is because, during the last 30 years, we have established a comprehensive system of administrative law. It bears some little resemblance to the *droit administratif* of France in that it fulfils a dual purpose. On the one hand it gives the subject an efficient remedy against a public authority. On the other hand it protects a public authority from being harassed by busybodies and cranks.

But it differs from the *droit administratif* in that it is all within the jurisdiction of the High Court: whereas in France the distinction is so complete that there is a different hierarchy of courts. Private law culminates in the *cour de cassation*: public law in the *conseil d'état*.

2 A spectacular advance

It is in the realm of remedies that public law has made the most spectacular advance. The Court of Appeal made a

[1] [1982] 3 WLR 604, 619.

preliminary skirmish on 30 June 1982, a little before I retired, in *O'Reilly v Mackman*.[1] But the main assault was made by the House of Lords in two cases decided on 25 November 1982 after I retired. They are *O'Reilly v Mackman*[2] and *Cocks v Thanet District Council*.[3]

i *The old remedies*

In order to understand the significance of these two decisions, you should know that for 100 years before 1950 the only remedies in public law known to the English courts were the old prerogative writs of certiorari, mandamus and prohibition. These were of very limited scope and suffered from many procedural disadvantages.

After 1950 there were advances on two fronts. One advance was to extend the remedy by prerogative writs so as to cover many more misdoings by public authorities: such as errors of law on the face of the record, and going outside their jurisdiction, and so forth. The other advance was to develop the remedy by ordinary actions so as to make the equitable remedies of declaration and injunction available against public authorities for breach of public law.

Each of these advances had its advantages and disadvantages. The complainant chose whichever suited him best. If he wanted to quash a decision of a public authority, he would go by certiorari. If he wanted to compel it to do its duty, he would ask for mandamus. If a declaration would suit his book – to declare what was its duty – he would issue a writ in an ordinary action. Likewise if he wanted an injunction to stop it breaking this duty, he would also issue a writ. Some of the most important cases in public law were decided in actions for declarations, such as *Barnard v National Dock Labour Board*,[4] *Pyx Granite Co Ltd v Ministry of*

[1] [1982] 3 WLR 604.
[2] [1982] 3 WLR 1096.
[3] [1982] 3 WLR 1121.
[4] [1953] 2 QB 18.

Housing and Local Government,[1] *Ridge v Baldwin*[2] and *Anisminic Ltd v Foreign Compensation Commission.*[3]

ii *The request to the Law Commission*

The procedures became so diverse that on 8 December 1969 the Law Commission

were formally requested by Lord Gardiner (the Lord Chancellor), in pursuance of section 3(1)(e) of the Law Commissions Act 1965,
'to review the existing remedies for the judicial control of administrative acts and omissions with a view to evolving a simpler and more effective procedure.'

iii *Limited to procedure*

Many regretted that these terms of reference were limited to procedure: but they need not have worried. By reforming procedure the way was laid open for the judges to reform the substantive law. In amending the law of procedure, the judges have reformed the substantive law as well. This has always been the case. Sir Henry Maine put it in this way:[4]

So great is the ascendancy of the Law of Actions in the infancy of Courts of Justice, that substantive law has at first the look of being gradually secreted in the interstices of procedure.

And Maitland's phrase has come down the years:[5]

The forms of action we have buried, but they still rule us from their graves.

iv *All remedies combined*

The Law Commission made their report in March 1976 (Law Com no 73).[6] It was implemented by Rules of Court (Order 53) in 1977 and given statutory force in 1981 by section 31 of the Supreme Court Act 1981. It combined all

[1] [1960] AC 260.
[2] [1964] AC 40.
[3] [1969] 2 AC 147.
[4] *Early Law and Custom,* 389.
[5] *Equity,* 296.
[6] Cmnd 6407.

the former remedies into one proceeding called Judicial Review. At one stroke the courts could grant whatever relief was appropriate. Not only certiorari and mandamus, but also declaration and injunction. Even damages. The procedure was much more simple and expeditious. Just a summons instead of a writ. No formal pleadings. The evidence was given by affidavit. As a rule no cross-examination, no discovery, and so forth. But there were important safeguards. In particular, in order to qualify, the applicant had to get the leave of a judge.

The statute is phrased in flexible terms. It gives scope for development. It uses the words 'having regard to'. Those words are very indefinite. The result is that the courts are not bound hand and foot by the previous law. They are to 'have regard to' it. So the previous law as to who are – and who are not – public authorities, is not absolutely binding. Nor is the previous law as to the matters in respect of which relief may be granted. This means that the judges can develop the public law as they think best. That they have done and are doing.

3 What are 'public authorities'?

The first thing to notice is that public law is confined to 'public authorities'. What are 'public authorities'? There is only one avenue of approach. It is by asking, in the words of section 31(2)(b) of the Supreme Court Act 1981: What is the 'nature of the persons and bodies against whom relief may be granted by such orders', that is, by mandamus, prohibition or certiorari?

These are divided into two main categories:

First, the persons or bodies who have legal authority to determine questions affecting the common law or statutory rights or obligations of other persons as individuals. That is the formula stated by Lord Justice Atkin in *R v Electricity Comrs, ex parte London Electricity Joint Committee Co (1920) Ltd*[1] as broadened by Lord Diplock in *O'Reilly v Mackman*.[2]

[1] [1924] 1 KB 171, 205.
[2] [1982] 3 WLR 1096, 1104.

122

Second, the persons or bodies who are entrusted by Parliament with functions, powers and duties which involve the making of decisions of a public nature. That goes back to the time of Chief Justice Holt who said in 1691:

This Court will examine the proceedings of all jurisdictions erected by Act of Parliament. And if they, under pretence of such Act, proceed to incroach jurisdiction to themselves greater than the Act warrants, this Court will send a certiorari to them, to have their proceedings returned here; to the end that this Court may see, that they keep themselves within their jurisdiction: and if they exceed it, to restrain them. And the examination of such matters is more proper for this Court.[1]

To which I would add the words of Lord Goddard CJ in *R v National Joint Council for Dental Technicians, ex parte Neate:*[2]

The bodies to which in modern times the remedies of these prerogative writs have been applied have all been statutory bodies on whom Parliament has conferred statutory powers and duties which, when exercised, may lead to the detriment of subjects who may have to submit to their jurisdiction.

But those categories are not exhaustive. The courts can extend them to any other person or body of a public nature exercising public duties which it is desirable to control by the remedy of judicial review.

There are many cases which give guidance, but I will just give some illustrations.

Every body which is created by statute – and whose powers and duties are defined by statute – is a 'public authority'. So Government departments, local authorities, police authorities, and statutory undertakings and corporations, are all 'public authorities'. So are members of a statutory tribunal or inquiry, and the board of visitors of a prison. The Criminal Injuries Compensation Board is a public authority. So also, I suggest, is a university incorporated by royal charter: and the managers of a state school. So is the Boundary Commission: and the Committee of Lloyd's.

[1] See *R v Inhabitants – in Glamorganshire* (1691) 1 Ld Raym 580.
[2] [1953] 1 QB 704, 707.

But a limited liability company incorporated under the Companies Acts is not a 'public authority', see *Tozer v National Greyhound Racing Club Ltd.*[1] Nor is an unincorporated association like the Jockey Club. You may ask: What about trade unions? No case has arisen on the point, but in view of the many statutes regulating their powers and duties, they may be a 'public authority'.

[1] (1983) Times, 16 May.

2 A notable difference

1 A dichotomy

The House of Lords have recently spoken of a 'dichotomy'. They did it in *Cocks v Thanet District Council*.[1] That word only means 'dividing a whole into two parts'. They have divided the functions of a public authority into two parts: one part is its public law function; the other part is its private law function. But how are you to decide between the two? Which is public? Which is private? Likewise its duties are divided into two. One part is its public law duties. The other part is its private law duties. But the division is very difficult to make. So difficult indeed that I can foresee an infinity of trouble arising from it. It makes me regret that the dichotomy was ever made. But still it has been done and you will all have to live with it in perpetuity.

Roughly speaking – very roughly – the public law functions of a public authority are those which involve the determination of questions and the making of decisions: but the private law functions are those which involve the carrying out of contracts or works or other operations by the public authority. At this stage of development, the best way is to look at some actual instances.

2 Actual instances

i *The Borstal boys take a yacht*

I have described the case of the Borstal boys, *Dorset Yacht Co*

[1] [1982] 3 WLR 1121.

v Home Office,[1] in *The Discipline of Law* (pages 250–253) but I would refer to it again now because it illustrates so well public law functions and private law functions.

Just to remind you of the facts: In September 1962 the motor yacht *Silver Mist* was lying at moorings in Poole Harbour. No one was on her. In the middle of the night seven Borstal boys got aboard her. They cut her adrift and did much damage. They were all from the Borstal institution at Portland. They were on a training exercise under three officers. They were quartered in an empty house on Brownsea Island. The three officers went to bed. But during the night seven of the boys (out of ten) got out and did the damage. The owner of the yacht sued the Home Office for damages.

In order to find out the public law function of the Home Office, you must bear in mind that the aim of Borstal training is to reform the boys by giving them considerable freedom. 'Open Borstals' are the order of the day. This requires delicate and difficult decisions in classifying the boys, in seeing whether they are suitable or not and also in deciding what is the appropriate treatment and supervision. It is one of the risks of the system – a conscious and deliberate risk – that boys will sometimes escape and do damage. When the Home Office make decisions in this sphere, they are public law decisions and do not give rise to a cause of action in private law. So there was no cause of action against the Home Office for allowing these boys to go out on this expedition to Brownsea Island.

Now I come to the private law function of the Home Office. It was the duty of the three officers to exercise proper supervision over the boys. If they failed to take proper precautions to prevent the boys from escaping, they were negligent in the execution of their duty. If this resulted in damage, the Home Office would be liable to an action in private law – an action for negligence.

[1] [1969] 2 QB 412, CA; affd. [1970] AC 1004, HL.

Lord Diplock said:[1]

A cause of action is capable of arising from failure by the custodian to take reasonable care to prevent the detainee from escaping, if his escape was the consequence of an act or omission of the custodian falling outside the limits of the discretion delegated to him under the statute.

The practical effect of this would be that no liability in the Home Office for 'negligence' could arise out of the escape from an 'open' Borstal of a trainee who had been classified for training at a Borstal of this type by the appropriate officer to whom the function of classification had been delegated upon the ground that the officer had been negligent in so classifying him or in failing to re-classify him for removal to a 'closed' Borstal. The decision as to classification would be one which lay within the officer's discretion. . . .

But to say this does not dispose of the present appeal, for the allegations of negligence against the Borstal officers are consistent with their having acted outside any discretion delegated to them and having disregarded their instructions as to the precautions which they should take to prevent members of the working party of trainees from escaping from Brownsea Island. Whether they had or not could only be determined at the trial of the action.

ii *The house gets cracked*

ANNS V MERTON LONDON BOROUGH COUNCIL[2]

In 1962 some developers were building a block of maisonettes. The plans showed that the concrete foundations were to be 3 feet thick. But the builders only made them 2 feet 6 inches thick. After a few years, cracks appeared. The builders could not pay for the damage. The owners sued the local council. They said that the council's inspector had not inspected the foundations at all or, if he had, he had done it badly.

Now the public law function of the local council was this: They had *power* under the statute to appoint inspectors but they had no duty to do so. It was for them to decide upon the scale of resources they would make available – how many inspectors they should have and how many inspections were to be made, and so forth. Decisions in that sphere were a

---

[1] [1970] AC 1004, 1069.
[2] [1978] AC 728.

public law function and did not give rise to a cause of action in private law.

But the actual inspecting of the foundations was a private law function. If the inspector, having assumed the task of inspecting, did not exercise reasonable care to ensure that the byelaws were complied with, the council would be liable in damages for negligence.

In that very case Lord Wilberforce (at page 756) gave an apt illustration from an American case, *Indian Towing Co Inc v United States*.[1] If a public authority was under a statutory duty to build a lighthouse and did not build it, that would be a failure in its public law function. It could be remedied by judicial review. But if it built the lighthouse and failed to keep the light in working order, that would be a failure in its private law function.

iii *Snow and ice on Pilgrim's Way*

HAYDON V KENT COUNTY COUNCIL[2]

In February 1973 snow fell and there was a hard frost. A steep path down from Pilgrim's Way had become very slippery and dangerous. A lady went down the footpath to work. She went very carefully because it was so slippery. But despite all her care, she slipped and broke her ankle.

She complained that the Kent County Council were at fault. The footpath had been dangerous for two days and they had done nothing about it.

The Kent County Council said that they gritted all the main roads. But they simply had not the men or the lorries to grit also all the footpaths. That was a public law decision and they were not liable to an action. I said (page 361):

If there was any error in the highway authority, it was an error which lay within the policy area, and not the operational level.

But if the men who were gritting main roads had overlooked one small stretch – by negligence on their part –

[1] (1955) 350 US 61.
[2] [1978] QB 343.

that would be a failure in private law for which an action would lie − if it was found to cause damage.

iv *An Italian family is homeless*

Much litigation has arisen out of the Housing (Homeless Persons) Act 1977. The first case we had was *De Falco v Crawley Borough Council.*[1] I opened my judgment in this way (at page 472):

Every day we see signs of the advancing tide. This time it is two young families from Italy. They had heard tell of the European Economic Community. Naturally enough, because it all stemmed from a Treaty made at Rome. They had heard that there was freedom of movement for workers within the Community. They could come to England without let or hindrance. They may have heard, too, that England is a good place for workers. In Italy the word may have got round that in England there are all sorts of benefits to be had whenever you are unemployed. And best of all they will look after you if you have nowhere to live. There is a special new statute there which imposes on the local authority a duty to house you. They must either find you a house or put you up in a guest house. 'So let's go to England,' they say. 'That's the place for us.'

In that telling I have used a touch of irony, but there is a good deal of truth behind it.

Now the De Falco family came to England from Italy. They stayed for a few weeks with the wife's brother at Horsham. Then the brother turned them out. They went to stay with another relation who after a month or two gave them notice to quit. They went to the Crawley Council and applied to be housed under the new Act. The obligation of the council depended on whether the family had become homeless intentionally or unintentionally. If *intentionally*, the council were only to provide temporary accommodation for them. If *unintentionally*, they had to provide permanent accommodation for them.

The council decided that they had become homeless *intentionally*. The De Falco family complained that the council's decision was erroneous and brought an action to

[1] [1980] QB 460.

challenge it. The Court of Appeal held that an action was maintainable. I said (page 476):

The applicant has an option. He can either go by action in the High Court or county court: or by an application for judicial review.

But two years later the House of Lords in *Cocks v Thanet District Council*[1] said that was wrong. They said that he could only go by judicial review. The reason was because the decision of the council on that point – whether their homelessness was intentional or unintentional – was a public law decision. But once they had decided it, their manner of exercising it was a private law duty. Lord Bridge of Harwich said (page 1125):

It is necessary to analyse the functions of housing authorities under the Housing (Homeless Persons) Act 1977. These functions fall into two wholly distinct categories. On the one hand, the housing authority are charged with decision-making functions. It is for the housing authority to decide whether they have reason to believe the matters which will give rise to the duty of inquiry or to the temporary housing duty. It is for the housing authority, once the duty of inquiry has arisen, to make the appropriate inquiries and to decide whether they are satisfied, or not satisfied as the case may be, of the matters which will give rise to the limited housing duty or the full housing duty. These are essentially public law functions. . . .

On the other hand, the housing authority are charged with executive functions. Once a decision has been reached by the housing authority which gives rise to the temporary, the limited or the full housing duty, rights and obligations are immediately created in the field of private law.

Lord Bridge went on to comment that in the *De Falco* case the decision of the Court of Appeal, of which he and I were both members, 'was influenced by a failure to appreciate the significance of the dichotomy of functions to which I have drawn attention in the two foregoing paragraphs.' Professor H. W. R. Wade has recently made the pertinent comment that 'since no one had previously heard of any such dichotomy, this failure was hardly surprising'.[2]

[1] [1982] 3 WLR 1121.
[2] (1983) 99 LQR 169.

v *The four prisoners at Hull prison*

O'REILLY V MACKMAN[1]

This next case is one solely on a public law function. It is now the leading case. These were the facts:[2]

Four men were in prison in Hull. They were all serving long sentences for serious crimes. O'Reilly is typical. He was serving 15 years for robbery. Over four days in September 1976 there was a riot in the prison, coupled with extreme violence. Men got on to the roof and stayed there day and night. They threw missiles and slates off the roof. They ransacked the canteen. They assaulted prison officers and staff. After the riot was quelled, many men were charged with offences against discipline contrary to the provisions of the Prison Rules. In each case the board of visitors held an inquiry. Take O'Reilly as an example. The board found him guilty on all charges. They ordered him to be kept in solitary confinement for 196 days and to lose remission of 510 days. Likewise with others.

Many of the men complained about the conduct of the board of visitors. They said that the board had failed to comply with the rules of natural justice.

The decision of the board of visitors was clearly a public law function. There was no private law about it at all.

vi *The new terminals in the river Thames*

TATE AND LYLE INDUSTRIES LTD V GREATER LONDON COUNCIL[3]

In 1966 the Greater London Council had statutory power to construct two new terminals in the river Thames. These were for the Woolwich Ferry. The terminals were piers which jutted out into the river. The object was for cars to be driven on and off the terminals. They were so designed that they caused silt to block up the way to the wharves of Tate and Lyle. This was a private law function and the Greater London Council were held liable in damages in an ordinary action.

---

[1] [1982] 3 WLR 604, CA; affd. [1982] 3 WLR 1096, HL.
[2] [1982] 3 WLR 604, 615.
[3] [1983] 2 WLR 649.

vii *A probationer constable resigns*

CHIEF CONSTABLE OF THE NORTH WALES POLICE V EVANS[1]

A young man was accepted as a probationer constable in the North Wales Police. The period of probation was two years. He did well but comments circulated about his private life. There were inquiries at a lower level but then he was summoned to an interview with the chief constable.

The chief constable told him that he (the chief constable) had made a mistake in accepting him and the chief constable gave him the opportunity to resign as an alternative to formally dispensing with his services. The probationer constable said, and his account was not disputed (page 1170):

> I asked if I could have a reason for this action but he refused outright. I was not informed of what was alleged against me nor afforded any opportunity to be heard by way of defence or explanation. I asked for time to consider and he said that I must let him know by 10 a.m. the following morning. I was not given any document recording this decision.

As a result of the chief constable's threat, he signed on the next day a formal letter of resignation.

He brought proceedings for judicial review on the basis that he had been treated unfairly and in a manner contrary to natural justice. His complaint was upheld by the Court of Appeal and the House of Lords. In the Court of Appeal I said (at page 1173):

> It is my opinion that the chief constable was not justified in dispensing with the services of Constable Evans or in requiring him to resign.

But the significant point for present purposes is that it was accepted by all the courts that the chief constable was a 'public authority', that in interviewing the probationer constable he was exercising a 'public function' and that it was his 'public duty' to act fairly and reasonably in exercising it. Lord Hailsham, the Lord Chancellor, said (at page 1160) as to the remedy of judicial review:

> This remedy, vastly increased in extent, and rendered, over a long period

[1] [1982] 1 WLR 1155.

in recent years, of infinitely more convenient access than that provided by the old prerogative writs and actions for a declaration, is intended to protect the individual against the abuse of power by a wide range of authorities, judicial, quasi-judicial, and, as would originally have been thought when I first practised at the Bar, administrative. It is not intended to take away from those authorities the powers and discretions properly vested in them by law and to substitute the courts as the bodies making the decisions. It is intended to see that the relevant authorities use their powers in a proper manner.

Since the range of authorities, and the circumstances of the use of their power, are almost infinitely various, it is of course unwise to lay down rules for the application of the remedy which appear to be of universal validity in every type of case. But it is important to remember in every case that the purpose of the remedies is to ensure that the individual is given fair treatment by the authority to which he has been subjected and that it is no part of that purpose to substitute the opinion of the judiciary or of individual judges for that of the authority constituted by law to decide the matters in question. The function of the court is to see that lawful authority is not abused by unfair treatment and not to attempt itself the task entrusted to that authority by the law.

Professor Wade suggests that the remedy by judicial review in that case was not appropriate and that the probationer constable's correct remedy was

an action for damages for the tort of intimidation, having been forced to act to his detriment under threat of unlawful injury.[1]

For once, however, I would differ from the Professor. It was, I think, very appropriate for the conduct of the chief constable to be challenged by way of judicial review, and to be condemned on the simple ground that it was, in the words of the Lord Chancellor, 'unfair treatment'. It was an extension of the law, no doubt, but I suggest a desirable extension. I would even go further. The appropriate remedy (instead of any declaration) would have been simply to award damages to the probationer constable, which would include compensation for the distress and injured feelings suffered by him.

[1] (1983) 99 LQR 172.

3 Public law functions

The new distinction between public law and private law is not only important on remedies. It is of the first importance in substantive law. Once you place a particular function into the box labelled 'public law', it is governed by entirely different principles from those in the box labelled 'private law'. I will state them.

i *The difference between public and private law*

In public law the central principle is that a public authority must properly perform the public function assigned to it by the law. It must not exceed the powers which have been entrusted to it: and it must duly perform the duties which have been laid upon it. If it does not do so, it is acting ultra vires. It can be called to account by any citizen who has a sufficient interest in the matter.

In private law there are several principles. In the law of contract that a man should keep his promises. In the law of tort that a man should take reasonable care not to injure his neighbour. If he does not do so, he is liable in damages by the remedy of a writ or by an action. And so forth.

ii *Support for the difference*

In support of this difference, I start with the proposition stated by Professor Wade in his treatise on *Administrative Law:*[1]

The simple proposition that a public authority may not act outside its powers (ultra vires) might fitly be called the central principle of administrative law.

I go on to the seed sown by Lord Diplock in the case of the Borstal boys, *Dorset Yacht Co v Home Office*, when he said:[2]

The public law concept of ultra vires has replaced the civil law concept of negligence as the test of the legality, and consequently of the actionability, of acts or omissions of government departments or public authorities done in the exercise of a discretion conferred upon them by

[1] (5th edn) p 38.
[2] [1970] AC 1004, 1067.

Parliament as the means by which they are to achieve a particular public purpose.

To which I would add the principle well stated by the Court of Appeal in its unanimous judgment in the case of the Boundary Commission, *R v Boundary Commission for England, ex parte Foot:*[1]

There are many Acts of Parliament which give ministers and local authorities extensive powers to take action which affects the citizenry of this country, but give no right of appeal to the courts. In such cases, the courts are not concerned or involved so long as ministers and local authorities do not exceed the powers given to them by Parliament. Those powers may give them a wide range of choice on what action to take or to refrain from taking and so long as they confine themselves to making choices within that range, the courts will have no wish or power to intervene. But if ministers or local authorities exceed their powers – if they choose to do something or to refrain from doing something in circumstances in which this is not one of the options given to them by Parliament – the courts can and will intervene in defence of the ordinary citizen. It is of the essence of parliamentary democracy that those to whom powers are given by Parliament shall be free to exercise those powers, subject to constitutional protest and criticism and parliamentary or other democratic control. But any attempt by ministers or local authorities to usurp powers which they have not got or to exercise their powers in a way which is unauthorised by Parliament is quite a different matter. As Sir Winston Churchill was wont to say, 'that is something up with which we will not put.' If asked to do so, it is then the role of the courts to prevent this happening. . . .

A long line of cases has established that if public authorities purport to make decisions which are not in accordance with the terms of the powers conferred on them, such decisions can be attacked in the courts by way of an application for judicial review; and furthermore, that even if such decisions on the face of them fall within the letter of their powers, they may be successfully attacked if shown to have been 'unreasonable'.

iii *Interpreting the statute*

In many cases the question of ultra vires depends on the true interpretation of a statute. The courts have to say, on its wording, whether the public authority has kept within the powers conferred on it or has duly performed the duties laid

[1] [1983] 2 WLR 458, 465, 474.

upon it. That is well illustrated by the important case of the fares on London's buses and tubes, *Bromley London Borough Council v Greater London Council*.[1] The speeches in the House of Lords cover 40 pages of analysis of the statute. All the laymen found them most indigestible. So did many lawyers.

Apart from interpretation there are several other principles which the courts have formulated. I set them out in *The Discipline of Law*. But I would bring them up to date.

iv *The duty to inquire fairly and impartially*

If a public authority holds an inquiry in pursuance of a public law duty, it must be conducted fairly or, as it is sometimes said, in accordance with the rules of natural justice. Its members must be free from bias: and it must give all concerned a fair hearing. If it does not do so, it goes outside its powers. This was upheld mightily in the great case of *Rookes v Barnard*.[2]

To this I would add a corollary. If a public authority dismisses one of its officers – or threatens him with dismissal and in consequence he resigns – then it must conduct itself fairly and reasonably. That appears from the recent case of *Chief Constable of the North Wales Police v Evans*[3] which I have described earlier.

v *The duty to decide in accordance with the law*

It is implicit in the powers conferred on a public authority that, in any determination that it may make, it will act in accordance with the law. If it goes wrong in point of law or misdirects itself in point of law, it goes outside its powers.

For many years there was a distinction between the kinds of error. If the public authority went outside its jurisdiction altogether, its decision was void. But if it made an error within its jurisdiction, it could not be avoided.

[1] [1982] 2 WLR 62.
[2] [1964] AC 1129.
[3] [1982] 1 WLR 1155.

That distinction has now gone. No tribunal or inquiry has any jurisdiction to make an error of law on which the decision of the case depends. This has now been affirmed by the House of Lords in the vastly important case of *O'Reilly v Mackman*[1] when Lord Diplock said (page 1108):

> The full consequences of the *Anisminic* case[2] . . . have been virtually to abolish the distinction between errors within jurisdiction that rendered voidable a decision that remained valid until quashed, and errors that went to jurisdiction and rendered a decision void ab initio provided that its validity was challenged timeously in the High Court by an appropriate procedure.

So we have no cause to trouble ourselves with errors within or without the jurisdiction: nor with void or voidable. That is a great relief.

vi *The duty to exercise a discretion reasonably*

Again, if a public authority is entrusted, as part of its public law function, with the exercise of a discretion, it must take into account all relevant considerations. It must not be influenced by any irrelevant consideration. And its discretion must be exercised reasonably – in this sense, that it must not be so unreasonable that no reasonable authority could have reached it. That was said by Lord Greene (Master of the Rolls) in his celebrated judgment in *Associated Provincial Picture Houses Ltd v Wednesbury Corpn*[3] and has been repeatedly affirmed since.

vii *The duty to come to a reasonable decision*

Yet again, if a public authority is required as part of its public law function to come to a decision on a matter of fact, its finding must be reasonable in the sense that it must not be so unreasonable that no reasonable person could come to it. This is the gist of Lord Radcliffe's remarks in *Edwards v Bairstow*[4] which were treated as applicable to cases of judicial

[1] [1982] 3 WLR 1096.
[2] [1969] 2 AC 147.
[3] [1948] 1 KB 223, 234.
[4] [1956] AC 14, 36.

review by me in *Ashbridge Investments Ltd v Minister of Housing*,[1] by Lord Diplock in *O'Reilly v Mackman*[2] and by Lord Bridge in *Cocks v Thanet District Council*.[3]

viii '*Reasonable*'

Time after time the courts, in seeing whether they should interfere with the decision of a public authority, say that they will only do so if the decision is 'so unreasonable that no reasonable man could come to it.' This is just an emphatic way of saying, as Lord Hailsham (Lord Chancellor) said in *Re W (An Infant)*[4] that:

Two reasonable parents can perfectly reasonably come to opposite conclusions on the same set of facts without forfeiting their title to be regarded as reasonable. The question in any given case is whether a parental veto comes within the band of possible reasonable decisions and not whether it is right or mistaken. Not every reasonable exercise of judgment is right, and not every mistaken exercise of judgment is unreasonable. There is a band of decisions within which no court should seek to replace the individual's judgment with his own.

The courts will only interfere with the decision of a public authority if it is outside the band of reasonableness.

It was well put by Professor Wade in a passage in his treatise on *Administrative Law*[5] and approved by the Court of Appeal in the case of the *Boundary Commission*:[6]

The doctrine that powers must be exercised reasonably has to be reconciled with the no less important doctrine that the court must not usurp the discretion of the public authority which Parliament appointed to take the decision. Within the bounds of legal reasonableness is the area in which the deciding authority has genuinely free discretion. If it passes those bounds, it acts ultra vires. The court must therefore resist the temptation to draw the bounds too tightly, merely according to its own opinion. It must strive to apply an objective standard which leaves to the deciding authority the full range of choices which the legislature is presumed to have intended.

[1] [1965] 1 WLR 1320, 1326.
[2] [1982] 3 WLR 1096, 1107.
[3] [1982] 3 WLR 1121, 1125.
[4] [1971] AC 682, 700.
[5] (5th edn) p 362.
[6] [1983] 2 WLR 458, 475.

ix *The duty to hold the balance fairly*

There has emerged of late a duty on a public authority – in carrying out its public law functions – to hold the balance fairly between competing sections of the public. Just as a trustee is under a duty to hold an even hand between beneficiaries and not favour one above the other, so also is a public authority under a duty to hold the balance fairly between the competing interests under its care. Because of the analogy with trusts, it is called a fiduciary duty. This important principle was upheld by the House of Lords in the London Transport fares case, *Bromley London Borough Council v Greater London Council.*[1] It is of much importance both in its legal and political aspects. So much so that it needs a special chapter of its own.

[1] [1982] 2 WLR 62.

3 Law and politics

1 London Transport

i *25 per cent off London fares*

BROMLEY LONDON BOROUGH COUNCIL V GREATER LONDON COUNCIL[1]

In 1981 there was much controversy over the fares on London Transport. These were the facts as I described them in my judgment (at page 64):

On May 7 of this year there was an election for the Greater London Council. In advance of the election, the Labour Party issued a manifesto. In it they promised that, if they won, they would within six months cut the fares on London's buses and tubes by 25 per cent. They did win the election. They kept their promise. They told the London Transport Executive to cut the fares by 25 per cent. The Transport Executive did as they were told. Within six months, on October 4, 1981, they cut the fares by 25 per cent. The travelling public were well pleased with the gift. It meant millions of pounds in their pockets instead of in the ticket machines. But not the ratepayers of London. They were required to contribute £69 million to pay for it. In order to enforce payment, the GLC made a supplementary precept. This was an order directed to all the 35 London boroughs commanding them to raise the necessary funds. They were to do it by making a supplementary rate on all the ratepayers. The London boroughs have most reluctantly obeyed. They have made the supplementary rate and have required their ratepayers to pay it. But meanwhile one London borough – Bromley – has challenged the validity of the whole procedure. They apply to the courts for an order of certiorari to quash the supplementary precept.

At the outset I would say that all three members of this court are

[1] [1982] 2 WLR 62.

interested on all sides. We are all fare-paying passengers on the tubes and buses and benefit from the 25 per cent cut in fares. My wife and I also have the benefit of senior citizens to travel free. We are all ratepayers in the area of Greater London and have to pay the increase in rates imposed by the supplementary precept. No objection is taken by any party to our hearing the case. Any Court of Appeal would be likewise placed.

The case was decided in the Court of Appeal and the House of Lords on the interpretation of the Transport (London) Act 1969. It was held that the GLC had acted ultra vires. I said (at page 68):

The council itself had no power to make resolutions to enforce a 25 per cent cut. That was a completely uneconomic proposition done for political motives – for which there is no warrant – including the supplementary precept. It was beyond their powers. It is ultra vires and void. It cannot be allowed to stand.

But in case I was wrong, I went on to state the fiduciary duty.

ii *The balancing exercise*

This was the principle as I saw it (at page 68):

The GLC owed a duty both to the travelling public and to the ratepayers. Its duty to the travelling public is to provide an integrated, efficient and economic service at reasonable fares. Its duty to the ratepayers is to charge them as much as is reasonable and no more. In carrying out those duties, the members of the GLC have to balance the two conflicting interests – the interest of the travelling public in cheap fares – and the interest of the ratepayers in not being overcharged. The members of the GLC have to hold the balance between these conflicting interests. They have to take all relevant considerations into account on either side. They must not be influenced by irrelevant considerations. They must not give undue weight to one consideration over another, lest they upset the balance. They must hold the balance fairly and reasonably. If they come to a decision which is, in all the circumstances, unjust and unreasonable, then the courts can and should interfere. This is shown by *Roberts v Hopwood* [1925] AC 578 when the Poplar councillors gave undue weight to giving their workers a minimum wage and insufficient weight to the interests of the ratepayers. Also by *Prescott v Birmingham Corpn* [1955] Ch 210 where the Birmingham Corporation gave undue weight to giving free travel to the elderly and insufficient weight to the interests of the ratepayers. But in *Luby v Newcastle-under-Lyme Corpn* [1964] 2 QB 64 the council got the balance right as between the tenants as a whole and individual tenants in particular. This line of cases is, in my opinion, more applicable to our present situation of conflicting interests than *Associated Provincial Picture Houses Ltd v Wednesbury Corpn* [1948] 1 KB 223.

This principle was accepted in the House of Lords. Lord Wilberforce said (at page 99):

[The GLC] acted in breach of its fiduciary duty. . . . It failed to hold the balance between the transport users and the ratepayers as it should have done.

Lord Brandon of Oakbrook said (at page 130):

It was the duty of the GLC to balance fairly against each other the interests of the travelling public on the one hand and those of the ratepayers in the London boroughs on the other.

iii *The GLC did not hold it fair*

This was my conclusion as I stated it (at page 70):

The GLC did not hold the balance fair. The 25 per cent was more than fair to the travelling public and less than fair to the ratepayers. Millions of passengers on the buses and tubes come from far outside the London area. They come every day. They get the benefit of the 25 per cent cut in fares without paying a penny increase on their rates at home. That is more than fair to them. It is a gift indeed to them given without paying a penny for it. Whereas thousands of ratepayers in London who pay the rates never use the buses or tubes at all. Bromley, for instance, has no tubes. It is less than fair to them. It is positively penal. It is not fair to make these ratepayers pay for these gifts to people who come from far afield.

2 The manifesto

i *Open to question*

In coming to my decision I commented upon the manifesto. I thought that the majority of the council gave too much weight to it. They regarded the election result as giving them a mandate. They regarded themselves as committed to it and that they were bound to honour it. This is what I said about it (at page 69):

In giving such weight to the manifesto, I think the majority of the council were under a complete misconception. A manifesto issued by a political party – in order to get votes – is not to be taken as gospel. It is not to be regarded as a bond, signed, sealed and delivered. It may contain – and often does contain – promises or proposals that are quite unworkable or impossible of attainment. Very few of the electorate read the manifesto in full. A goodly number only know of it from what they read in the newspapers or hear on television. Many know nothing whatever of what it contains. When they come to the polling booth, none of them vote for the manifesto. Certainly not for every promise or proposal in it. Some may be influenced by one proposal. Others by another. Many are not influenced by it at all. They vote for a party and not for a manifesto. I have no doubt that in this case many ratepayers voted for the Labour Party even though, on this one item alone, it was against their interests. And vice versa. It seems to me that no party can or should claim a mandate and commitment for any one item in a long manifesto. When the party gets into power, it should consider any proposal or promise afresh – on its merits – without any feeling of being obliged to honour it or being committed to it. It should then consider what is best to do in the circumstances of the case and to do it if it is practicable and fair.

Both Lord Diplock and Lord Brandon of Oakbrook expressed a similar view.

By my words I raised a hornets' nest. The hornets swarmed out and stung me with venom. They accused me of being political. Whereas all I had done was to state what I believe is a principle of constitutional law.

ii '*Out, Out, Out*'

Not only in regard to the manifesto but also in the decision itself, some political groups attacked me. They treated me as if I alone was responsible and as if I had inflicted an injustice on the travellers by London buses and tubes. It was useless for me to say that it was not me but the House of Lords, and that they had decided it strictly on the interpretation of the statute. They blamed it all on me.

During this time I addressed the students of University College, London, of which I was the Visitor. Those inside were welcoming. But a mob of students outside were vociferous in condemnation of me. Throughout my talk, there were refrains of 'Out, Out, Out.' When I left the hall they rushed at me. A dozen strong students protected me – but the protestors hurled flour at me and the car.

3 Council tenants

i *They want to buy their houses*

R V SECRETARY OF STATE FOR THE ENVIRONMENT EX PARTE NORWICH CITY COUNCIL[1]

Soon afterwards there was another case which involved party politics. This was in the city of Norwich. It was about the sale of council houses to tenants. This is what I said (at page 583):

This case raises party politics. There is no hiding it: each side in the case has been influenced by its political views. But all these are put aside in this court. The issues are to be decided according to law and none else. It is about the sale of council houses. They have built them for the purpose of housing those in need. They have received housing subsidies from the government for the purpose. But they have become the subject of much controversy. . . .

Now Parliament has passed the Housing Act 1980. It gives council tenants the right to buy their houses at a big discount. Sometimes at half price. Some local councils think this is undesirable. It means that the houses are taken out of their housing stock. They are no longer available for the young marrieds and others who are desperately in need of accommodation.

The city of Norwich has been caught up in this conflict. It is a fine cathedral city with a population of 120,000. The city council owns about 25,000 dwellings – about half of all those in the city. When the Act of 1980 came into force many tenants claimed the right to buy their council houses. But there seemed to be endless delays. The tenants became very upset. They complained to the Secretary of State about the slowness. The Secretary of State tried to get the city council to hurry things up, but not with any great success. At length he took very drastic action. He took all the sales out of the hands of the council and into his own hands. The council dispute his right to do this. They have come to the court asking that the order of the Secretary of State be quashed.

The statute gave the Minister a 'default power'. It enabled him to take over the function himself – to do it all himself by

[1] [1982] 2 WLR 580.

144

his own civil servants – and to charge the cost to the local authority. As to this I said (at page 590):

This 'default power' enables the central government to interfere with a high hand over local authorities. Local self-government is such an important part of our constitution that, to my mind, the courts should be vigilant to see that this power of the central government is not exceeded or misused. Wherever the wording of the statute permits, the courts should read into it a provision that the 'default power' should not be exercised except in accordance with the rules of natural justice. That follows from such cases as *Board of Education v Rice* [1911] AC 179 and *Ridge v Baldwin* [1964] AC 40. After all, the minister is dismissing the local authority for default in carrying out their duty. He is replacing them by his own civil servants. He is making them pay all the costs and depriving them of the interest they would have received. Simple fairness requires that this should not be done unless they are told what is alleged against them and they have had an opportunity of answering it.

Apart from this, the very decision of the minister himself is open to judicial review. If the minister does not act in good faith, or if he acts on extraneous considerations which ought not to influence him, or if he misdirects himself in fact or in law, the court will in a proper case intervene and set his order aside.

ii *Protect the individual*

So the Court of Appeal looked into the matter. It upheld the order of the Minister. This is what I said (at page 592):

The concern of this court, as always, is to protect the individual from the misuse or abuse of power by those in authority. The individual here is the tenant. He has been given by Parliament the right to buy the house in which he lives. Yet in the exercise of that right he has met with intolerable delay. The responsibility for that delay is, beyond doubt, the responsibility of the Norwich City Council. They acted – or failed to act – in complete good faith. But they were misguided. And they must answer for it. . . . The council here showed too little concern for the rights of the tenants. They should have given them higher priority. They were unreasonable not to do so.

What is the remedy? What recourse have the tenants for redress? None by coming to the courts. Nothing could be done effectively by mandamus. The statute has provided a remedy. It has enabled the Secretary of State to make a 'default order'. It is a very great power to be used only after careful consideration. The Secretary of State here did give it careful consideration. He gave the council every opportunity to mend their ways. He gave them ample notice of what was alleged against them. He heard all that they had to say before he made his order. He gave them clear warning of the consequences. His order, strong as it was, was within his statutory powers. It cannot be upset in this court.

4 Remedies

1 Private law functions

i *No dispensation from the ordinary law*

The discourse on private law functions can be much shorter. Public authorities, including Ministers of the Crown, enjoy no dispensation from the ordinary law of tort and contract – except insofar as the statute gives it to them. They are liable like any other person for breach of contract, trespass, nuisance, negligence, and so forth. They are also liable for the negligence or other conduct of their servants within the course of their employment and the scope of their authority. Their relations with their servants – being under contract – are regarded as part of their private law functions. They come within the employment legislation. Even if they hold an inquiry about the dismissal of a servant – in circumstances contrary to the rules of natural justice – they are not liable to the process of judicial review, see *R v British Broadcasting Corpn, ex parte Lavelle*.[1] But there are some relationships, where the employee is not a mere servant but an officer holding a public office, where the remedy of judical review may be available, see *Malloch v Aberdeen Corpn*.[2] The speech of Lord Wilberforce gives illustrations of the difficulty of drawing the line. He said (page 1595):

... A comparative list of situations in which persons have been held entitled or not entitled to a hearing, or to observation of rules of natural

[1] [1983] 1 WLR 23.
[2] [1971] 1 WLR 1578.

justice, according to the master and servant test, looks illogical and even bizarre. A specialist surgeon is denied protection which is given to a hospital doctor; a university professor, as a servant, has been denied the right to be heard, a dock labourer and an undergraduate have been granted it; examples can be multiplied (. . .). One may accept that if there are relationships in which all requirements of the observance of rules of natural justice are excluded (and I do not wish to assume that this is inevitably so), these must be confined to what have been called 'pure master and servant cases', which I take to mean cases in which there is no element of public employment or service, no support by statute, nothing in the nature of an office or a status which is capable of protection. If any of these elements exist, then, in my opinion, whatever the terminology used, and even though in some inter partes aspects the relationship may be called that of master and servant, there may be essential procedural requirements to be observed, and failure to observe them may result in a dismissal being declared to be void.

That list by Lord Wilberforce is striking proof of the difficulties to which the 'new dichotomy' may give rise – between public and private law.

ii *Statutory authority a defence?*

There is one point which needs special mention. Very often public authorities execute works under statutory authority which cause damage to innocent persons. They then plead the statutory authority as a reason for not paying compensation. We had to consider this when a big oil refinery was built in South Wales and caused nuisance by noise and smell to all the persons in the neighbourhood. The case was *Allen v Gulf Oil Refining Ltd.*[1] I ventured to state the principle in my judgment. In it I referred to private undertakers but it also applies to public authorities. This is what I said (at pages 168–169):

I have considered this case on the construction of the statute according to the principles laid down in the railway cases of the 19th Century. But I venture to suggest that modern statutes should be construed on a new principle. Wherever private undertakers seek statutory authority to construct and operate an installation which may cause damage to people living in the neighbourhood, it should not be assumed that Parliament intended that damage should be done to innocent people without

[1] [1980] QB 156.

148

redress. Just as in principle property should not be taken compulsorily except on proper compensation being paid for it so, also, in principle property should not be damaged compulsorily except on proper compensation being made for the damage done. No matter whether the undertakers use due diligence or not, they ought not to be allowed – for their own profit – to damage innocent people or property without paying compensation. They ought to provide for it as part of the legitimate expenses of their operation, either as initial capital cost or the subsequent revenue. *Vaughan v Taff Vale Rly Co* (1860) 5 H & N 679, exposes the injustice of the Victorian rule. A landowner had a wood of eight acres before the railway came. The railway company got a private Bill and built the railway. Sparks from an engine burnt down the wood. He was denied any compensation at all. To avoid such injustice, I would suggest that, in the absence of any provision in the statute for compensation, the proper construction of a modern statute should be that any person living in the neighbourhood retains his action at common law; and that it is no defence for the promoters to plead the statute. Statutory authority may enable the promoters to make the installation and operate it but it does not excuse them from paying compensation for injury done to those living in the neighbourhood.

I realise that there is a difficulty about an injunction. No court would wish to grant an injunction to stop a great enterprise and render it useless. But that difficulty is easily overcome. By means of Lord Cairns' Act, the Chancery Amendment Act 1858, the court can award damages to cover past or future injury in lieu of an injunction: see *Leeds Industrial Co-operative Society Ltd v Slack* [1924] AC 851.

In *Allen v Gulf Oil Refining Ltd* the House of Lords watered this down. They said that it was the duty of the authority 'to carry out the work and conduct the operation with all reasonable regard and care for the interests of other persons'.[1] But in practice the result may well be the same.

2 Which remedy to use?

i *Judicial review the normal recourse*

In view of the new dichotomy between public law and private law, practitioners will often have to decide which remedy to use. This was the crucial point in the important case of *O'Reilly v Mackman*.[2]

[1] [1981] AC 1001, 1011.
[2] [1982] 3 WLR 604, CA; affd. [1982] 3 WLR 1096, HL.

I have told you already of this case which arose out of the riots at Hull prison. Several of the men complained that the board of visitors had acted unfairly in that they had failed to comply with the rules of natural justice.

The first men applied for judicial review in the nature of certiorari. They succeeded, see *R v Board of Visitors of Hull Prison, ex parte St Germain.*[1] Later on, other men issued writs asking for a declaration. They were too late for certiorari. So they attempted to go by action. One judge held that they could. Another judge held that they could not. The issue came before the Court of Appeal. I said:[2]

Now that judicial review is available to give every kind of remedy, I think it should be the normal recourse in all cases of public law where a private person is challenging the conduct of a public authority or a public body, or of anyone acting in the exercise of a public duty. I am glad to see that in *R v Inland Revenue Comrs, ex parte National Federation of Self-Employed and Small Businesses Ltd* [1981] 2 WLR 722, 737, Lord Diplock has endorsed the principle which I ventured to set out in *R v Greater London Council, ex parte Blackburn* [1976] 1 WLR 550, 559:
I regard it as a matter of high constitutional principle that if there is good ground for supposing that a government department or a public authority is transgressing the law, or is about to transgress it, in a way which offends or injures thousands of Her Majesty's subjects, then any one of those offended or injured can draw it to the attention of the courts of law and seek to have the law enforced, and the courts in their discretion can grant whatever remedy is appropriate.

I have often quoted that principle because it is of such importance.

ii *Safeguards against abuse*

I also pointed out that judicial review has safeguards against abuse which are not available in ordinary actions. In particular, the need to obtain the leave of a judge in order to pursue the complaint.

Then I mentioned the reasons why judicial review is to be the normal remedy. I said (at page 621):

None of these safeguards against abuse are available in an ordinary action – issued as of course – without leave – against a public authority or a

[1] [1979] QB 425.
[2] [1982] 3 WLR 604, 620.

public body. Some complainants – or their advisers – have seized upon this. They have brought actions at law instead of judicial review. Instances are ready to hand. An action was brought in the county court for damages against a local authority for breach of the Housing (Homeless Persons) Act 1977: see *Thornton v Kirklees Metropolitan Borough Council* [1979] QB 626. An action was brought in the Chancery Division for a declaration against the Home Office under the Immigration Act 1971: see *Uppal v Home Office* (1978) Times, 21 October. If such actions were to be permitted (as an alternative to judicial review) it would open the door to great abuse. Nearly all these people are legally-aided. If they were allowed to proceed by ordinary action, without leave, I can well see that the public authorities of this country would be harassed by all sorts of claims – long out of time – on the most flimsy of grounds.

iii *The end result*

So I came to this conclusion (at page 622):

Wherever there is available a remedy by judicial review under section 31 of the Supreme Court Act 1981, that remedy should be the normal remedy to be taken by an applicant. . . . It is an abuse to go back to the old machinery instead of using the new streamlined machinery. It is an abuse to go by action when he would never have been granted leave to go for judicial review.

The decision was affirmed by the House of Lords where Lord Diplock said:[1]

It would in my view as a general rule be contrary to public policy, and as such an abuse of the process of the court, to permit a person seeking to establish that a decision of a public authority infringed rights to which he was entitled to protection under public law to proceed by way of an ordinary action and by this means to evade the provisions of Order 53 for the protection of such authorities.

This is a remarkable change – as Professor Wade has recently pointed out in the *Law Quarterly Review*.[2] He says that owing to the introduction of judicial review

the law has now revolved through a full circle: the action by writ for a declaration or injunction (which the courts have done so much to encourage as an alternative to the prerogative remedies over the last 30 years) is now found to be an abuse of the process of the court.

1 [1982] 3 WLR 1096, 1110.
2 (1983) 99 LQR 167–168.

iv *But not the only remedy*

It must be remembered that judicial review is only the *normal* remedy. There may still be cases where it is appropriate for a remedy to be sought by ordinary writ and declaration, even in a public law matter, as in *Air Canada v Secretary of State for Trade*.[1]

It is to be hoped that the new dichotomy will not lead to a procedural wrangle – so that a plaintiff does not really know where he stands. If he goes by judicial review – and that is mistaken – the court can allow the proceedings to proceed as if he began by writ. But the converse does not apply. If he begins by writ – and is mistaken – his proceedings will be struck out. Recent cases have shown up the difficulties. To avoid them I would like to suggest that a plaintiff who is aggrieved has a constitutional right to proceed by writ (seeking a declaration or injunction). A writ should not be regarded as an abuse of the process of the court except in plain cases where it is obvious that the plaintiff could and should have gone by judicial review.

[1] [1983] 2 WLR 494.

5 Postscript

I would end this discourse as I ended in *O'Reilly v Mackman:*[1]

I cannot refrain from referring to a few words I said in 1949 at the end of my Hamlyn Lecture, *Freedom under the Law* (1949) page 126:
Just as the pick and shovel is no longer suitable for the winning of coal, so also the procedure of mandamus, certiorari, and actions on the case are not suitable for the winning of freedom in the new age. They must be replaced by new and up-to-date machinery, by declarations, injunctions, and actions for negligence. . . . We have in our time to deal with changes which are of equal constitutional significance to those which took place 300 years ago. Let us prove ourselves equal to the challenge.

Now, over 30 years after, we do have the new and up-to-date machinery. I would say with Lord Diplock in *R v IRC, ex parte National Federation of Self-Employed and Small Businesses Ltd* [1981] 2 WLR 722, 737:
To revert to technical restrictions . . . that were current 30 years or more ago would be to reverse that progress towards a comprehensive system of administrative law that I regard as having been the greatest achievement of the English courts in my judicial lifetime.

So we have proved ourselves equal to the challenge. Let us buttress our achievement by interpreting section 31 in a wide and liberal spirit. By so doing we shall have done much to prevent the abuse or misuse of power by any public authority or public officer or other person acting in the exercise of a public duty.

[1] [1982] 3 WLR 604, 623.

Section Six

Trade Unions

Introduction

In this section I deal at some length with trade unions and the law. This is because I know of no book on it which has been written for the general reader. All have been written by lawyers for lawyers. They soon become submerged in technicalities. Yet it is a subject of the first importance for a large part of our people who are not lawyers. It is important for all employers and workmen, for all members of trade unions and non-members, for Members of Parliament and all who are concerned with the welfare of our society. It has for the last 100 years been the subject of acute political controversy. Statutes have been passed or repealed according to which government was in power. There have been recent statutes which have already been considered and still need further consideration by the courts. Still more legislation is proposed. So I thought it might be useful if I told you in my own words something of the story. I do so especially as I have been closely involved in it for the last 30 years.

1 Up to the 1906 Act

1 The background

i *Are trade unions above the law?*

I have been accused of prejudice against them. On one or two occasions, when off the judicial bench, I have said that 'trade unions are above the law'. Whereupon I have been accused of being politically prejudiced against them. I deny the charge. If you should look into the cases in which I have taken part, you will see that sometimes the judgments have been in favour of trade unions: and sometimes against them. In every case I have decided in accordance with the law as I believe it to be. When I have said that 'trade unions are above the law' that is just shorthand for saying that trade unions and their leaders have been granted by Parliament a wide exemption from the ordinary law of the land. They are in many cases immune from suit in the courts.

If you know your history, you will know that in this field for 100 years law and politics have been mixed up together. Politics have influenced the law, and the law has influenced politics. Many of the cases that come before the courts are fraught with political consequences. The very decision of them becomes the subject of political controversy. The columnists comment on them. Pressure groups press for legislation to overrule them. All this is unavoidable. But none of it means that the judges themselves are political.

As I myself have been accused, I would say that I have never been a member of a political party. I have never voted at a parliamentary election. I have refused invitations to any meeting, fête or dance sponsored by a political party. I regard this of the first importance so that all should know that I am independent of any political party whatsoever.

ii *Disputes should be settled by arbitration*

All over England in recent years the prayer has gone up: 'Let justice be done between the trade unions and the public.' To my mind, justice could have been done in every dispute if the two sides could have agreed to have their disputes settled by arbitration. But in many cases – such as the recent water strike – one side or the other refuses arbitration. Each thinks it can get better terms by standing out until the other side gives in. They do not heed the advice given by Archbishop William Temple. He took the Christian precept of love towards your neighbour and gave this illustration:[1]

Imagine a Trade Union Committee negotiating with an Employers' Federation in an industrial crisis on the verge of a strike. This Committee is to be actuated by love. Oh, yes, by all means, but towards whom? Are they to love the workers or the employers? Of course – both. But then that will not help them much to determine what terms ought to be either proposed or accepted. . . . Love, in fact, finds its primary expression through justice which, in the field of industrial disputes, means in practice that each side should state its case as strongly as it can before the most impartial tribunal available, with determination to accept the award of that tribunal. At least that puts the two parties on a level, and is to that extent in accordance with the command 'Thou shalt love thy neighbour as thyself.'

iii *A giant's strength*

Throughout my time trade unions have been increasing in power. The courts have had little control over them: because the trade unions and their leaders have been given, by statute, immunity from legal process. This immunity was fair enough in early days. Employers used to exploit their workmen by paying low wages, subjecting them to harsh conditions, and dismissing them at a week's notice. It was

[1] Temple *Christianity and the Social Order.*

159

only by the men combining together in trade unions that these conditions could be remedied. But latterly the trade unions appear to many to have taken undue advantage of this immunity. It has been used to enforce excessive demands, such as to increase wages beyond those which the industry can afford, especially in regard to nationalised undertakings. In the course of this the trade unions have inflicted immeasurable hardship and injury on thousands and thousands of innocent people. They have stopped services essential to the life of the community. So much so that everywhere the cry went up, with Shakespeare:[1]

> 'O! it is excellent
> To have a giant's strength, but it is tyrannous
> To use it like a giant.'

iv *The weapon used*

The trade unions have a mighty weapon to hand. They make demands. They threaten 'industrial action' unless their demands are met. They say they will use their 'industrial muscle' to twist the arm of the employers.

What is the meaning of this? It means they will use all the power at their disposal to gain their ends. They will call men out 'on strike', that is, not to go to work. They will tell them to 'work to rule', or to 'go slow', that is, not to do their work properly. They will 'black' goods, that is, refuse to handle them as they ought to do. They will 'black' customers, that is, not allow any dealings with them. They will set up 'picket lines' which others will not, or dare not, cross. They will call out men in other industries (who are not affected) to come out 'in sympathy' with those who are affected. And so forth.

v *What the common law says*

If it were not for the statutes, most of this industrial action would be illegal. The common law has developed much in my time. In its modern form I stated the principle in *Torquay*

---

[1] *Measure for Measure*, Act II, sc. 2.

Hotel Co Ltd v Cousins.[1] I repeated it in *Acrow (Automation) Ltd v Rex Chainbelt Inc.*[2] This is the principle:

I have always understood that if one person deliberately interferes with the trade or business of another, and does so by unlawful means, that is, by an act which he is not at liberty to commit, then he is acting unlawfully, even though he does not procure or induce any actual breach of contract. If the means are unlawful, that is enough.

That principle leaves open the question: What is to be regarded as 'unlawful means'? It is certainly unlawful to induce a person to break a contract. It is also unlawful to prevent or hinder him in the performance of a contract. The House of Lords in the recent case of *Merkur Island Shipping Corpn v Laughton*[3] approved what I said in *Torquay Hotel Co Ltd v Cousins:*[4]

The interference (which is unlawful) is not confined to the procurement of a *breach* of contract. It extends to a case where a third person *prevents* or *hinders* one party from performing his contract, even though it be not a breach.

It follows that 'unlawful means' includes intimidation, inducing breach of contract, preventing or hindering the performance of a contract, collective boycott, and 'blacking'. All these are unlawful at common law.

iv *The right to strike*

It is often said that the men have a right to strike. That is much too broad a proposition. As I said in *The Discipline of Law*, pages 180–182, they only have a right to strike so long as they give proper notice of their intention to cease work: and this notice must be at least as long as a proper notice to terminate the employment altogether. A lightning strike or a walk-out by the men is not lawful. It is a breach of their contract of employment. Anyone who persuades or induces

---

[1] [1969] 2 Ch 106, 139.
[2] [1971] 1 WLR 1676, 1682
[3] [1983] 2 WLR 778, 786.
[4] [1969] 2 Ch 106, 138.

them to do so is guilty of a wrong at common law. It is the use of unlawful means.

2 The attainment of immunity

i *Two cases in 1901*

For the moment I would, however, revert to the common law as it stood in 1901. In that year there were two decisions of the House of Lords which were very adverse to trade unions. One was *Taff Vale Rly Co v Amalgamated Society of Railway Servants*[1] where it was held that a trade union could be sued for the wrongs done by its members. The other case was *Quinn v Leathem*[2] where it was held that if two or more people combine to injure a person in his trade by unlawful means they could be sued for damages.

ii *The 1906 Act is passed*

These decisions gave rise to much political controversy. Eventually there was a general election in which the Liberals gained the ascendancy. Labour combined with Liberals to pass the Trade Disputes Act 1906. It reversed the *Taff Vale* case by enacting in section 4 that a trade union could not be sued for wrongs done by its members. It reversed *Quinn v Leathem* by giving considerable immunity from suit. The statute in several places used words which have become known in some circles as 'the golden formula'. They are: 'An act done by a person in contemplation or furtherance of a trade dispute.'

iii *'The golden formula'*

Section 3 of the 1906 Act is so important that I set it out in full:

An act done by a person in contemplation or furtherance of a trade dispute shall not be actionable on the ground only that it induces some

[1] [1901] AC 426.
[2] [1901] AC 495.

other person to break a contract of employment or that it is an interference with the trade, business, or employment of some other person, or with the right of some other person to dispose of his capital or his labour as he wills.

The immunity given by 'the golden formula' is very extensive. It received a severe shock in 1964 by the decision of the House of Lords in *Rookes v Barnard*.[1] That decision was politically unacceptable to the Labour Government so the immunity was restored by the Labour Government in the next year in the Trade Disputes Act 1965.

iv *The ordinary person*

By the spring of 1970 the country as a whole had turned against trade unions, or rather, against the way they had abused their 'giant's strength'. They thought it was tyrannous to use it like a giant. At the general election in June 1970, they voted the Conservatives back into power.

[1] [1964] AC 1129.

2 The Industrial Relations Act 1971

1 The Act is passed

i *A Bill is presented to Parliament*

The Conservative Government undoubtedly had a mandate from the electorate to curb the powers of trade unions and their leaders. They introduced a major Bill in Parliament. The architect of it was the Solicitor-General, Sir Geoffrey Howe QC. It was designed to regulate industrial relations in two ways in particular:

first, by having a register of trade unions and giving immunity to those who registered;

second, by setting up the National Industrial Relations Court (which I will call the Industrial Court) to enforce the law.

ii *It has a stormy passage*

The Bill had a stormy passage through Parliament. It was bitterly opposed by the Labour party. It was passed into law as the Industrial Relations Act 1971. It came into force on 28 February 1972. From the beginning it was boycotted in several quarters. Most of the trade unions refused to register under it. They did not treat the Industrial Court as a court of law. They regarded it as a tool of the Government.

iii *A tool of the Government*

The Industrial Court was manned by a High Court judge

and two or more lay members. But the trade unions refused to nominate any members to it. It was given powers equivalent to those of the High Court but it was not the High Court. It was a separate tribunal of its own. It sat in a separate building of its own. Its members sat informally round a table. They had neither wigs nor robes. It had none of the dignity or authority of the High Court. Its opponents worked up feeling against it. They suggested that it was not a regular court of justice at all. It was, in their view, a tool used by the Government to enforce a repressive law. No wonder it was regarded with hatred by those whom it affected. No wonder they moved heaven and earth to do away with it. They refused to acknowledge its authority. They would not appear before it, nor argue before it. If it made orders, they would not obey. They would rather go to prison – confident that, if they did so, there would be a general strike which would bring down the Government.

iv *The Act is put to the test*

Within a few weeks the Act was put to the test. At all major ports the dockers took industrial action. The employers sought to protect their businesses. They applied to the Industrial Court. It led to a leading case called *Heatons'* case. It was, from the political point of view, most important. So you must forgive me if I explain it in detail.

2 *Heatons'* case – a crucial decision

HEATONS TRANSPORT (ST HELENS) LTD V TGWU[1]

i *The dockers are angry*

At one time goods used to be carried by sea in sacks or bags or crates and loaded by cranes on to ships. But by the year 1970 this method was being replaced by a system called the 'container revolution'. Thenceforward goods were carried in big steel containers in purpose-built ships called 'container ships'. This affected greatly the workers in the docks. They

[1] [1973] AC 15.

saw their jobs disappearing before their very eyes. No longer did they unload wagons on the quay. No longer did they fill the slings or work the cranes. No longer did they stack or stow in the holds. Only a few men were needed to work the lifting-gear of the containers.

The containers, of course, had to be filled and emptied – or, as the men put it, 'stuffed' or 'stripped' – but this was done by other men, not dock workers but men at warehouses outside the dock area. The dockers were so angry that they decided to 'black' all lorries carrying goods from these warehouses to the docks.

ii *Heatons are 'blacked'*

Heatons were road hauliers. Their warehouse was in St Helens, some distance from the ports. On Monday 20 March 1972, one of their drivers took his lorry to the docks at Liverpool. A man at the entrance asked to see his union card. The driver produced it. It was not stamped. The man said: 'You're on the black list. We can't unload you.' He was not allowed to take his lorry into the docks. Day after day the same thing happened.

iii *The 'blacking' was unofficial*

This black list was entirely unofficial. It had been prepared by the dock shop stewards at Liverpool docks. They had prepared it on their own without any authority from any committee of the union or any officer of the union. The 'blacking' was done on the instructions of the shop stewards without any direction or approval by anyone higher up.

There was similar 'blacking' at Hull. It was all done by the shop stewards on their own. The officers of the union tried to restrain the shop stewards but failed. The Industrial Court paid a tribute to the officers of the union at Hull and said:[1]

We have been greatly impressed and assisted by the oral evidence which union officials have given in this case. They have advised their Hull shop stewards to cease 'blacking' Panalpina, but, regrettably, without any

[1] [1973] AC 15, 45.

effect. We have no doubt that this advice is sincerely given and that the officials concerned genuinely hope that it will be heeded.

But it was not heeded. The 'blacking' continued.

iv *Heatons go against the union*

Heatons were so aggrieved that they went to the Industrial Court and complained – not against the shop stewards, but against the trade union itself. It was the Transport and General Workers' Union, the biggest union in the land. It had never recognised the 1971 Act. It had never registered as a trade union. It did not appear before the Industrial Court. Nor was it represented. Yet, in its absence, the Industrial Court made order after order against it, restraining *the union itself* from 'blacking' Heatons' lorries.

v *But not against the shop stewards*

The orders of the court were directed against the trade union itself, not against the shop stewards. So the shop stewards were not bound by the court's orders. They continued their unofficial action without any authority from the officers of the union. On Sunday 9 April 1972 the shop stewards called a mass meeting of the dock workers. Six thousand attended. They voted overwhelmingly to continue the 'blacking'. And they did continue.

vi *The union is fined £55,000*

In March and April 1972 the Industrial Court held that the union itself was guilty of contempt of court on the ground that the union itself had continued the 'blacking'. The court fined the union at first £5,000 and then a further £50,000, but still the 'blacking' continued.

At this stage the union at last got lawyers to represent them. They went to the Industrial Court and asked for a review of the fines. The court refused. The union appealed to the Court of Appeal.

vii *The Court of Appeal quash the fines*

The Court of Appeal allowed the appeal. It was on 13 June 1972. It set aside the fines. These are the passages in the Law Report which show the grounds of the decision. After referring to the rules of the union and their handbook, I said (at page 48):

I find no authority in a shop steward – or in a shop stewards' committee – to take industrial action on his or their own initiative. The matter must first be put before one of the official committees of the union before it can be made responsible. It must at least be approved by the district committee of the union. That is the lowest body to which the rules permit industrial action to be delegated: see rules 3(9) and 6(15) and (16). It is no good getting the approval of an officer of the union. It must be by an official committee of the union.

Then at the end of my judgment, I said (at page 51):

If this trade union had been registered under the Act, it would undoubtedly have gone clear. Its rules would have provided expressly – as, in my opinion, these do impliedly – that the shop stewards have no authority to call for industrial action on their own initiative. If registered, the shop stewards would be guilty of unfair industrial practices, but the union would not: see section 96(1)(a). Why then should the union be mulcted in heavy fines and large compensation, simply because it was not registered? If the legislature had intended that an unregistered union should be so penalised, it should have said so in terms. It should have said that an unregistered union – in contrast to a registered union – is to be liable for the actions of its shop stewards, whether authorised or not. For that is what it comes to. But Parliament has not said so. By keeping silent on its liability for shop stewards, Parliament has left it to the courts to decide. And we must decide it according to law, not influenced in the least by any political considerations. . . .

According to the law as I believe it to be, a union, registered or unregistered, is not responsible for the conduct of its shop stewards when they call for industrial action, if in so doing those shop stewards are acting outside the scope of their authority. On the evidence in this case I hold that the shop stewards at Liverpool and Hull were acting on behalf of their own work groups and not on behalf of the union. They were acting outside the scope of their authority from the union. They are undoubtedly liable themselves, but the union is not.

I would, therefore, allow the appeals in all these cases. I would set aside the fines and order them to be repaid. I would set aside the final orders, remarking only that it is a pity the union did not from the very outset appear before the court and put its case. . . .

viii *A coach-and-six through the Act*

The decision came as a profound shock to the Government. Next day, 14 June 1972, *The Times* on its front page in a bold headline said:

APPEAL COURT'S RULING ON SHOP STEWARDS SEEN AS BLOW TO GOVERNMENT AIMS

Then it said:

Senior ministers, shocked by a Court of Appeal ruling that the TGWU was not legally responsible for its shop stewards blacking container lorries, yesterday assumed that the issue would be taken to the House of Lords. . . .

Another headline was:

MINISTERS SHOCKED BY JUDGMENT

and *The Times* went on to give the views of others:

Trade union politicians both on the left and the right had no doubt that the judgment has driven a coach-and-six through the Industrial Relations Act. For them Lord Denning and his colleagues had inflicted a profoundly significant defeat on the Government, particularly on Sir Geoffrey Howe QC, the Solicitor-General, who devised the Act and led for the Government in proceedings before the National Industrial Relations Court. . . .

In a leading article headed THE DENNING DECISION *The Times* paid a glancing tribute to our impartiality:

If there are any who really believe that the judiciary is systematically prejudiced against their interests, they now have before them a notable instance of contradiction of that belief.

3 The three dockers

CHURCHMAN V JOINT SHOP STEWARDS' COMMITTEE[1]

i *Employers go against the shop stewards*

That decision in *Heatons'* case meant that the Act would become a dead letter unless something was done. What was

[1] [1972] 1 WLR 1094.

to be done? The employers still had a shot in their locker. Although they could not go against the trade union, could they not go against the shop stewards? After all, it was the shop stewards who instigated and carried out the 'blacking' of Heatons. The Court of Appeal had said that the shop stewards were responsible. Why not go against them?

ii *Three dockers picket a depot*

The occasion was ready to hand – not against the shop stewards at Liverpool, but in London. There was a depot at Chobham Farm. It was some distance from the docks. Men were employed there to strip and stuff containers. They received comparatively low wages. Dock workers claimed the right to do the work – at their own high wages. Now all the men – both those at the depot and those at the docks – were members of the same union, the Transport and General Workers' Union. The dockers had their own shop stewards. Three of them picketed the depot. They stopped lorries entering it. This mightily upset the men working in the depot. It meant that they would lose their jobs. So the men in the depot went to the Industrial Court for protection. The court made an order against the three shop stewards, restraining them from stopping the lorries. The three did not attend the court. Nor were they represented.

I have told you a little of the story in *The Due Process of Law*, pages 36–39, but in view of its importance I will tell more of it now.

iii *The three are committed to prison*

On 14 June, the very day after the decision of the Court of Appeal in *Heatons'* case, the Industrial Court made a committal order against the three dockers. The President of the Court, as reported in *The Times* of 15 June said:

The three men had not appeared. Since they had not been ordered to attend court they were acting within their rights. But as the court itself had said – and as the Court of Appeal had said yesterday – failure to attend was most ill-advised. The conduct of the three had gone far beyond anything which could appropriately be disposed of by fines. There was no alternative to committing them to prison. Accordingly the court would sign warrants for their arrest and detention. But the court wished them to have every opportunity to explain their conduct and to appeal to the Court of Appeal if they considered that they were being treated unjustly.

Therefore the warrants would not issue until 2 pm on Friday. . . .

iv *All dockers stop work*

So the deadline was 2 pm on Friday 16 June. But the dock workers of England did not wait until then. As soon as the news broke that the three were to be committed to prison, the dockers of England stopped work. Thirty-five thousand of them at all the major ports. It was in protest against the threatened imprisonment of the three. The country was at crisis point.

v *The Official Solicitor comes in*

Then there came a *deus ex machina*. You know, of course, that phrase. It means literally 'a god (let down upon the stage) from the machine'. The 'machine' was part of the furniture of the stage in an ancient Greek theatre. The phrase means today 'the intervention of some unlikely event to extricate one from difficulties.'

The 'god' in this case was no other than the Official Solicitor. The 'machine' was his room on the top floor of the Law Courts.

vi *How did he come into it?*

Many people have wondered how the Official Solicitor came into it. I wrote a note at the time of all that happened. I summarised it in a statement I made in court. I give it now in a little more detail.

The deadline, as I have said, was 2 pm on Friday 16 June. As soon as I got back from lunch at 1.55 pm, Mr Peter Pain of counsel came to see me. He explained that he had been in consultation with members of the Transport and General

Workers' Union all the morning. He had some papers and thought there might be some points to be urged against the committal, but he could not get any instructions from anyone to put them forward. They had been trying to get in touch with the three dockers, but it would seem that they had been deliberately keeping out of the way. He said that the union would not instruct him to apply. He felt that, as the freedom of the individual was at stake – as well as the national interest – someone ought to bring the matter before the Court of Appeal at the earliest possible moment.

Lord Justice Buckley and Lord Justice Roskill came in. I told them what had been said. After discussing other possibilities, I reminded them that when a person, who was in prison for contempt, would not apply for release, the Official Solicitor might do so, and that the Official Solicitor might represent the men. I spoke to the Official Solicitor on the telephone. I asked if he would come. He said, 'Yes.' He came. I said that I believed he had authority to act in some cases for men who were detained, and I wondered if he could act in the case of the three dockers. He said at once that he could do so under the general authority given to him by the Lord Chancellor's instructions. He told us that he already knew about the case and had retained counsel. Then he went off to consult counsel again.

vii *The committal orders are set aside*

Everyone acted very quickly. At 3.15 pm on that very afternoon counsel appeared before us. Not only for the Official Solicitor but also for the workers in the depot. We read the evidence. We heard arguments. We gave judgment allowing the appeal. We quashed the order for committal. In giving reasons, I said:[1]

It seems to me that the evidence before the Industrial Court was quite insufficient to prove – with all the strictness that is necessary in such a proceeding as this, when you are going to deprive people of their liberty – a breach of the court's order.

[1] [1972] 1 WLR 1094, 1100.

172

viii *One of the greatest victories*

Our decision ended the crisis – for the time being. That was on Friday 16 June. Early the next week there were mass meetings of dockers at all the major ports in the country. They voted overwhelmingly to return to work. At a meeting of over 5,000 dock workers on Tower Hill on Monday 19 June, as reported in *The Times* the next day, Mr Steer – one of the three dockers – said:

We consider this one of the greatest victories in industrial history in this country. Furthermore, if any other trade unionist, no matter where he comes from, is placed in prison for daring to have the temerity to defend his living, then we will come out on strike in his support. Our policy of no compromise has led to victory. We can be proud, as our stand has made the biggest loophole in the most pernicious piece of legislation passed this century.

The Times itself on its front page added this comment:

Although flushed with victory . . . unofficial dockers' leaders gave a clear warning that any further use of the law would provoke another immediate country-wide strike.

4 The five dockers

MIDLAND COLD STORAGE LTD V TURNER[1]

i *Another crisis looms*

The opportunity soon arrived. This time there was trouble at a cold store run by Midland Cold Storage at Hackney, East London. Dock workers claimed the right to do the work there instead of the existing men. Shop stewards of dockers organised pickets to stand outside the gates of the cold store. The pickets took the names of firms and numbers of any vehicles crossing the picket lines. These firms were then 'blacked' by dock workers all over the country. Dockers refused to load or unload vehicles belonging to those firms. The proprietors of the cold store applied to the Industrial

[1] [1972] ICR 230, Times, 22 July.

Court. On 10 July 1972, that court made an order requiring the dockers to refrain. They did not do so. So on 21 July, proceedings were brought before the court against five dockers on the picket lines. The five dockers did not appear. Nor were they represented. But Mr Vinelott QC and Mr Alexander appeared for the Official Solicitor as amicus curiae.

ii *Five dockers jailed*

The Industrial Court made an order committing the five dockers to prison. Next day *The Times* had a big black heading:

FIVE DOCKERS JAILED FOR CONTEMPT: 'NO INTENTION OF OBEYING COURT'

It reported the judgment of the President of the Court (Sir John Donaldson):

. . . Midland and their workers are entitled to be protected from these men who have constituted themselves judge and jury in their own cause. If the court cannot protect them by orders, it has no alternative but to resort to physical restraint.

Each member of this court has reached this conclusion with regret. The purpose of this court is to promote good industrial relations and none of us imagines for one moment that the making of committal orders will achieve this result. But the issue is far greater even than good industrial relations. The public at large, through a properly elected Parliament, has set up the Industrial Court. It has given this court the power and the duty of protecting the rights of all workers, unions and employers in accordance with law. The issue is whether these men are to be allowed to opt out of the rule of law. Can they pick and choose, relying upon it for the protection of their homes and families but rejecting it when, even temporarily, it obstructs their industrial objectives? It is a very simple issue, but vastly important, for our whole way of life is based upon the acceptance of the rule of law.

iii *Intense activity behind the scenes*

Once again the dockers all over the country came out on strike. The major ports were paralysed. What was to be done?

The feeling among some observers was that the order of the Industrial Court was open to question. They had imprisoned the five dockers indefinitely. They ought, it was said, only to have fined them or committed them for a few days. Something should be done to get them released as soon as possible. There was intense activity behind the scenes.

iv *An application is arranged*

On Tuesday 25 July my clerk received a message that an application might be made to the Industrial Court at 2 pm that day about the five dockers. The reason was because the Official Solicitor had decided himself to see the five dockers at Pentonville Prison and, if they refused to apologise or purge their contempt, he was going to apply to the Industrial Court to review the sentence of committal. If the Industrial Court refused to release the dockers, he was going to appeal to the Court of Appeal. He was expected to come at about 2.15 pm, if he could manage it. I told my clerk that we should be ready to hear it.

v *But no application is made*

As it turned out, however, the Official Solicitor did not, on that Tuesday, make any application to the Industrial Court to review the order for committal, nor did he make any appeal to the Court of Appeal. This must have been because a better way had been thought of, as now appears. The intense activity behind the scenes had led to this sequence of events which led to the release of the five.

vi *In the morning* – Heatons' *case is reversed*

On the very next morning, Wednesday 26 July, the House of Lords gave their decision in *Heatons'* case.[1] They reversed the Court of Appeal. They held that the trade union was responsible for the disobedience of the shop stewards to the order to stop the 'blacking'. They restored the fines of

[1] [1973] AC 15.

175

£55,000 imposed by the Industrial Court. It is no secret that the decision of the House of Lords was given in great haste. They were correcting the typescript up to the last moment.

vii *In the afternoon – the release of the five*

On the afternoon of the self-same day, Wednesday 26 July, the Official Solicitor applied to the Industrial Court for the release of the five dockers. The President of that Court said that none of the five had asked the Official Solicitor to make the application, nor did they approve of his doing so. But then the President went on to say – as reported in *The Times* on Friday 28 July:

> . . . If there had been no other factor the court does not see how, consistently with its duty, it could order the release of the five men. But a new factor has emerged – the decision earlier today of the House of Lords in the Heatons' Transport appeals. The Lords' judgment makes it clear that the primary method of enforcement contemplated by the Industrial Relations Act is against the funds of organisations rather than against individuals. That has been the court's view. . . .
>
> This afternoon the situation is entirely changed. The Transport Union is again accountable for the 'blacking' organised by its shop stewards. . . .
>
> The men themselves deserve little consideration. The unions do. . . .
>
> In the end we have concluded that, in the light of the House of Lords' decision and the consequent support which they (the Midland firm and their employees) may now expect from the unions, justice to them can still be done if these men are released. . . .

viii *The tension is eased*

So the five were released. The tension was eased. Most of the dockers went back to work. All hopes then turned to a committee which had been formed to advise on the docks. There were two chairmen – Lord Aldington and Mr Jack Jones. During that very week they issued a report in which they recommended: 'Up to £4,000 severance pay for dockers and a pledge to encourage new job opportunities' (*The Times*, Friday 28 July). After some time they managed to achieve peace. Where the courts had failed, they had succeeded.

5 The political consequences

i *They were immense*

The political consequences were immense. The Industrial Relations Act had been shattered. The Government had set up the Industrial Court to enforce the Act. Yet it had been shown by events to be powerless. It had made orders committing to prison at first three dockers and afterwards five dockers. These orders had been ineffective. The dockers had all been released. Never again could the Industrial Court hope to enforce its orders committing persons to prison.

ii *I am shaken to the core*

I know that in Government circles the downfall of the Act was attributed to the Court of Appeal in *Heatons'* case. Some time afterwards I was told by one in a high place:

Your decision was a disaster for the country, which will last till the end of the century.

I was shaken to the core. But I was not downcast. I just thought:

Thank goodness, the judges of the Court of Appeal are independent.

No government dare seek to influence them.

3 The 1974 and 1976 Acts

1 The trade unions triumphant

i *Swift legislation*

In March 1974 there was a general election. Labour was returned to power. They had promised to repeal the hated 1971 Act, and they did so. They acted swiftly. Within four months, in July 1974, they had enacted the Trade Union and Labour Relations Act 1974. The very first section (section 1(1)) said:

The Industrial Relations Act 1971 is hereby repealed.

The statute used 'the golden formula' in section 13 so as again to give immunity to trade union leaders for 'an act done by a person in contemplation or furtherance of a trade dispute' and by an amendment in section 3(2) in the 1976 Act they extended this immunity even further.

ii *A famous victory*

So the trade unions and their leaders had won all along the line. They had destroyed the Industrial Relations Act 1971. They had got almost complete exemption from the courts of law. It was a famous victory for them. But the ordinary man might well ask: What good came of it? As Robert Southey, the poet, said after the Battle of Blenheim:

> 'And everybody praised the Duke,
> Who this great fight did win.'

'But what good came of it at last?'
Quoth little Peterkin.
'Why that I cannot tell,' said he,
'But 'twas a famous victory.'[1]

2 The Court of Appeal take a hand

i *They limit immunity*

So in 1976 the trade unions were triumphant. Their 'golden formula' was serving them well. But then the Court of Appeal took a hand. In case after case it sought to restrict the immunity to reasonable limits. Much depended upon the true interpretation of the words in 'the golden formula' – 'in furtherance of'. The Court of Appeal said that those words only availed the trade union leaders when the act was one which could *reasonably* be considered to be 'in furtherance of' a trade dispute. And also by saying that 'secondary action' would not be protected. These points are somewhat technical. They can best be understood by reference to three cases where the Court of Appeal granted injunctions against leaders of trade unions. I start with an early one of which I told you in *The Discipline of Law*.

ii *Televising the Cup Final*

BRITISH BROADCASTING CORPN V HEARN[2]
The Cup Final at Wembley is the sporting event of the year. It was to be televised all over the world on 21 May 1977. One transmission was to be to South Africa. It was by way of the Indian Ocean satellite. A pressure group took strong objection to the policy of apartheid in South Africa. So did a trade union of broadcasting staff. They asked the British Broadcasting Corporation ('BBC') to stop the transmission of the Cup Final to South Africa. The BBC refused. The trade union then decided to take 'industrial action'. They told the technicians not to transmit via the Indian Ocean

---

[1] *After Blenheim.*
[2] [1977] 1 WLR 1004.

satellite. They claimed that it was 'in contemplation of a trade dispute'.

The Court of Appeal issued an injunction against the trade union leader. They held that there was no 'trade dispute'. In the course of my judgment I gave this illustration (page 1011):

Take the case which I put in the course of argument: If printers in a newspaper office were to say: 'We don't like the article which you are going to publish about the Arabs – or the Jews – or on this or that political issue – you must withdraw it. If you do not do so, we are not going to print your paper.' That is not a trade dispute. It is coercive action unconnected with a trade dispute. It is an unlawful interference with the freedom of the press. It is a self-created power of censorship. It does not become a trade dispute simply because the men propose to break their contracts of employment in doing it.

So the Cup Final was televised to South Africa.

iii *Advertisements in newspapers*

ASSOCIATED NEWSPAPERS GROUP LTD V WADE[1]

Mr Forman, the owner of the *Nottingham Evening Post*, was a very independent man. He did not want his place to be a 'closed shop'. His men were free to join a trade union or not, as they pleased. The trade union did not like this. They insisted that he should recognise it for the purpose of collective bargaining. When he refused, the trade union brought extreme pressure on him. They studied the pages of the *Nottingham Evening Post*. They took down the names of the various advertisers in the newspaper. They then wrote to the advertisers and told them not to advertise in that newspaper. Many obeyed. But 16 brave firms stood out. They included Boots, the famous Nottingham firm of chemists. They continued to advertise in the *Nottingham Evening Post*. Thereupon the union took action against the courageous 16. The union told all their members all over the country not to handle or publish advertisements for those 16.

[1] [1979] 1 WLR 697.

The object of the union was to injure the *Nottingham Evening Post*. Mr Wade, the general secretary of the union, said in his affidavit (page 707):

> The object of this campaign is manifestly to put pressure on the advertisers and thereby bring pressure to bear on *The Post* by drying up or severely diminishing its advertising revenue.

The Court of Appeal granted an injunction to prevent the union from 'blacking' those advertisers.

iv *Interference with press freedom*

From that case two principles of great importance emerged. The first was that the action by the trade union was 'unlawful means'. I said (page 709):

> . . . A trade union has no right to use its industrial strength to invade the freedom of the press. They have no right to interfere with the freedom of editors to comment on matters of public interest. They have no right to interfere with the freedom – and duty – of public authorities to recruit staff; or otherwise inform the public of matters of interest or concern to them. They have no right to interfere with the freedom of commercial firms to advertise their wares. These freedoms are so fundamental in our society that no trade union has any right to interfere with them. Interference with the freedom of the press is so contrary to the public interest that it is to be regarded as the employment of unlawful means. . . .

v *'Furtherance' must be limited*

The second principle was that some limit must be put upon the words 'in furtherance of'. I said in the same judgment (page 712):

> It has been repeatedly said that these words 'in furtherance of' must be limited in some way. Else they would give trade unions a power to inflict tremendous injury on entirely innocent persons without any redress whatever. Those who advocate this power assert that trade unions always act responsibly. But the immunity extends not only to trade unions, but also to unofficial and unauthorised groups of all kinds: and these, as we all know, may act without any responsibility at all. So the law must put some limit on the words.

vi *Mr Alexander's argument*

In the search for some limitation, we had a most valuable argument by Mr Robert Alexander QC. I said that it was worth recording, and I recorded it. Then, after referring to the 1976 Act, I said (page 712):

So immunity is given now when pressure is brought upon a first supplier so as to induce him not to supply goods to the employer – and likewise a first customer. But Mr Alexander submitted that the immunity should not be given any further down the chain of supply. It should not be granted, he suggested, to interfere with supplies by the second supplier to the first supplier. Least of all by the third supplier to the second supplier or lower down the chain.

Mr Goldblatt very fairly acknowledged that these submissions were fairly close to the right answer.

I added: 'I agree.'

vii *Secondary picketing is unlawful*

This is how I went on:

But I would put it simply on the question of remoteness. Some acts are so remote from the trade dispute that they cannot properly be said to be 'in furtherance' of it. . . . The trade union may believe it to be in furtherance of it, but their state of mind is by no means decisive. It is the fact of 'furtherance' that matters, not the belief in it. . . .

Then, after a few instances, I said:

Thus when strikers choose to picket, not their employers' premises, but the premises of innocent third persons not parties to the dispute – it is unlawful. 'Secondary picketing' it is called. It is unlawful at common law and is so remote from the dispute that there is no immunity in regard to it.

viii '*Black or be blacked*'

This is how I concluded (page 714):

This is the first case in which we have had to consider the ultimatum 'black or be blacked'. By its very terms, it puts a pistol at the heads of innocent third persons who are not parties to the dispute at all. They are told they must damage the employers or else they will suffer damage themselves. This threat may be so remote from the dispute itself that it cannot properly be said to be 'in furtherance' of it. The wanton infliction of damage on innocent third persons cannot be tolerated by the law: unless the leaders of the trade union can bring themselves within the statutory immunity. On the evidence so far in this case, I am not satisfied that they can bring themselves within the statutory immunity. The threat 'black or be blacked' was unlawful. Let it not be uttered again. . . .

ix 'Copy' for newspapers

EXPRESS NEWSPAPERS LTD V McSHANE[1]

This is the leading case. It concerns journalists. They are all members of a big union called the National Union of Journalists. But they are widespread. Some work for local newspapers in the provinces. Others work for the national newspapers in London. Yet others work for the Press Association in London. The Press Association is a big agency for the collection of news. It collects news and distributes 'copy' both to the local newspapers and the national newspapers.

Now the local journalists in the provinces wanted more pay. The provincial owners said that they could not afford it. The union called out their local journalists on strike. That had little effect because the provincial newspapers got news from other sources, including the Press Association in London. So the union called on their members in the Press Association not to send out 'copy' to the provincial newspapers or the national newspapers. Only half of their members in the Press Association agreed, so 'copy' still got through to the provincial newspapers. Thereupon the union took a further step. They called on their members on the national newspapers. In particular, they called on the journalists on the *Daily Express* and told them not to accept 'copy' coming from the Press Association. So the *Daily Express* could not print their news. The *Daily Express* then applied for an injunction against the trade union leaders. The Court of Appeal granted it.

x 'Furtherance' is not a subjective concept

That story is a good illustration of the difference between 'primary action' and 'secondary action'. When the union

[1] [1979] 1 WLR 390.

183

called on their members on the provincial newspapers, that was primary action. It was taken against their own employers about their own pay. But when they called on their members in the Press Association who had no complaint, that was secondary action. And when they called on their members on the *Daily Express* – who also had no complaint at all – that was further secondary action. The Court of Appeal took the view that the secondary action was unlawful. This is what I said (page 396):

It is said on behalf of the trade union leaders that 'furtherance' depended on their state of mind. If they genuinely and honestly *believed* that the 'blacking' would advance the cause of the provincial journalists, then their acts were done 'in furtherance of' the dispute. The judge did not accept that submission. Nor do I. 'Furtherance' is not a merely subjective concept. There is an objective element in it.

So we granted an injunction. The Press Association sent out their 'copy'. The newspapers received it. The freedom of the press was maintained. So far, so good.

3 A speech gets me into trouble

i *It was far-off in Canada*

That decision in *Express Newspapers v McShane* was given on 21 December 1978. It was taken to the House of Lords. But meanwhile – before it got there – my wife and I, in April 1979, went to London, Ontario. I received an Honorary Doctorate of Civil Law at the University of Western Ontario. At the ceremony I told an academic audience:

The greatest threat to the rule of law is posed today by the big trade unions. One of the biggest problems is how to restrain the misuse or abuse of power.

I had no thought that my words would get beyond the hall in which I was speaking. But they did. They were sent apace to London, England. Journalists awaited us in Toronto. At Heathrow they gathered in swarms with photographers. They followed us in cars down to Whitchurch.

ii *A general election was pending*

Why did they make all this fuss? Only because there was a general election pending. The journalists reported that the Prime Minister, Mr Callaghan, 'led a storm of Labour and trade union protests about Lord Denning's remarks'; that Mr Foot, the Deputy Leader, said that Lord Denning 'had made an ass of himself'; and that the Haldane Society, which they described as a Left-wing group of about 500 practising and academic lawyers, said that Lord Denning should resign because of the 'extreme anti-trade union attitude reflected in a series of recent decisions.'

In reply, Conservative lawyers accused Mr Foot of leading a dangerous and irresponsible Left-wing campaign to undermine the authority of the judges.

iii *There is a change of Government*

I am quite sure that my remarks did not influence the general election. But the conduct of the trade unions did. They had gone too far. They had abused their powers and had put innocent people to the greatest distress, damage and inconvenience. That was one of the reasons why people voted for a Conservative Government.

4 New legislation imperative

1 The Lords give unlimited immunity

i *The Government approved of the Court of Appeal*

In May 1979 a Conservative Government came to power. It had a mandate which was to curb the power of the trade unions. It was to bring them under the rule of law. The Conservatives devoted themselves to this task under the lead of Mr James Prior. He wanted to avoid the mistakes which led to the downfall of the Industrial Relations Act 1971. So he took much care to conciliate the Trades Union Congress. It was said that he would have been glad to have affirmed the decision of the Court of Appeal in the leading case of *Express Newspapers Ltd v McShane* of which I have told you.

ii *But the Lords did not*

But his plans were dashed to pieces by the House of Lords. In December 1979 they delivered a devastating blow. They reversed the Court of Appeal. They held that under the Trade Union Acts of 1974 and 1976 passed by the Labour Government all secondary action was lawful. Their decision is reported in *Express Newspapers Ltd v McShane*.[1] Lord Diplock used words which were entirely contrary to what I had said in the Court of Appeal. This is what he said (page 686):

. . . the test of whether an act was done 'in . . . furtherance of' is a purely

[1] [1980] AC 672.

186

subjective one. If the party who does the act honestly thinks at the time he does it that it may help one of the parties to the trade dispute to achieve their objectives and does it for that reason, he is protected by the section.

Inasmuch as every trade union leader always thinks his action will help one of the parties to the dispute, that means that, it being entirely subjective, the immunity was virtually complete.

iii *Dire consequences are foreseen*

Lord Diplock realised the dire consequences of this ruling. He said so himself (page 687):

It is, I think, these consequences of applying the subjective test that, not surprisingly, have tended to stick in judicial gorges: that so great damage may be caused to innocent and disinterested third parties in order to obtain for one of the parties to a trade dispute tactical advantages which in the court's own view are highly speculative and, if obtained, could be no more than minor.

iv *They are swallowed*

Yet the House of Lords accepted these consequences. They held that the test was purely subjective, or at any rate Lord Diplock did. This gave the trade union leaders carte-blanche to take any secondary action they liked – so long as their leaders thought it might help them in the dispute. That was the crucial decision. It made legislation imperative.

v *'A leaky umbrella'*

On 18 December 1979, *The Times* came out with a leading article very critical of the House of Lords. It criticised their decision in *Express Newspapers v McShane* and also in the *Rossminster* case[1] that same week. At the end of the article, *The Times* used a sentence about the House of Lords which was most expressive:

If our liberties had to be protected by them, they would prove a leaky umbrella.

[1] [1980] AC 952.

The article is so perceptive that I venture to quote from it here:

A LEAKY UMBRELLA

'Once great power is granted, there is a danger of it being abused. Rather than risk such abuse, it is . . . the duty of the courts so to construe the statute as to see that it encroaches as little as possible upon the liberties of the people of England.' On the surface, it seems that some violence was done to that principle – the words are Lord Denning's – in the House of Lords last week. Two cases of considerable importance to civil liberties were decided by the law lords. In both, the application of an illiberal law was upheld. In each, a decision of the Court of Appeal, presided over by Lord Denning, was reversed.

Throughout the history of the English legal system there have existed two broad strands of judicial approach. There have been those judges who have taken the view that, without usurping the functions of Parliament, a judge has the duty to interpret the law, as far as he can, in a way which accords with social and personal justice, which upholds rather than destroys the civil liberties of the individual, which looks with suspicion and not equanimity on the increasing encroachment of the state and other power-groups in the lives of citizens. Lord Denning is the most distinguished living and Lord Mansfield the most distinguished historic example of such a judicial activist.

There is another kind of judge who sees his task as maintaining the authority of the state, interpreting Acts of Parliament narrowly, supporting the words of the law in preference to the justice of the case, and affirming that it is for Parliament to change a law that turns out to be unjust or absurd, and not for judges to achieve that result through statutory interpretation. In recent years, the House of Lords has, in general, followed that path, and Lord Devlin has recently, in *The Judge* (Oxford University Press), presented a powerfully argued case in support of judicial conservatism.

There is something to be said for both approaches, though our admiration goes to Lord Denning. . . .

2 The great steel strike

Before the Conservatives had presented any Bill to Parliament, there was a destructive strike in the steel industry. It was the first in its history. It had widespread repercussions. It came before the courts.

i *Public and private sectors*

DUPORT STEELS LTD V SIRS[1]

The steel industry is divided into two sectors. The 'public sector' which is run by the nationalised corporation, the British Steel Corporation, and the 'private sector' which is run by private firms such as Hadfields Ltd of Sheffield. All the men in both sectors are members of one large trade union. The men in the public sector were dissatisfied with their wages. The men in the private sector were content with theirs. The union leaders called a strike of the men in the public sector. So the public sector shut down whilst the private sector kept producing steel. This reduced greatly the effectiveness of the strike. So the union called out their members in the private sector. It was on a Wednesday. The strike was to start on the Sunday. The employers came in haste to the courts. They issued a writ on Thursday 24 January 1980. Mr Justice Jones heard it on Friday 25 January. He refused an injunction.

ii *The Court of Appeal grant an injunction*

We held a special Saturday sitting. We granted an injunction. I said (pages 150–151):

This action is timed to take place at six o'clock tomorrow morning.

There is evidence of the disastrous effect which this action will have, not only on all the companies in the private sector, but on much of British industry itself. The private sector, as I have said, has a turnover – if it continues to work – of £1,500,000,000 a year. The turnover in the private sector is about £30,000,000 a week. If the men are called out in the private sector, all these companies would have to shut down at enormous loss. Not only will they have to shut down, but all the firms which they supply will not be able to carry on with their work. They will not be able to make their steel. British Leyland, who depend on 80 per cent of their supplies from the private sector, will have to shut down much of their works too. Not only that: we will lose trade here in this country, and our competitors abroad will clap their hands in anticipation of being able to send their products into England: because our industry is at a standstill.

[1] [1980] 1 WLR 142.

189

In these circumstances, it is not surprising that 16 of the big private steel companies in this country have come to the courts hoping they can get here in time – to restrain the three principal members of this union (. . .) calling this disastrous strike, which is going to injure British industry so much.

I concluded (page 154):

. . . To call out these private steel workers, who have no dispute at all with their employers, would have such a disastrous effect on the economy and well-being of the country that it seems to me only right that the court should grant an injunction to stop these people being called out tomorrow morning: to stop all this picketing: and to stop all these people who are preventing the movement of steel up and down the country.

iii 'Scargill defies Lord Denning'

Our decision was most unwelcome to the union. On Monday 28 January the *Evening Standard* had a black headline in huge letters:

SCARGILL DEFIES LORD DENNING

Then it said:

LORD DENNING versus Arthur Scargill. The Yorkshire miners' leader today made a dramatic call for trade unionists to defy the Master of the Rolls and his steel strike ruling.

Mr Scargill said Lord Denning's ruling that secondary picketing of private sector steel firms must end was 'absolutely deplorable'. He went on: 'Lord Denning has given a judgment which is in line with Tory Party philosophy and trade union members involved in this dispute should recognise that.

They have a simple choice to make. They either accept the decision of three men in wigs sitting in a remote part of London or accept the advice and instruction of their trade union.

I hope they accept the advice of their trade union, come out on strike, continue to picket, and win their dispute.'

He said the ruling should be 'completely ignored' and added that Yorkshire miners would now black all deliveries of steel to collieries and Coal Board workshops.

Mr Scargill . . . has previously spoken passionately for the steelmen's strike at a mass meeting. . . .

190

iv *The union, however, obey*

On Wednesday 30 January *The Times* reported that the union had voted to obey the Court of Appeal's instruction. But, although obeying it, the union was bitterly critical of the ruling. *The Times* quoted the words of Mr William Sirs, the General Secretary of the union. He is highly respected and is a magistrate himself. This is the quotation:

> Whatever was in Lord Denning's judgment is being applied as per Lord Denning. As a magistrate I want to follow the letter of the law. I want the members to do that.
>
> I would not be impressed if they did not. But they have been law-abiding citizens. They have agreed to accept even the law of Lord Denning.

Although obedient to the ruling, the union, however, moved very quickly to get our decision reversed.

v *The Lords quickly reverse us*

In that self-same week, the union took the case to the House of Lords. The Lords heard it – and decided it – in record time. Five days after our judgment the House of Lords allowed a petition by the defendants for leave to appeal. The following day, Friday 1 February, they heard the appeal. They allowed it straightaway. They gave their written reasons on Thursday 7 February. They reversed the Court of Appeal.

vi *'Good law? Bad justice'*

On Saturday 2 February, the very next day after the decision, *The Times* thundered again against the House of Lords. They had a leading article headed:

GOOD LAW? BAD JUSTICE

I venture to quote from it:

> Yet again the Law Lords have resisted the temptation to equitable but creative interpretation of law dangled before them by Lord Denning. How far they have rejected his arguments we shall not know until the

judgments are published. When they come they will certainly be read with interest. The speed and unanimity of their decision, and Lord Diplock's comment that there were no significant differences between this case and that of McShane, suggest that the rejection is emphatic. . . . The clear practical unfairness of yesterday's decision, however well-based on the statute, makes legislation imperative in any case. Its immediate result is that the private steelmen are to be called out again, in order to put pressure on the Government. . . .

We are sometimes told by scholarly lawyers that Magna Carta has no longer any force in British courts; that it is not binding. The private steel employers will have had that scholarly point brought home to them in the most vivid way. 'To no one will we sell, deny or delay rights or justice.' When it comes to trade union law the House of Lords holds, repeatedly and perhaps correctly, that no rights or justice exist under British statutes.

vii *The reasons*

A week later the House of Lords gave their reasons. Lord Diplock said of the conduct of the trade union (page 161):

There may be some who would deplore this conduct; harsh words descriptive of it may come readily to the tongue; but it seems to me that, whatever else may be fairly said about it, it cannot be said with any plausibility that it was not done in furtherance of the existing trade dispute with B.S.C.

So the 'secondary action' was held to be lawful. The union acted quickly. They called the workers in the private sector out on strike. The men obeyed this call. They did no work. There was much disruption and much bitterness. Some of the works were closed down. Companies were wound up. A tragedy which had lasting consequences.

viii *The Government has to act*

The decision of the House of Lords made legislation imperative. The Government had to act. They issued a consultative paper. They eventually issued a Bill which became the Employment Act 1980.

5 The 1980 Act

1 Section 17 on secondary action

i *A tortuous section*

The Act contained one section especially to deal with secondary action. It is section 17. It is a deplorable section. We considered it in *Hadmor Productions Ltd v Hamilton*, where I said:[1]

On reading through the Employment Act 1980, and especially section 17 on secondary action, I confess to a sense of bewilderment. It is the most tortuous section I have ever come across. After a careful re-reading, I think I can discern the general legislative purpose of section 17. It is to retain the statutory immunity for primary action, but to remove the immunity for secondary action. It means that trade union officials who call out men in a dispute with their employer are not liable for acts directed against the employer (primary action), but they are liable for acts directed against his customers or suppliers or other traders (secondary action).

ii *Its tortuosity*

These are the twists which make up the tortuosity. It is like a piece of string made of several strands of thread:

(a) the strand which gives immunity to some kinds of secondary action;

(b) the strand which gives no immunity for other kinds of secondary action;

(c) the strand which goes to define those kinds of secondary action which have immunity;

[1] [1981] 3 WLR 139, 151.

(d) the strand which goes to define those kinds which have no immunity.

Then you twist those strands together to make a piece of string; then you tie the string into knots; then you present it to the lawyers to unravel. They take hours about it.

iii *Flags of convenience*

So far there have been only two cases on the section. Each of them concerned a 'flag of convenience'. This arises when shareholders living in a maritime country (like England or Holland) form a one-ship company in a foreign country such as Panama or Liberia. The vessel is bought in the name of that company and registered under the flag of that country. It is highly convenient for the shareholders because it enables them to avoid the safety regulations of their own country and the high wages of their own seamen. They recruit seamen from countries such as India or Hong Kong where wages are low.

iv *The ITF previously 'blacked' them successfully*

An important trade union objects strongly to these 'flags of convenience'. It is the International Transport Workers' Federation, shortly known as 'ITF'. When a vessel comes into an English port – and is ready to depart – the union instructs the tugmen and lock-keepers to 'black' the vessel. They will not help her to leave unless the demands of the ITF are met. The seamen (from India or Hong Kong) have no complaint. They are only too glad to have employment at the low wages. But the union 'blacks' the vessel. In the first case under the previous Acts, we granted an injunction to stop the 'blacking'.[1] I told you about it in *The Discipline of Law*, pages 192–193. But in a later case the House of Lords overruled us.[2] They held that the 'blacking' was immune.

---

[1] *Star Sea Transport Corpn v Slater, Laughton and Collarbone, The Camilla M* [1979] 1 Lloyd's Rep 26, CA.
[2] See *NWL Ltd v Woods* [1979] 1 WLR 1294.

v *But not now under the 1980 Act*

This kind of 'blacking' came under close scrutiny in two recent cases in the Court of Appeal: *Marina Shipping Ltd v Laughton*[1] and *Merkur Island Shipping Corpn v Laughton*.[2] The latter has very recently been affirmed by the House of Lords.[3] All the courts condemned the tortuosity of section 17. After examining it in depth, they held that this kind of 'blacking' was 'secondary action' which was no longer immune. Injunctions were granted restraining it. Just as we had done in *The Camilla M*. So we were restored after all. In the House of Lords Lord Diplock said:[4]

I appreciate that this will have the consequence of making it more difficult for I.T.F. to continue to apply its policy of 'blacking' vessels sailing under flags of convenience without a blue certificate from I.T.F. It may also make blacking more difficult in other industries where contracts and sub-contracts are common, but your Lordships have not needed to go into that in the instant appeal. One thing is plain as to the intention of Parliament in enacting section 17 of the Act of 1980; it was to impose restrictions upon the circumstances in which 'blacking' could be procured without incurring liability in tort. The only function of this House in its judicial capacity is to ascertain from the language that the draftsman used the extent of those restrictions.

2 Need for clarity

i *Lack of it condemned*

In *Merkur's* case the present Master of the Rolls (Sir John Donaldson) condemned the obscurity of section 17. He said: '. . . it has taken us hours to ascertain what is and what is not "offside"'. Lord Diplock in the House of Lords said that it was 'most regrettably lacking in the requisite degree of clarity.' I have set out the passages in full on page 110 of this book.

---

[1] [1982] QB 1127.
[2] [1983] 2 WLR 45.
[3] [1983] 2 WLR 778.
[4] [1983] 2 WLR 778, 790.

ii *Leave it to the judges*

In the 1982 Act the Government has left section 17 as it stands. This means that the judges will have to disentangle it in case after case. They will seek to make the law intelligible when Parliament has made it unintelligible. If I may venture a forecast, I suggest that the law may turn out to be much as the Court of Appeal stated it in *Express Newspapers Ltd v McShane* and *Duport v Sirs*, and not as the House of Lords stated it in those cases. But you must go by the section. You must spend hours and hours in studying it. You will be quite uncertain whether you have got the right answer. You will have to wait and see what the House of Lords say.

6 The closed shop

1 Trade union power

i *Power to expel*

The trade unions get much of their strength by means of their power over their men. Their rules give them power to expel a member or to discipline him if he does not obey a strike call. This means that many a man will have to take part in a strike even though he disagrees with it. He may want to go on working for his employer and earn his wages, yet he dare not do so because he would be disciplined by his union and, if it is a closed shop, he would lose his job.

ii *A newcomer must join*

Everyone knows what a 'closed shop' is. It means a factory or workshop or firm in which all the workmen are members of a trade union. It is closed to everyone except the members. Any newcomer who comes to work there must join the union. If the newcomer refuses to do so, the others, already being members of the union, will insist on his dismissal. They tell the employer, 'Sack him or we will go on strike.' The employer gives in. He dismisses the man. Or the man gives in and joins the union.

iii *So must old hands*

Sometimes the shop is not 'closed' at the outset. It has been open to all comers: but then, over the years, a large number of the men have become members of a trade union – but a few have stayed out. Then the men who are already members decide to 'close' the shop if they can do so. They argue in this way: 'We have obtained good pay and conditions from the employer by the negotiations conducted on our behalf by our union. Why should these others get the benefit of the negotiations when they are not members of the union and have not paid the subscriptions to it?' So they tell the employer: 'Sack those who are not members, or we will go on strike.' The employer does so. He dismisses them. Or the men give in and join the union.

iv *Lawful at common law*

That sort of compulsion was nearly always effective. The employer would rather dismiss the recalcitrant employee than have a strike by the others. Such a dismissal was lawful, as the Court of Appeal held in *Morgan v Fry*.[1] Rather than be dismissed, the man joined the trade union. So the closed shop was enforced and was lawful.

2 The statutes

i *The 1971 Act*

When the Conservative Government came into power, they passed the Industrial Relations Act 1971. One part of it dealt with the 'closed shop'. The Act placed great difficulties in the way of the 'closed shop'. It virtually abolished it. It gave every worker the right as between himself and his employer to be a member of such trade union as he might choose, or of *no* trade union. If a man applied for work, the employer could not stipulate that he should belong to this or that trade union, or to any trade union at all. Although the statutory provisions were well intended, nevertheless it has been authoritatively stated that

they met with considerable resistance from trade unions and in practice its closed shop provisions were circumvented by many employers and

[1] [1968] 2 QB 710; see *The Discipline of Law*, pp 181–182.

unions. The closed shop continued much as before. [Green Paper quoted by the European Court of Human Rights in the case of the three railwaymen, *Young, James and Webster v United Kingdom*.[1]]

ii *The 1974 and 1976 Acts*

When the Labour Government came into power, they repealed the Industrial Relations Act 1971 and passed the 1974 Act. They afterwards amended it by the 1976 Act. It contained elaborate provisions which were specially concerned with closed shops. The purpose was to make it lawful for the employer to enforce a closed shop if he did it in accordance with an agreement with a trade union – called a 'union membership agreement'.

iii *'Union membership agreement'*

This was an agreement by which the employer and the trade union agreed that in order to be employed a man must be a member of an appropriate trade union. Where there was such an agreement, if a man refused to join a union and was dismissed as a consequence, his dismissal was to be regarded as fair. There was, however, an exception. The 1974 Act contained a provision under which a man could object

on grounds of religious belief to being a member of any trade union whatsoever or on any reasonable grounds to being a member of a particular trade union. [See Schedule 1, paragraph 6(5).]

But the 1976 Act limited this so that he could only object 'on the ground of religious belief to being a member of any trade union whatsoever' [see section 1(e)]. That meant that in practice no man could ever object. No religion, so far as I know, objects to a man joining a trade union.

So under the 1974 and 1976 Acts the closed shop was effectively closed. It was shuttered and barred against anyone who was not a member of an appropriate trade union.

[1] [1981] IRLR 408, 413, para 26.

iv *If there is no such agreement*

But, if there is no such agreement, every man in the shop has the right to join a trade union – or to refuse to join one – as he pleases. If his employer objects to trade unions – and the man, nevertheless, joins a trade union – and the employer dismisses him, then the dismissal is to be regarded as unfair. If the trade union wishes the man to join the union – and the man refuses – and the union gets the employer to dismiss him, then again his dismissal is to be regarded as unfair.

3 The Acts of 1980 and 1982

Much of this has been altered by the Employment Acts of 1980 and 1982. In these Acts, the Government has made a determined effort to bring our legislation on the closed shop into accord with the European Convention on Human Rights.

i *Ballot of members*

The concept of a 'union membership agreement' is retained. When there is such an agreement it is lawful for employers and unions to enforce a closed shop. But such an agreement is only valid if it has been approved by a ballot of the employees. The ballot must be so conducted that everyone can cast his vote in secrecy if he wishes. It must also be given an overwhelming majority in favour of approval. It must be either (a) not less than 80 per cent of those entitled to vote, or (b) not less than 85 per cent of those who voted.

ii *How far is the ballot binding?*

If the approval is given by the required majority, so that there is a 'union membership agreement', then the union and the employer can operate a closed shop. But there is this important loophole open to a man – which is included no doubt so as to ensure compliance with the freedom guaranteed by the European Convention. It is in section 58 of the 1978 Act, as amended by section 7 of the 1980 Act and section 3 of the 1982 Act. He is entitled to refuse to join a trade union

if the employee genuinely objects on grounds of conscience or other deeply-held personal conviction to being a member of any trade union whatsoever or of a particular trade union.

It seems to me that that loophole may be wide enough for any man to escape so long as he has a genuine objection to joining a trade union. I should think that the industrial tribunals will be readily persuaded that he objects because of a 'deeply-held personal conviction'.

Furthermore, by sections 4 and 5 of the 1980 Act, if a man is unreasonably expelled from a union or is unreasonably refused membership of a union, he can make complaint to an industrial tribunal. He can get a declaration as to its validity and, if he suffers loss, he can get compensation.

iii *When there is no ballot*

If there has been no ballot – or if a ballot has not resulted in a sufficient majority – then there is no binding 'union membership agreement'. In those circumstances the 1980 and 1982 Acts give the man the right to join the trade union of his choice. It means that there can be no closed shop. Either the man can join a trade union or not, as he pleases. He is not to be dismissed because he either refuses to join, or desires to join, a trade union. In other words, the closed shop is no longer applicable.

Those are the principal provisions of the Acts in this regard. Of course, there is much more to be found in the Acts. All I do in this book is to pick out the salient points: and refer to the principal cases decided thus far.

7 Trade Unions go 'poaching'

1 The Bridlington principles

Trade unions are often in conflict with one another. They are rivals. Each trade union wants to maintain and increase its membership. It objects to its rivals 'poaching' its members. What is to be done?

It is a problem which has vexed the trade union movement for many years. As long ago as 1939 there was a congress of trade unions at Bridlington. They agreed upon a code of conduct. It was designed to minimise conflict between trade unions. The code of conduct has ever since been called the 'Bridlington principles'. Whenever there was a conflict about a member, the two unions had to consult between themselves: and decide between them to which union he should belong. If they could not agree, the dispute had to be referred to the Trades Union Congress (TUC) for adjudication. The decision of the TUC was final.

The important thing to notice is that these Bridlington principles apply only to the two trade unions. The man himself is not a party to them. They are not incorporated into his terms of membership. He has no voice in the decision of any dispute between the two trade unions. He is a pawn in the struggle between them. They fight for his body. Here are two cases which illustrate it.

2 Mr Cheall's case

CHEALL V ASSOCIATION OF PROFESSIONAL EXECUTIVE
CLERICAL AND COMPUTER STAFF[1]

i *His membership is terminated*

Mr Cheall was employed by Vauxhall Motors as a security
officer. He was deeply inbued with the loyalties and
traditions of the trade union movement. He was a member
of the Transport and General Workers' Union (TGWU) for
many years. But he got dissatisfied with it: and after a while
he sent in his resignation. After three or four weeks he joined
a rival union called the Association of Professional Executive
Clerical and Computer Staff (APEX). They welcomed him
with open arms. But, in so doing, they infringed the
Bridlington principles. TGWU complained to the TUC.
The disputes committee heard both unions. They decided in
favour of TGWU – without paying any regard to what Mr
Cheall said as he was not a party. The committee awarded
that APEX should exclude Mr Cheall, and advised him to
rejoin TGWU. Mr Cheall wrote a letter to Mr Len Murray,
the TUC General Secretary, protesting against the award of
the disputes committee. He said:[2]

. . . I want to point out that the result is unjust, undemocratic and
unacceptable . . . I appreciate that there is no appeal procedure laid down
on the findings of the disputes committee, for a union or members
concerned. This in itself is not democratic. This proves what I said at the
meeting, that Bridlington is totally out of date, and is inadequate to meet
present-day requirements.

APEX, however, did as the TUC told them. They
terminated the membership of Mr Cheall. But he did not
obey the award. He did not rejoin TGWU. He got legal aid
and brought proceedings in the courts, claiming that APEX
had wrongly purported to terminate his membership.

---

[1] [1982] 3 WLR 685, CA; revsd. [1983] 2 WLR 679, HL.
[2] [1982] 3 WLR 685, 690, CA.

ii *The Court of Appeal uphold his complaint*

The Court of Appeal (by a majority) held that APEX were themselves at fault by expelling him from the union without giving him a hearing and when there was no reasonable cause for expelling him. This is what I said:[1]

> . . . If a man has a right to join a trade union for the protection of his interests, it must follow that he has the right not to be expelled from it, or to have his membership terminated, except for reasonable cause and in accordance with the requirements of natural justice. I said as much in *Nagle v Feilden* [1966] 2 QB 633, 646 and I repeat it here. What good is it for a man to have a right to *join* a trade union, if he can be *expelled* the very next day for no cause or arbitrarily or capriciously without any reasonable cause? And, if there is some cause alleged against him on which it is said to be reasonable to exclude him, surely he must have notice of what the cause is, and be given a reasonable opportunity of dealing with it? These two are therefore the conditions on which he can be expelled or his membership be terminated: First, there must be reasonable cause. Secondly, it must be done in accordance with natural justice.

iii *The argument the other way*

I realise that there was a considerable argument the other way. This is how I put it (page 695):

> The argument to the contrary is this: it is said that rule 14 is necessary so as to keep order in industrial relations. If it were not for the Bridlington principles there would be chaos. Trade union would fight against trade union, poaching members, and so forth. Either might call a strike. Strikes are common in inter-union disputes. The conflict would do great damage to our industrial structure. That is a point of view which is entitled to respect. But it is not accepted even amongst the experts in industrial relations. In this very case expert evidence was called the other way.

iv *A stand must be made on principle*

And then I came to my own conclusion in this final paragraph:

> I take my stand on something more fundamental. It is on the freedom of the individual to join a trade union of his choice. He is not to be ordered

[1] [1982] 3 WLR 685, 693, CA.

to join this or that trade union without having a say in the matter. He is not to be treated as a pawn on the chessboard. He is not to be moved across it against his will by one or other of the conflicting parties, or by their disputes committee. It might result, when there is a 'closed shop', in his being deprived of his livelihood. He would be crushed between the upper and nether millstones. Even though it should result in industrial chaos, nevertheless the freedom of each man should prevail over it. There comes a time in peace as in war – as recent events show* – when a stand must be made on principle, whatever the consequences. Such a stand should be made here today. I hold the trade union A.P.E.X. was wrong to terminate the membership of the plaintiff. I would allow the appeal, accordingly.

* When speaking of 'recent events' I was referring, of course, to the Falklands crisis.

v *The Lords reverse us*

The case went to the House of Lords. Very recently, on 30 March 1983, they overruled the Court of Appeal. They held that it was lawful for the union to expel Mr Cheall. The House affirmed the validity of the Bridlington principles. Lord Diplock said:[1]

I know of no existing rule of public policy that would prevent trade unions from entering into arrangements with one another which they consider to be in the interests of their members in promoting order in industrial relations and enhancing their members' bargaining power with their employers; nor do I think it a permissible exercise of your Lordships' judicial power to create a new rule of public policy to that effect. If this is to be done at all it must be done by Parliament.

vi *What a pity!*

Then Lord Diplock went on to say:

Different considerations might apply if the effect of Cheall's expulsion from A.P.E.X. were to have put his job in jeopardy, either because of the existence of a closed shop or for some other reason.

To me, this seems a difficult distinction to draw because the justice of the case – as between himself and the union – would appear to be the same whether or not his job

[1] [1983] 2 WLR 679, 685–686.

was put in jeopardy. But then there is this final sentence of Lord Diplock:

My human sympathies are with Mr Cheall, but I am not in a position to indulge them; for I am left in no doubt that upon all the points that have been so ingeniously argued, the law is against him. . . .

What a pity!

3 On the milk round

TAYLOR V CO–OPERATIVE RETAIL SERVICES LTD[1]

The Co–op in Worcester employed 80 or 90 milk rounds-men. There was a 'union membership agreement' by which they were to belong to one or other of two trade unions. Each of them was appropriate for the men to join. Mr Taylor belonged to one of them (the 'first' union) but he got dissatisfied with it. He left and joined the other union (the 'second' union). The first union complained to the TUC disputes committee. The hearing was only between the two unions. Mr Taylor was no party to it at all. The disputes committee decided in favour of the first union. They advised that Mr Taylor should rejoin the first union. He refused to do so. Thereupon the first union told the employers to dismiss him. The employers did as they were told. They dismissed him. He brought proceedings against the employers before the industrial tribunal. He failed because there was a 'union membership agreement' under which his dismissal was to be regarded as fair dismissal. He appealed to the Employment Appeal Tribunal, and thence to the Court of Appeal. But in all the courts in England he was held to have no claim. That was because of the 1974 and 1976 statutes.

[1] [1982] ICR 600.

8 The European Convention

1 The 1974 and 1976 Acts were in breach of it

Both of those cases were decided under the 1974 and 1976 statutes. Now the position has been entirely altered. It is because of the European Convention and the decision of the European Court at Strasbourg. Ever since 1950 the United Kingdom has adhered to the European Convention on Human Rights: and is bound to implement it. Article 11 says that:

Everyone has the right . . . to form and to join trade unions for the protection of his interests.

If the United Kingdom Government pass legislation which is in conflict with that right, then it can be brought before the European Court at Strasbourg: and that court can order the United Kingdom Government to pay compensation to the injured party.

It is now settled that the Acts of 1974 and 1976 were in breach of the European Convention on Human Rights.

2 The three railwaymen

YOUNG, JAMES AND WEBSTER V UNITED KINGDOM[1]

It was so settled in the case of the three railwaymen. I have told you of it before but I would remind you of it now. In

[1] [1981] IRLR 408.

1975 British Rail (the employers) made a 'union membership agreement' with the three railway unions. It made
British Rail a 'closed shop'. By it no man was to be
employed by British Rail unless he was a member of one of
those trade unions.

Before the agreement 8,000 members of British Rail (out
of 250,000) were not members of one of those trade unions.
After the agreement (making it a 'closed shop'), all but 54
joined one of those trade unions. 54 refused. Owing to their
refusal, British Rail dismissed them.

i *No remedy in England*

One of them – Mr James – complained to an industrial
tribunal in England. He alleged that his dismissal was unfair.
But the tribunal held that, under the legislation, they were
bound to regard his dismissal as fair. This was based on the
1974 Act, as amended by the 1976 Act. It was similar to the
cases of Mr Cheall and Mr Taylor of which I have told you.

The other two – Mr Young and Mr Webster – were in
like position. They accepted that under the existing
legislation their dismissal was to be regarded as fair.

ii *But a remedy at Strasbourg*

In those circumstances they applied to the European
Commission of Human Rights, who referred it to the
European Court at Strasbourg. After a full hearing, the court
held by 18 votes to 3 that there had been a breach of Article
11 of the Convention. The court held that, in the
circumstances of these cases, compulsion to join a particular
union was contrary to the Convention. They said:[1]

However, a threat of dismissal involving loss of livelihood is a most
serious form of compulsion and, in the present instance, it was directed
against persons engaged by British Rail before the introduction of any
obligation to join a particular trade union.

In the court's opinion, such a form of compulsion, in the circumstances of the case, strikes at the very substance of the freedom

[1] [1981] IRLR 408, 417, paras 86–87.

guaranteed by Article 11. For this reason alone, there has been an interference with that freedom as regards each of the three applicants.

The court held that in the circumstances the United Kingdom should pay compensation to the three applicants for the loss of their jobs.

3 In the long run

i *Mr Taylor too*

Now go back to Mr Taylor's case at page 206. It seems to me that Mr Taylor would now be entitled to compensation. This is how I concluded my judgment in his case:[1]

Mr Taylor was subjected to a degree of compulsion which was contrary to the freedom guaranteed by the European Convention on Human Rights. He was dismissed by his employers because he refused to join a trade union which operated a closed shop. He cannot recover any compensation from his employers under English law because, under the Acts of 1974 and 1976, his dismissal is to be regarded as fair. But those Acts themselves are inconsistent with the freedom guaranteed by the European Convention. The United Kingdom Government is responsible for passing those Acts and should pay him compensation. He can recover it by applying to the European Commission, and thence to the European Court of Human Rights. But I see no reason why his employers should pay him compensation. They only did what the trade unions compelled them to do. He cannot sue the trade unions. They are immune from suit. This means that the appeal must be dismissed. He cannot recover any compensation in these courts. But, if he applies to the European Court of Human Rights, he may in the long run – and I am afraid it may be a long run – obtain compensation there. So in the end justice may be done. But not here.

ii *The United Kingdom Government has now made compensation*

The United Kingdom Government, however, acted so as to provide compensation for Mr Taylor and the three railwaymen and others in like position. Under a scheme introduced with the Employment Act 1982 compensation is available to those dismissed because of a closed shop – and who had no legal remedy when the 1974 and 1976 Acts were in force. In a

[1] [1982] ICR 600, 610.

news item on 21 June 1983 *The Times* said that more than 400 people had applied, of whom 207 were found eligible. £261,086 was paid out to 54. The highest payment was £10,659.

4 Conclusion

It does seem that in the Employment Acts of 1980 and 1982 the United Kingdom Government has made every effort to bring the law into accord with the European Convention. Those Acts are, however, very obscure. We are told that in the new Parliament there is to be more legislation on trade unions. It is to be hoped that the existing statutes will be revised at the same time: so that they may be clear and intelligible to all who have to act on them.

Section Seven

Conflicts in the Courts

Introduction

During my last four years as Master of the Rolls, the newspapers used to count up the number of cases in which I had recently been reversed by the House of Lords. They used to say, for instance, 'Lord Denning has been reversed 10 times.' They ignored the fact that I never sat alone. In every case I had two Lords Justices sitting with me and usually agreeing with me with reasoned judgments of their own. It was the whole Court of Appeal which was reversed – not me alone. I will tell you of the more important. In many of them the facts are fascinating. So I have set them out.

I have also set out the reasons given by the judges – both in the Court of Appeal and the House of Lords. I hope you will forgive the many extracts. I have done it so that you – both students and practitioners – can form your own opinion. Which of the reasons do you prefer? If you think that the law – as laid down by the House of Lords – needs amending, I hope you will write to the Law Commission and say so. It is their statutory duty 'to receive and consider any proposals for the reform of the law which may be made or referred to them' (section 3(1)(a) of the Law Commissions Act 1965). Your proposals will, I am sure, be well worth considering.

1 Locus standi

1 The Fleet Street casuals

R V INLAND REVENUE COMMISSIONERS, EX PARTE NATIONAL
FEDERATION OF SELF–EMPLOYED AND SMALL BUSINESSES LTD[1]

This case raised the whole question of locus standi. I
discussed the subject in *The Discipline of Law* Part 3, pages
113–144. Now I bring it up to date. I tell of this case as I did
in my judgment.[2]

i *Mickey Mouse and Company*

The men are called the 'Fleet Street casuals.' There are about 6,000 of
them. They do casual work for newspapers. They love a bit of humour.
When signing their pay dockets, they do not sign their true names. They
use fictitious names and addresses. One favourite is 'Mickey Mouse of
Sunset Boulevard'. Another is 'Sir Gordon Richards of Tattenham
Corner'. But they do not sign in these names merely for fun. They use
them for a serious purpose. It is to hide their true identities: so that they
should not be discovered by the taxmen. By this means the 'Fleet Street
casuals' have defrauded the revenue of about £1 million a year.

The employers did not know their true names. But the trade unions
did. There are three trade unions controlling this newspaper trade:
NGA, NATSOPA and SOGAT. Every casual worker has to be a
member of one of these trade unions: because they operate a closed shop.
Each union has the names and addresses of all its casuals. When a man
seeks work, he has to go to the 'call office' of the union. He is then given a
'call slip' authorising him to go to a particular newspaper for work. He
does his work; receives his pay; signs his pay docket as 'Mickey Mouse'

[1] [1980] QB 407, CA; revsd. [1982] AC 617, HL.
[2] [1980] QB 407, 418–425, CA.

214

or other fictitious name and address; and goes home. This device defeats the revenue authorities completely. They do not know the true names of these men. The trade unions do. They have a complete list of the men, their names and addresses, and the shifts worked by them. In many ways the trade unions fill the role of the men's employers. But the revenue authorities have no access to these lists. They have no power to compel the unions to disclose the true names and addresses. So they cannot assess them to tax on their earnings.

ii *They are given an amnesty*

A year or two ago the revenue authorities found out about these false signatures. So did the BBC. They had a programme on 'Panorama' exposing these frauds. The revenue authorities were perplexed. They wondered what was the best way to deal with the problem. They would have liked to have legislation to deal with it. But in the absence of new legislation, they felt that they had to make a special arrangement with those concerned. It looks as if these casuals threatened to take industrial action if their names were disclosed and they were made to pay up their past taxes. So the revenue authorities had discussions with the employers and the trade unions. They came to a special arrangement. It was this: The men were to give their true names for the future and pay their future taxes: but they were given an *amnesty* for much of the past. They were to be let off most of the past tax of which they had defrauded the revenue. . . .

2 The Federation bring proceedings

i *By judicial review*

News of the amnesty was given in the newspapers and on the television. Many were shocked by it. Especially some self-employed and small shopkeepers – good men and true who pay their taxes. They asked themselves: 'Why should these "Fleet Street casuals" – who have defrauded the revenue – be given this preferential treatment? Why should they be let off when any one of us (if he did any such thing) would have been pursued to the uttermost farthing?'

So these small men, through their federation, 50,000 of them, took legal advice. On it they have taken advantage of a new procedure called 'judicial review'. They have come to the courts and ask for this relief: (i) A declaration that the Board of Inland Revenue acted unlawfully in granting an amnesty to casual workers in Fleet Street, and (ii) an order of mandamus directed to the board to assess and collect income tax from the said casual workers in Fleet Street, according to the law.

ii *The Revenue object*

. . . The Revenue object to these proceedings being taken against them. They say that no one has any standing to come to the courts to complain of their actions. No one at all. Not an ordinary citizen. Not even a taxpayer who is aggrieved by them. Not even the 50,000 of them in this federation. Maybe the Attorney-General might do so, but he has never been known to proceed against a government department. The Divisional Court has upheld the contention of the revenue. The self-employed and small shopkeepers, as taxpayers, appeal to this court. . . .

iii *The amnesty assumed to be unlawful*

Now in the course of the proceedings, the revenue made a concession – or rather, the Court of Appeal believed it to be a concession. Mr Patrick Medd, as we understood it, invited us to proceed on the assumption that, in granting an amnesty, the revenue acted unlawfully. He recognised that they have no dispensing power: they have no power to make tax concessions without the authority of Parliament. No one, not even the Crown, can dispense with the laws of England. So, even assuming that the amnesty was unlawful, the revenue submitted that the federation had no locus standi.

3 The Court of Appeal's view

i *A genuine grievance*

. . . The only question, on that assumption, is whether these self-employed and small shopkeepers can complain of such unlawfulness. Have they a 'genuine grievance'? They think that the 'Fleet Street casuals' are being given preferential treatment – over and above that afforded to other taxpayers – because they have available the weapon of 'industrial action' open to them. They have no industrial muscle. They have no one against whom to strike.

One thing I must say. If these self-employed and small shopkeepers cannot complain, there is no one else who can. The unlawful conduct of the revenue (assuming it is unlawful) will go without remedy. The revenue authorities will have obtained a dispensing power without it being authorised by Parliament. And that, by a defect in our procedure – because no one has a locus standi to complain.

Rather than grant the revenue such a dispensing power, I would allow the whole body of taxpayers a locus standi to complain. Assuredly the Attorney-General will not complain on their behalf. He never does complain against a government department. And as the whole body is too cumbersome, I would allow the body of taxpayers (50,000 of them) represented by the federation to complain.

ii *A parallel is found*

They have a genuine grievance which finds a parallel in the grievance of the beneficiaries in *Vestey v Inland Revenue Comrs* [1979] Ch 177, 197–198, where Walton J said:

'I conceive it to be in the national interest, in the interest not only of all individual taxpayers – which includes most of the nation – but also in the interests of the revenue authorities themselves, that the tax system should be fair. . . . One should be taxed by law, and not be untaxed by concession. . . . A tax system which enshrines obvious injustices is brought into disrepute with all taxpayers accordingly, whereas one in which injustices, when discovered, are put right (and with retrospective effect when necessary) will command respect and support.'

Those eloquent words were quoted and stressed by Lord Wilberforce in 1979 when the case reached the House of Lords [1979] 3 WLR 915, 926, 931. Adapting them here I would say that if the revenue authorities are found to be exercising a dispensing power – not given to them by Parliament – then it is open to a representative body of taxpayers – representative of the whole – to come to the courts to complain of it: and to seek a declaration as to the rights or wrongs of it. . . .

iii *Not mere busybodies*

My conclusion is therefore that these self-employed and small shop-keepers are not mere busybodies. They are not spending their funds on this litigation out of spite or malice. They have a genuine grievance because, as they see it, the 'Fleet Street casuals' are getting out of paying their back taxes: because of their 'industrial muscle'. They feel that this is unfair and should be put right. They ask the courts to consider their grievance and say whether it is well-founded or not. I think they should be heard. They should not be brushed off as having no suffcient interest. I would allow the appeal accordingly.

Lord Justice Ackner agreed with me but Lord Justice Lawton dissented.

4 The view of the Lords

i *They reverse the Court of Appeal*

The House of Lords reversed the Court of Appeal on the ground that it was wrong to consider locus standi as a preliminary point on its own. It was necessary to consider, not only the federation as a group who had a grievance, but also the nature of the grievance: and to see whether, taking the two together, there was sufficient material to call upon the Board of Inland Revenue for an answer.

ii *But only because the assumption was mistaken*

The important point to note is that the revenue were no longer prepared to assume that the granting of the amnesty was unlawful. The Lord Advocate expressly stated:[1]

> The appellants do not accept, even for the purposes of argument, that they in any way acted unlawfully in this matter. The Court of Appeal wrongly thought this was conceded. The evidence gives no basis, moreover, for suggesting that the inspector in any way succumbed or might have succumbed to pressure from the trade unions. The appellants' decisions were entirely proper and sensible decisions in the exercise of their statutory functions.

That was the turning point. In the Court of Appeal I had based my judgment on the concession. I said:[2]

> I must confess that, if it were not for the concession made by Mr Medd I should have been disposed to say that, as a matter of discretion, the application should be refused.

So in the end there was no difference between the House of Lords and me.

iii *Outdated technical rules are gone*

The reasoning of each of their Lordships is worthy of study in depth. The principal reason was because there was no evidence whatever that the Board of Inland Revenue had

[1] [1982] AC 617, 623, HL.
[2] [1980] QB 407, 424, CA.

done anything unlawful or ultra vires. Lord Diplock made it clear that, if there had been any substance in the charge of conduct which was unlawful or ultra vires, then the federation would have had a locus standi. He said:[1]

It would, in my view, be a grave lacuna in our system of public law if a pressure group, like the federation, or even a single public-spirited taxpayer, were prevented by outdated technical rules of locus standi from bringing the matter to the attention of the court to vindicate the rule of law and get the unlawful conduct stopped. The Attorney-General, although he occasionally applies for prerogative orders against public authorities that do not form part of central government, in practice never does so against government departments. It is not, in my view, a sufficient answer to say that judicial review of the actions of officers or departments of central government is unnecessary because they are accountable to Parliament for the way in which they carry out their functions. They are accountable to Parliament for what they do so far as regards efficiency and policy, and of that Parliament is the only judge; they are responsible to a court of justice for the lawfulness of what they do, and of that the court is the only judge.

---

[1] [1982] AC 617, 644, HL.

2 Liberty of the subject

1 The military style operation

i *The* Rossminster *case*[1]

This case raised the whole question of the liberty of the subject. When I wrote *The Due Process of Law*, the *Rossminster* case had been decided by the Court of Appeal and was under appeal to the House of Lords. I would invite you to read once again the dramatic story of the 'military style operation'. It is in *The Due Process of Law* pages 115–122. I said (at page 116): 'It may be that our decision will be set aside by the House of Lords.'

ii *We are upset*

It was set aside by the majority of their Lordships but there was a strong dissent by Lord Salmon. May I remind you of what happened. The officers of the Inland Revenue went to a circuit judge and told him on oath that they had reasonable grounds for suspecting that the Rossminster group had been guilty of an offence in connection with tax and that evidence of it could be found on the premises. On the faith of it, the circuit judge signed a search warrant. Armed with this, the revenue early one morning raided the offices of the Rossminster group and took away 12 van loads of documents. The Court of Appeal held that the warrant was bad because it did not specify any particular tax offence: that

[1] *Inland Revenue Comrs v Rossminster Ltd* [1980] AC 952.

in consequence the seizure of the documents was bad and that the revenue authorities had exceeded the power given to them by the statute.

The House of Lords allowed the appeal on the ground that the revenue authorities were authorised by Parliament to do what they did. It was not necessary for them to specify any particular offence. The general suspicion of *a* tax offence was enough.

iii *A breath-taking inroad*

Lord Scarman was very unhappy about it. He said it was 'a breath-taking inroad' (at pages 1021–1022):

My Lords, I agree that these appeals should be allowed and add some observations only because of the importance of the issues raised, and because I share the anxieties felt by the Court of Appeal. If power exists for officers of the Board of Inland Revenue to enter premises, if necessary by force, at any time of the day or night and then seize and remove any things whatsoever found there (which they have reasonable cause to believe may be required as evidence for the purposes of proceedings in respect of any offence or offences involving any form of fraud in connection with, or in relation to, tax) it is the duty of the courts to see that it is not abused: for it is a *breath-taking inroad* upon the individual's right of privacy and right of property. Important as is the public interest in the detection and punishment of tax frauds, it is not to be compared with the public interest in the right of men and women to be secure in the privacy of their homes, their offices, and their papers. Yet if the law is that no particulars of the offence or offences suspected (other than that they are offences of tax fraud) need be given, how can the householder, or occupier of premises, hope to obtain an effective judicial review of the entry, search and seizure at the time of the events or shortly thereafter? And telling the victim that long after the event he may go to law and recover damages if he can prove the revenue acted unlawfully is cold comfort – even if he can afford it.

It is therefore with regret that I have to accept that, if the requirements of section 20C of the Taxes Management Act 1970 . . . are met, the power exists to enter, and search premises, and seize and remove things there found and that the prospect of an immediate judicial review of the exercise of the power is dim. Nevertheless, what Lord Camden CJ said in *Entick v Carrington* (1765) 19 State Tr 1029, 1066, remains good law today:

'No man can set his foot upon my ground without my licence, but he is liable to an action, though the damage be nothing. . . . If he admits the fact, he is bound to show by way of justification, that some positive law has empowered or excused him.'

Yet Lord Scarman did allow his breath to be taken away. He went on to hold, with reluctance, that the requirements of the statute had been met, so that there was a 'positive law' which empowered the revenue to do what they did. So did all the other Law Lords except Lord Salmon. The revenue got access to all the documents.

iv *Lord Salmon dissents*

Lord Salmon dissented. He said (at page 1020):

. . . This, however, is by no means any ordinary case. It is a case of great constitutional importance which can seriously affect individual liberty. . . . In my view, the judge misconstrued section 20C by thinking that it laid down that what he had been told on oath by the officer of the Inland Revenue was sufficient to allow the warrants to be issued.

v *'A leaky umbrella'*

In a leading article *The Times* made this comment in their issue of 18 December 1979:

Lord Salmon's reasoning on the facts is more convincing than that of his colleagues.

It so happened that in the same week the House of Lords decided the case of *Express Newspapers Ltd v McShane.*[1] It was a trade union case of which I have already told you in the section on trade unions. The House reversed the Court of Appeal in that case as well as in the *Rossminster* case.[2] *The Times* were very critical of the House of Lords. They headed their leading article significantly 'A leaky umbrella' and ended it:

If our liberties had to be protected by them, they would prove a leaky umbrella.

You can read further extracts from it on page 188 of this book.

[1] [1980] AC 672.
[2] [1980] AC 952.

2 Another important point

i *Is there a remedy against the Crown?*

In the *Rossminster* case, the House of Lords decided another important point. It was about the remedies available to the subject against the Crown. The Court of Appeal realised that under section 21 of the Crown Proceedings Act 1947 they could not grant an injunction against the Crown. Nor could they make an interim declaration. So they made a final declaration. I said (at page 976):

> The question was raised whether we could, under our new procedure, grant a declaration. I wish we could grant an interim declaration but it has been decided by this court that we cannot do so. That was decided in *International General Electric Company of New York Ltd v Customs and Excise Comrs* [1962] Ch 784. All we can do is make a final declaration. So be it. If that be the only way, I would do it. This is a case where speed is of the essence. This is a case where the freedom of the individual is involved. It is a case where his right to his personal property is involved. It demands immediate remedy. It demands immediate decision. So I think we should decide it now, even upon the affidavit evidence we have before us. Upon that evidence, it is a proper case under this new procedure (which is now entrusted in our hands) in which to make a declaration.
>
> It has this drawback. It means that in any subsequent proceedings or in a pending action the matter will be said to be finally adjudged. The revenue may seek hereafter to say: 'We did reasonably require all these documents and we did not exceed our powers.' But the result of the declaration will be – and I think both counsel agree to this – that the matter is finally adjudged now. Justice demands that we should decide it quickly – as we do – and give a decision now. I would hold that this seizure was bad and that the revenue officers exceeded the powers given to them by the statute.

ii *Deaf Parliamentary ears*

But the House of Lords took a different view. They held that we had no power to make a declaration. Lord Diplock said (at page 1014):

> My Lords, this serves once again to draw attention to what, for my part, I regard as a serious procedural defect in the English system of administrative law: it provides no means of obtaining interlocutory

relief against the Crown and its officers. The useful reforms effected by the amendment to the Rules of Court by substituting the new Order 53 for the old system of prerogative orders, could not overcome this procedural defect, which would require primary legislation. Such legislation has been recommended in the Report of the Law Commission on which the revision of Order 53 was based. It is greatly to be hoped that the recommendation will not continue to fall upon deaf parliamentary ears.

As far as I know the parliamentary ears are still deaf. There is no means of obtaining interlocutory relief against the Crown and its officers.

iii *Four years later*

Now for the sequel. You know the saying, 'The proof of the pudding is in the eating.' So also the proof of the 'military style operation' is whether it gave rise to a prosecution for a tax offence. The revenue authorities got the documents. They took four years examining them. They then decided not to take criminal proceedings. On 30 June 1983 the Attorney-General told the House of Commons:

The board has decided, on the advice of leading counsel and after consultation with me, that no criminal proceedings will be instituted against Rossminster Ltd or any of the other companies or individuals from whose premises documents were taken under warrant on 13 July 1979, or against any of their employees.

The board will now be taking steps to deal with the liabilities for tax and, where appropriate, for interest and penalties that have come to light in the course of the investigation.

It would appear therefore that the documents did not disclose sufficient evidence to warrant criminal proceedings: and that the revenue were not justified in their 'military style operation'.

3 The *Mareva* up to date

1 The juristic principle

In *The Due Process of Law* I told of the *Mareva* injunction at pages 133–151. I told you about *The Siskina*[1] in which the House of Lords douched it with cold water. But it has proved itself to have been the greatest piece of judicial law reform in our time. It has since been vindicated by the legislature. In the recent case of *Z Ltd v A–Z and AA–LL*[2] the Court of Appeal examined the juristic principle underlying it. I will tell you of it. It shows the worth of this new jurisdiction.

i *Ruritania – a pseudonym*

I said in my judgment:[3]

... Ruritania is an imaginary country. The name was invented by Anthony Hope in his novel *The Prisoner of Zenda*. I will use it so as to conceal the identity of a real country and its people. There was a large company with its head office in Ruritania: and a London office here. It had its main banking account with a bank in Hentzau. Then some conspirators got to work to defraud the Ruritanian company. Telexes and cables were sent purporting to come from the company's head office in Ruritania. These authorised huge sums to be transferred from the company's bankers in Hentzau to London, and paid to suppliers of goods. The telexes and cables were forged. No goods had been supplied. The moneys went into the hands of the conspirators. The Ruritanian company was defrauded of £2,000,000. The moneys were believed to

[1] [1979] AC 210.
[2] [1982] QB 558.
[3] [1982] QB 558, 570–578.

have been paid into divers accounts at various banks in London, and used to buy motor cars and other things. When the fraud was discovered, the Ruritanian company was anxious to trace the moneys into the various banking accounts, and also the goods. It was important that any dealings should be stopped before the conspirators knew that the fraud had been discovered. It was so urgent that, before issuing a writ, the Ruritanian company made application to the commercial judge seeking orders against any of those who might possibly have had a part in the fraud, and against any of the estate agents and solicitors who might, quite innocently, have taken part in the transfers, and against the banks who might still be holding any of the money. They went before the commercial judge, Bingham J, and got a *Mareva* injunction to stop any dealings with the assets, save in so far as they exceeded £2,000,000. This was followed immediately by a writ in which the Ruritanian company claimed damages against 17 defendants for conspiracy to defraud and against 18 defendants (including the five great clearing banks) for 'specific discovery, interrogatories and injunctions all to preserve the subject matter of the action herein'. The Ruritanian company got *Anton Piller* orders, and also orders for interrogatories. They also got *Mareva* injunctions against the first 17 defendants. By these means the Ruritanian company succeeded in recovering £1,000,000 out of the £2,000,000. Since then a settlement has been made by which the Ruritanian company has recovered, we are told, a good deal of the balance. But the action has been kept alive because the five clearing banks desire the law to be elucidated. They want to know what is the position of innocent third parties, like themselves, when served with notice of a *Mareva* injunction. This has never been investigated before: and we are grateful to counsel for the assitance they have given.

ii Mareva *fully established*

The *Mareva* injunction is now an established feature of English law. The principles applicable to it – as against the defendant – have been stated in numerous cases from 1975 to 1981. They have been given statutory force by section 37(3) of the Supreme Court Act 1981, which says:

'The power of the High Court . . . to grant an interlocutory injunction restraining a party to any proceedings from removing from the jurisdiction of the High Court, or otherwise dealing with, assets located within that jurisdiction shall be exercisable in cases where that party is, as well as in cases where he is not, domiciled, resident or present within that jurisdiction.'

Those words 'otherwise dealing with' are in my opinion to be given a wide meaning. They are not to be construed as ejusdem generis with 'removing from the jurisdiction'. . . . Giving them this wide meaning, they bear out what I said in *Rahman (Prince Abdul) bin Turki al Sudairy v Abu-Taha* [1980] 1 WLR 1268, 1273:

'So I would hold that a *Mareva* injunction can be granted against a man even though he is based in this country if the circumstances are such that there is a danger of his absconding, or a danger of the assets being removed out of the jurisdiction or disposed of within the jurisdiction, or otherwise dealt with so that there is a danger that the plaintiff, if he gets judgment, will not be able to get it satisfied.'

iii *Effect against the banks*

. . . Once a bank is given notice of a *Mareva* injunction affecting goods or money in its hands, it must not dispose of them itself, nor allow the defendant or anyone else to do so – except by the authority of the court. If the bank or any of its officers should knowingly assist in the disposal of them, it will be guilty of a contempt of court. For it is an act calculated to obstruct the course of justice. . . .

You may ask: Suppose the defendant sued the bank for dishonouring a cheque, what would be the answer of the bank? In my opinion the *Mareva* injunction makes it unlawful for the bank to honour the cheque. 'It is plain that a contract to do what it has become illegal to do cannot be legally enforceable. There cannot be default in not doing what the law forbids to be done': see *Denny, Mott and Dickson Ltd v James B Fraser & Co Ltd* [1944] AC 265, 272, per Lord Macmillan. . . .

The juristic principle is therefore this: As soon as the bank is given notice of the *Mareva* injunction, it must freeze the defendant's bank account. It must not allow any drawings to be made on it, neither by cheques drawn before the injunction nor by those drawn after it. The reason is because, if it allowed any such drawings, it would be obstructing the course of justice – as prescribed by the court which granted the injunction – and it would be guilty of a contempt of court.

I have confined my observations to banks and bank accounts. But the same applies to any specific asset held by a bank for safe custody on behalf of the defendant. Be it jewellery, stamps, or anything else. And to any other person who holds any other asset of the defendant. If the asset is covered by the terms of the *Mareva* injunction, that other person must not hand it over to the defendant or do anything to enable him to dispose of it. He must hold it pending further order. . . .

iv *Discovery*

In order to make a *Mareva* injunction fully effective, it is very desirable that the defendant should be required in a proper case to make discovery.

If he comes on the return day and says that he has ample assets to meet the claim, he ought to specify them. Otherwise his refusal to disclose them will go to show that he is really evading payment. There is ample power in the court to order discovery: see *A J Bekhor & Co Ltd v Bilton* [1981] QB 923. I am sorry that the majority of the court there reversed Parker J and differed from Griffiths LJ, but it was only on the special facts.

Nowadays in any flagrant case the courts not only grant a *Mareva* injunction. They make also an *Anton Piller* order and an order for discovery of documents. It is a revolutionary procedure but very effective as the *Ruritania* case shows.

4 Who can get a *Mareva*?

There are two cases in which the House of Lords reversed the Court of Appeal which caused me much disappointment. They are the *Gouriet* case of which I told you in *The Discipline of Law* pages 137–143 and *The Siskina*. In both cases the House of Lords proceeded on the footing that the High Court had no power to grant an 'interlocutory injunction except in protection or assertion of some legal or equitable right'. Mr Gouriet had no such right. Nor had the cargo-owners in the *Siskina*. Although it was most just and convenient that an injunction should be granted (as I hope my discourse showed) nevertheless the House of Lords held it was not permissible.

1 Can the police get a *Mareva*?

i *The old lady's bank account*

This very conflict came up again in May 1982 in a most interesting case. It is *Chief Constable of Kent v V*.[1] The Chief Constable of Kent sought to freeze the sums in a bank account. He had no legal or equitable right to the sums but yet an injunction was granted.

There was an old lady living in Tunbridge Wells. She had a good deal of money to her credit in Grindlays Bank. A man was charged with wrongfully extracting money from her account. It was alleged that he drew 21 cheques on her account amounting to £16,001 and that he paid them into

[1] [1982] 3 WLR 462.

his own bank account: and that he also paid in moneys which he had got from other people, and he had drawn upon them from time to time. So you could not tell which was which.

He had been charged but not tried. So nothing was to be taken against him. The allegations were not to be taken as true.

ii *The Chief Constable applies for an injunction*

The Chief Constable of Kent feared that the man might draw out the moneys from the bank so that they would be beyond recall. He issued a writ and applied ex parte for an injunction to restrain him from drawing out money from the bank account.

iii *Selling video cassettes*

In my judgment I first told of *West Mercia Constabulary v Wagener.*[1] I said:[2]

Wagener put advertisements in local newspapers advertising video cassettes for sale at low prices, and asking for cheques to be sent in advance. A lot of customers sent cheques. Wagener paid them into his bank account. But he never sent any cassettes to the customers. The whole thing was suspected of being a fraud. But the police did not know the names of the customers. So the Chief Constable himself applied for an injunction to 'freeze' the bank account. Forbes J granted an injunction.

iv *A suitcase full of banknotes*

I went on to say (at page 465) that Forbes J put this case:

Suppose a bank robber steals a million pounds in easily negotiable notes. He puts them into a suitcase and deposits them in a luggage office or in a bank. If the police reasonably believe that they have been stolen or fraudulently obtained, they could, on getting a search warrant or by consent, seize the suitcase and the notes in it. The police could hold them just as any other goods that are believed to have been stolen or fraudulently obtained.

[1] [1982] 1 WLR 127.
[2] [1982] 3 WLR 462, 464.

v *Lifting the latch*

Then I took a logical step:

Next, suppose that, instead of the thief putting them into a suitcase, he pays them into his own bank account. His account may already be in credit, so that the stolen notes go to swell his credit balance. It may be in overdraft, so that they serve to pay off the overdraft and put him in credit. In either case, in so far as the notes can be traced into his bank account – and are still available to his credit – I am of opinion that the court, at the instance of the police, can and should freeze his bank account. If this be so when currency notes are stolen, so also it is when money is abstracted by forgery from the account of the true owner and put by the forger into his own account. This freezing is done so as to ensure that the moneys can in due course be restored to the rightful owner. I cannot believe that a thief can get away with his stolen hoard by the simple device of paying it into his own bank account. So long as it can be traced, it can be frozen. It may be that 150 years ago the common law halted outside the banker's door, but for the last 100 years, since the fusion of law and equity, it has had the courage to lift the latch, walk in and examine the books: see *Banque Belge Pour L'Etranger v Hambrouck* [1921] 1 KB 321, 335 by Atkin LJ and *Re Diplock* [1948] Ch 465, 520 by Lord Greene MR.

2 Is the remedy limited?

i *Some timorous souls*

I knew that Lord Justice Slade took a different view. So I continued:

Some timorous souls are fearful of this extension. They say that the police have no cause of action known to the law so as to come under RSC Ord 29, r 2, and that is where Forbes J went wrong in the *West Mercia* case [1982] 1 WLR 127, 131: and that the police have no legal or equitable right such as to warrant an injunction under RSC Ord 29, r 1. . . .

But I sought to overcome this objection by reference to section 37(1) of the Supreme Court Act 1981 which came into force on 1 January 1982. It says:

The High Court may by order (whether interlocutory or final) grant an injunction or appoint a receiver in all cases in which it appears to the court to be just and convenient to do so.

231

ii *A good and sensible test*

In view of this section I ventured to say with some boldness (at page 466):

It is no longer necessary that the injunction should be *ancillary* to an action claiming a legal or equitable right. It can stand on its own. The section as it now stands plainly confers a new and extensive jurisdiction on the High Court to grant an injunction. It is far wider than anything that had been known in our courts before. There is no reason whatever why the courts should cut down this jurisdiction by reference to previous technical distinctions. Thus Parliament has restored the law to what my great predecessor Sir George Jessel MR said it was in *Beddow v Beddow* (1878) 9 Ch D 89, 93 and which I applied in *Mareva Compania Naviera SA v International Bulkcarriers SA* [1975] 2 Lloyd's Rep 509, 510: 'I have unlimited power to grant an injunction in any case where it would be right or just to do so: . . .'. Subject, however, to this qualification: I would not say the power was 'unlimited'. I think that the applicant for an injunction must have a sufficient interest in a matter to warrant him asking for an injunction. Whereas previously it was said that he had to have a 'legal or equitable right' in himself, now he has to have a locus standi to apply. He must have a sufficient interest. This is a good and sensible test. It is the selfsame test of locus standi as the legislature itself authorised in section 31(3) of the Supreme Court Act 1981. Next, it must be just and convenient that an injunction should be granted at his instance as, for example, so as to preserve the assets or property which might otherwise be lost or dissipated. On this principle I think that the *Siskina* case [1979] AC 210 would be decided differently today. The cargo-owners had plainly a sufficient interest: it would have been most just and convenient to have granted an injunction, as I pointed out in the Court of Appeal in the *Siskina* case [1979] AC 210, 228E. It was most unjust for the House of Lords to refuse it.

iii *Have the police a 'sufficient interest'?*

I then considered the duty of the police:

I turn therefore to the crucial question in this case: has the Chief Constable a sufficient interest to apply for an injunction? We considered the position of the police in *R v Commissioner of Police of the Metropolis, ex parte Blackburn* [1968] 2 QB 118, 136, where I said:

'I hold it to be the duty of the Commissioner of Police of the Metropolis, as it is of every chief constable, to enforce the law of the land. He must take steps so to post his men that crimes may be detected; and that honest citizens may go about their affairs in peace.'

To this I would now add that it is his duty, once he knows or has reason to believe that goods have been stolen or unlawfully obtained, to do his best to discover and apprehend the thief and to recover the goods. Corresponding to that duty he has a right – or at any rate an interest – on behalf of the public to seize the goods and detain them pending the trial of the offender and to restore them in due course to the true owner. In pursuance of that duty – and of that right and interest – he can apply to the magistrate for a search warrant and to a High Court judge for an injunction.

So I hold that the Chief Constable here has a sufficient right and interest to warrant his applying to the court.

iv *Does it apply to a bank account?*

It was of course necessary to apply this reasoning to a bank account. This I did by giving this illustration:

Go back to the suitcase full of stolen currency notes – belonging to many persons who are not yet ascertained. If the thief deposits the suitcase with his bank, he is entitled to demand back his suitcase at any time and the bankers must deliver it to him at his request – unless there is an order of the court to prevent them doing so. Surely the police can get an injunction to stop the bank delivering it to him. Just as they can go to a magistrate and get a search warrant, surely they can go to a High Court judge and get an injunction. If that be correct for the currency notes in the suitcase, it must also be correct when they are paid into the thief's bank account. On an application by the police setting out their reasonable grounds, the High Court can grant an injunction to prevent the thief drawing on his bank account and the bank from honouring his cheques, so that in due course the moneys can be restored to the true owner. Such an injunction is vital as an ancillary support to an order for restitution under section 28 of the Theft Act 1968. That section enables the court of trial, on convicting the man, to order the stolen goods or their proceeds, direct or indirect, to be restored to the true owner. It would be a mockery of the law if he could always evade a restitution order by disposing of the goods or their proceeds pending his trial. The court must have power to grant an injunction to stop him from doing so.

v *Lord Justice Slade dissents*

I must point out here that Lord Justice Slade dissented. He said (at page 477):

At the risk of deserving the description of a timorous soul I find myself driven to the conclusion that (whether or not it might be desirable) the police themselves have no power under the common law to 'detain' intangible assets, even if they have reasonable grounds for supposing that they are traceable to property which has been obtained from another in breach of the criminal law. If, after full consideration of all the consequences, they think it desirable that they should have this right or that new special powers to seek relief by way of injunction, in cases like the present, should be conferred on them, then they should in my opinion seek such power from Parliament and not from the court.

I trust that if the view of Lord Justice Slade is right, Parliament will soon legislate to give the police the necessary power. I hope too that the general restriction imposed by the House of Lords (which limits injunctions to the protection of 'some legal or equitable right') will be lifted.

5 *Anton Piller* up to date

In *The Due Process of Law* I told you of the *Anton Piller* order. It is at pages 123–130. It is a new feature which runs parallel to the *Mareva* injunction. I sought to develop it in a case about video cassettes, but the House of Lords disagreed with me. Parliament has now put the position right. It is a matter of such importance that I would tell you about it. The case is *Rank Film Distributors Ltd v Video Information Centre.*[1] I take the facts from my own judgment.[2]

1 Video cassettes

i *A pirate king makes cassettes*

'It is, it is a glorious thing, to be a Pirate King,' said W. S. Gilbert: but he was speaking of ship pirates. Today we speak of film pirates. It is not a glorious thing to be, but it is a good thing to be in for making money. Film pirates plunder the best and most recent cinema films. They transpose them on to magnetic tape: and then sell video cassettes on the black market.

A film pirate works like this. He gets hold of a technician in a cinema or in a ship or an aircraft – any place where cinematograph films are projected on to a screen. The pirate then bribes the technician. He pays him, say, £100. The technician then 'borrows' a film for a night. It is simple enough. Instead of putting the film into the cupboard, as he should, he puts it into his own case. He hands the celluloid film to the pirate. Overnight the pirate takes the film to his 'laboratory'. He has

[1] [1982] AC 380.
[2] [1982] AC 380, 403–411.

235

there a machine for transferring the film from celluloid on to magnetic tape. It only takes an hour or so. Next morning the pirate returns the film to the technician. He puts it into the cupboard. No one is any the wiser. The pirate has during the night made a 'master tape'. He uses it for making video cassettes. He then sells these cassettes on the black market. There are many buyers available. A lot of people nowadays have video cassette recorders. Universities have them. Hotels have them. Private homes have them. They can use the cassette so as to reproduce the film when they like or wherever they like.

This black market makes huge inroads into the legitimate business of the film companies. They have been put to great expense in producing the best films: they have the copyright which gives them the sole and exclusive right to reproduce them. Yet here are the pirates plundering it – stealing all the best films.

By far the biggest buyers come from the Middle East and Africa. The newspapers have drawn attention to it. In the *Evening Standard* of April 17, 1979, there appeared an article with the headline:

LONDON'S £1M VIDEO PIRATES

'One world-beating success that is not likely to feature in the trade figures is the emergence of London as the international centre for a black market in video cassettes.

Trade in these recordings, made without payment of copyright, and carried on through a network of London box numbers, is estimated to be worth up to £1,000,000 a year.

Crates full of pre-recorded cassettes are being shipped out of London to the Middle East. . . .

The recent emergence of London as a world centre is due to the large number of Middle Eastern and African travellers who meet here, and who have an insatiable appetite for an alternative to the poor quality programmes put out by their own television networks.'

The pirates have good salesmen about. For instance, in February 1979 an executive of a film company was in Iran. He stayed a night in a hotel in Kuwait. Someone came up to him and said:

'Are you going to London? Here is a list of films which you can buy on video cassettes in London. Call the telephone number 937–0555 and ask for Ms Sue. The price of the tape will be £50 per hour running time.'

The film companies followed up that clue and others. Eventually they discovered the 'laboratory' where a pirate used to transpose the celluloid films on to magnetic tape. It was in a house in a suburb of London – half-an-hour out on the Underground. . . .

236

ii *The piracy is a criminal offence*

Such is the outline. The affidavits give the story in much more detail. But the evidence is quite sufficient to warrant the inference that here there was a conspiracy to defraud at common law – that still exists: see section 5(2) of the Criminal Law Act 1977 – and that those concerned were engaged in offences of making and selling infringing copies contrary to section 21 of the Copyright Act 1956.

But the criminal law does not provide an adequate remedy for the film companies. The Committee to consider the Law on Copyright and Designs (1966) (Cmnd 6732), presided over by Whitford J, reported that '. . . the criminal provisions are of little use and little used': see paragraph 708. The criminal law is too slow and the penalties too small. Section 21 creates only a summary offence: and the penalties have not been increased by the legislature. . . .

iii *Recourse to the civil courts*

So in waging this war against this crime, the film companies have had recourse to the civil courts: and especially to the Chancery Division of the High Court. They sought the advice of counsel, Mr Laddie, and he suggested that they should apply for an ex parte order – before the defendant was served with the writ – so as to take the trader by surprise before he got rid of his stock and any incriminating documents. The first such application came up for close consideration by Templeman J in *EMI Ltd v Pandit* [1975] 1 WLR 302. His judgment set a most valuable initiative. It was followed by this court in *Anton Piller KG v Manufacturing Processes Ltd* [1976] Ch 55 and extended in *EMI Ltd v Sarwar* [1977] FSR 146. Those cases were heard ex parte. In this case we have heard both sides. As a result, I think that we should affirm those decisions and also those that have followed them. It is an innovation which has proved its worth time and time again. So long as the evidence is strong enough, it is now commonplace for orders to be made against a householder ex parte, not only to restrain him from making or distributing infringing copies, but also so as to require him to permit his premises to be searched, and to require the infringing copies to be produced, also the invoices and documents disclosed, and furthermore for him to give the names and addresses of makers who supply him. In nearly every case the householder complies with the order. He raises no objection. He could object, if he wished to do so, but this is at the risk of proceedings being taken against him for contempt. Rather than take the risk, he complies with the order.

2 Self-incrimination

i *Privilege is claimed against self-incrimination*

So much being settled, most of the discussion before us turned on a new point which has not been raised before. It concerns privilege against self-incrimination. The order against the defendants in this case required them to answer interrogatories and to give discovery of documents. . . . The defendants took objection to giving that discovery. (One of them) in his affidavit claimed privilege from self-incrimination. He said:

'I now refer to that part of the order that orders me to make available on oath certain information to the plaintiffs and to make discovery of certain documents to the plaintiffs. I would wish, if I am so permitted, to decline to provide such information and discovery on the basis that it would tend to criminate me or to expose me to a penalty.'

This privilege has never been claimed before in any action for infringement of copyright. If it exists, it will apply not only in *Anton Piller* cases but in all cases of infringement of copyright, even where an order is made inter partes for discovery. So the point is of much importance. . . .

ii *I would not allow him the privilege*

There is plain evidence here that the defendants have done great wrong to the plaintiffs. They have stolen the plaintiffs' copyright in hundreds of films and have not paid a penny for it. Yet these wrongdoers glory in their wrongdoing. They get legal aid, and supported by it they say that, by reason of their wrongdoing, they have a privilege against self-incrimination. They rub their hands with glee and say to the injured plaintiffs: 'You cannot ask us any questions. You cannot see any of our documents. We have a privilege by which we can hold you at bay and tell you nothing. You cannot prove any damages against us – not more than minimal. You cannot get an account of our profits.'

To allow wrongdoers to take advantage of their wrongdoing in this way is an affront to justice itself. It is a great disservice to the public interest. It should not be allowed. If this illicit traffic is to be stopped, strong measures are needed. Whitford J has much experience in cases of this kind. He has made a strong order, and I agree with it. I would dismiss this appeal.

My two colleagues did not agree with me. They would allow the privilege.

iii *The Lords uphold the majority*

The House of Lords felt that the privilege against self-incrimination was so well established that it was capable of being invoked. But Lord Russell of Killowen (at page 448) made a plea for legislation:

Inasmuch as the application of the privilege in question can go a long way in this and other analogous fields to deprive the owner of his just rights to the protection of his property I would welcome legislation somewhat on the lines of section 31 of the Theft Act 1968: the aim of such legislation should be to remove the privilege while at the same time preventing the use in criminal proceedings of statements which otherwise have been privileged.

iv *Parliament quickly puts things right*

The House of Lords gave their decision on 8 April 1981. The Lord Chancellor and his department acted quickly. There was going through Parliament the Supreme Court Bill. It was passed on 28 July 1981. It contained a special section 72 on the lines suggested by Lord Russell. The privilege was taken away in civil proceedings for

infringement of rights pertaining to any intellectual property or for passing off

and 'intellectual property' was defined as meaning

any patent, trade mark, copyright, registered design, technical or commercial information or other intellectual property.

So the law is now as I thought it should be.

6 Delay in arbitrations

I come now to a big conflict in my time between the Court
of Appeal and the House of Lords. It arose out of a number of
cases where parties to a commercial dispute had agreed to go
to arbitration. The complainants made a claim for damages
and started an arbitration against the respondents. But the
complainants were guilty of inordinate and inexcusable
delay. So much so that a fair trial became impossible. The
respondents applied to stop the proceedings. The Court of
Appeal stopped three of them. But the House of Lords
allowed two of those three to go on.

These are the facts in outline of the three cases.

1 Three striking cases

i *The* Bremer Vulkan[1]

Here there was 12 years' delay. It was a case between German
shipbuilders and Indian buyers. The contract was governed
by German law but provided for arbitration in London. It
included a time bar barring any claim for defects. *It barred
them after 12 months*. The claim went to arbitration in
London. The arbitration was not started for five years. The
buyers sought to avoid the time bar (of 12 months) by saying
that it did not apply to arbitration in London. The

---

[1] *Bremer Vulkan Schiffbau und Maschinenfabrik v South India Shipping Corpn Ltd* [1981]
AC 909.

arbitration dragged on so long that after 12 years the German shipbuilders applied to stop the arbitration from going any further.

ii *The* Splendid Sun[1]

Here there was eight years' delay. In 1969 the *Splendid Sun* carried 10,400 tons of maize from Mexico to Venezuela. On arriving at the discharging port she grounded and suffered damage in over $200,000. The owners said it was the charterers' fault for not nominating a safe port. The charterers said it was the master's fault for bad navigation. In 1969 two experienced arbitrators in the City of London were appointed. Nothing happened for eight whole years. Then in 1978 the owners delivered points of claim. The charterers applied to stop the arbitration from going any further.

iii *The* Hannah Blumenthal[2]

Here there was 11 years' delay. This was a case about the sale of a ship in 1969. The sellers were Norwegian. The buyers were German. The agreement contained a clause for arbitration in London. It contained an express provision that the vessel

. . . shall be delivered and taken over as she is at the time of delivery, after which the sellers *shall have no responsibility* for possible faults or deficiencies of any description.

Two years later the German buyers made complaints and two arbitrators were appointed. In 1980, after 11 years had passed and many delays, the German buyers sought to revive the arbitration. The Norwegian sellers applied to stop the proceedings.

---

1 *André & Cie SA v Marine Transocean Ltd* [1981] QB 694.
2 *Paal Wilson & Co A/S v Partenreederei Hannah Blumenthal* [1982] 3 WLR 49, CA; varied [1983] 1 Lloyd's Rep 103, HL.

2 A new development

i *The Court of Appeal would stop the arbitrations*

In the first case – the *Bremer Vulkan* – in the Court of Appeal I said in my judgment:[1]

When I was young, a sandwich-man wearing a top-hat used to parade outside these courts with his boards back and front, proclaiming 'Arbitrate, don't litigate.' It was very good advice so long as arbitrations were conducted speedily: as many still are in the City of London. But it is not so good when arbitrations drag on for ever.

These cases mark a new development in the law of arbitrations. It is parallel to the development 11 years ago when we started to strike out actions at law for want of prosecution. . . .

Now in the year 1979 we are invited to make a like development in regard to arbitrations. Three recent cases now show that, in arbitrations, as well as in courts of law, cases may last 'so long as to turn justice sour'. They show, too, that an arbitrator has far less power than a judge. If the parties drag their feet, the arbitrator can do nothing to quicken them up. He cannot dismiss a claim for want of prosecution. He cannot strike out a dilatory plea which is put in just to gain time. He must abide the pleasure of the parties. He has no sanctions with which to enforce his orders. Seeing that he can do nothing, the question is: can these courts do anything about it? . . .

In the end I think we should make the new development which we are invited to make. We should develop the law as to arbitrations on the same lines as we did 11 years ago for the law of actions. The judges in the courts below – Donaldson J and Lloyd J – have pointed the way. Both are most experienced in the ways of arbitrations. By their opinions we set great store. They have struck out these three commercial claims for want of prosecution. I would do the same. . . .

Lord Justice Roskill said (at page 954):

. . . I see little or no difficulty in attaching to an agreement to arbitrate as a legal incident of such a contract an implied obligation in point of law upon the claimant who, like a plaintiff in the action, has the conduct of the case not to be guilty of such dilatory conduct in the prosecution of his claim as will defeat the whole purpose of the agreement to arbitrate by making a fair hearing before the arbitration tribunal impossible because of the lapse of time involved. . . .

[1] [1981] AC 909, 933–941.

ii *But the Lords would let them go on*

In this *Bremer Vulkan* case the House of Lords – by three to two – reversed the Court of Appeal on the ground that the obligation was mutual. It was the duty of the respondents to keep the arbitration going: they could not complain of delay by the claimants. Lord Diplock said:[1]

... Where the arbitration agreement is in a clause forming part of a wider contract and provides for the reference to arbitration of all future disputes arising under or concerning the contract, neither party knows when the agreement is entered into whether he will be claimant or respondent in disputes to which the arbitration agreement will apply. If it creates any contractual obligation to proceed with reasonable dispatch in all future arbitrations held pursuant to the clause – and I will consider later what that obligation is – the obligation is, in my view, mutual; it obliges each party to co-operate with the other in taking appropriate steps to keep the procedure in the arbitration moving, whether he happens to be the claimant or the respondent in the particular dispute.

... Respondents in private arbitrations are not entitled to let sleeping dogs lie and then complain that they did not bark.

3 The Court of Appeal is outspoken

The Court of Appeal were most outspoken in their criticisms of the House of Lords. I have never known anything like it. I will take three extracts:

i *My judgment in the* Splendid Sun:[2]

This mutual obligation comes as something of a surprise to everyone: especially to the denizens of Essex Court and St Mary Axe. Nothing of the kind was propounded before the judge, nor before us in the Court of Appeal. It appears for the first time in the speech of Lord Diplock in the House of Lords. It is, I suppose, too late for any words of mine to make any difference. It is for us to come to terms with it. It is said to be based on an implication. As such it goes beyond anything that I have hitherto understood. To my way of thinking, the implication is neither obvious, nor reasonable, nor necessary. Nor does it accord with reality. If the claimant does not pursue his claim – if he makes no application to the arbitrator – it is said that the respondent is bound himself to do so. Who

1 [1981] AC 909, 983, 988.
2 [1981] QB 694, 701.

ever heard of a respondent doing any such thing? Take this very case. It was not the charterers who were claiming any money. It was the owners. If they wanted to pursue their claim, they should have taken steps to put in their points of claim – or to apply for directions. It was not for the charterers to do so. Just as the owners started the arbitration by taking the first step. So they should have continued it by taking the second or succeeding steps as they came around to be done. As we all know, the cases are legion in which arbitrators are appointed and nothing more is heard of the case. Sometimes it is settled. At other times the claimant simply lets it drop: and the respondent does nothing. Does that mean that the claimant can revive it five, eight, 15 or 20 years later on? I cannot believe that the House of Lords intended any such thing. I think that we must have misunderstood the ruling in some way or other. Take this very case. If there really is a mutual obligation, the charterers, at the end of 1969, ought themselves to have roused the sleeping shipowners or have applied to the arbitrators for directions: and, as they did not do so, they are now in 1981 being faced with an arbitration – when all their evidence is lost. It would be most unjust to put such an obligation on the charterers – which no one had ever thought of before.

ii *Lord Justice Kerr in the* Hannah Blumenthal:[1]

It follows that the stark issue which faces the court is whether parties to an arbitration agreement are to be held to their agreement to arbitrate in such circumstances, whereas an action based on the same dispute would in the same circumstances unhesitatingly be struck out. Unless rigorously compelled by binding authority, I cannot accept that such an extraordinary dichotomy must follow as a matter of law, when our systems of litigation and arbitration are both basically adversarial in their nature, and when both are obviously directed to the common end of doing justice. It hardly needs emphasising that a fundamental characteristic of our common law system has always been the development of legal doctrine with the flexibility of pragmatic common sense, but the acceptance of this dichotomy would to my mind be wholly out of line with this tradition. . . .

The reality, I feel bound to say, is that until the decision by a majority of the House of Lords in the *Bremer Vulkan* case in January 1981, I do not think that it would have occurred to any practitioner, arbitrator or businessman familiar with arbitrations that our law is powerless in situations such as the present. I think that I can also properly say that from my own knowledge this decision has been received with the greatest concern, not only in the City and the Temple, but also abroad among practitioners and institutions who look to this country as an

[1] [1982] 3 WLR 49, 66, 67.

important venue for international commercial arbitrations. It is not surprising, as we were told by counsel, that it has already resulted in attempts to take advantage of references to arbitration which were thought to be long defunct by seeking to make capital out of their revival. It is also not surprising that the new Hong Kong Arbitration Ordinance which has been introduced into the Legislative Council as the result of proposals by the Hong Kong Law Reform Commission, and which will, I understand, be shortly enacted, includes a provision which neutralises this decision by empowering the court to order the termination of arbitratons, and prohibit further proceedings, where there has been undue delay by a claimant in instituting or prosecuting his claim, if the court is satisfied that the delay will give rise to a substantial risk that it is not possible to have a fair trial of the issues.

iii *Lord Justice Griffiths in the* Hannah Blumenthal:[1]

. . . As a result of the dilatory conduct of the buyers' solicitors and also, but to a much lesser extent, the sellers' solicitors, if this arbitration proceeds the arbitrator will be faced with the task of attempting to decide the dispute upon oral conversations alleged to have taken place in 1969. I entirely agree with Mr David Johnson, for the sellers, that as a matter of common sense the arbitration ought not to be allowed to proceed because after a lapse of 12 years it is a totally unrealistic exercise to attempt to decide with any precision what was said so long ago, and consequently there is a grave risk that justice will not be done.

If this dispute had been commenced as an action in the High Court, I have no hesitation in saying that it would have been struck out for want of prosecution. The delay has been inordinate and inexcusable, the sellers must be prejudiced in attempting to meet the buyers' allegations so long after the event, and there is a serious risk that there cannot be a fair trial of the issue in the sense that justice cannot be done between the parties after this lapse of time.

If I had not had the advantage of reading Lord Diplock's speech in *Bremer Vulkan Schiffbau und Maschinenfabrik v South India Shipping Corpn Ltd* [1981] AC 909, I should have fallen into the same error as the judge at first instance, the Court of Appeal and the two of their Lordships who expressed dissenting opinions in the House of Lords in that case. It would have appeared to me to be wholly divorced from reality and the expectation of commercial men that those facing claims should be under the same obligation to keep the claims moving against them as was imposed upon those who made the claims. Take the present case. The contract under which the ship was sold expressly excluded any 'responsibility for possible faults or deficiency of any description', yet

[1] [1982] 3 WLR 49, 61–62.

here are the buyers seeking to avoid the consequences of that express term by saying they were induced to enter into the contract by an oral representation which they first notified to the sellers some three years after the sale. The sellers might well be excused for thinking it was just a try on and be reinforced in that view by the apparent lack of enthusiasm of the buyers' solicitors to bring the matter before the arbitrators. Against this background, if the sellers' solicitor had written to the sellers to say that as the buyers' solicitors were proceeding so slowly he was going to prod them into action, I again agree with Mr Johnson that the sellers would probably have said to their solicitor, 'Whose side are you on?'

However this may be, I understand the decision in the *Bremer Vulkan* case in the House of Lords to impose mutual obligations on the parties to an arbitration to put an end to delay, and that the respondents in an arbitration are not entitled to complain of the complainants' delay as a ground for repudiating the arbitration. Lord Diplock [1981] AC 909, 988, ended his speech with these words: 'Respondents in private arbitrations are not entitled to let sleeping dogs lie and then complain that they did not bark.'

It may by now have appeared that my enthusiasm for the decision of the House of Lords in the *Bremer Vulkan* case is somewhat less than whole-hearted, but this does nothing to diminish my determination to follow it loyally unless it can legitimately be distinguished. From time to time every judge will be confronted with the decision of a higher court with which he does not agree, but there are limits to the judicial ingenuity which it is permissible to employ to avoid the consequences of the unpopular decision, particularly when it is a decision of the House of Lords.

4 The Lords adhere to their view

i *The facts were accepted*

Despite these outspoken criticisms, the House of Lords adhered to their view. The second case – *The Splendid Sun* – did not go to the Lords. When the third case – the *Hannah Blumenthal* – reached them, Lord Diplock again presided, but on this occasion, at his request, the leading speech was given by Lord Brandon of Oakbrook. He made it clear that on the facts he agreed with the judges below. He said:[1]

[1] [1983] 1 Lloyd's Rep 103, 108.

My Lords, Mr Justice Staughton at first instance, and all three members of the Court of Appeal on appeal from him, were of the opinion that there had been such inordinate delay by the buyers and the sellers in their preparation for the arbitration and the bringing of it to a hearing that a fair trial of the dispute between the parties was no longer possible. There was, in my view, ample material on which the two courts below could properly reach this conclusion, and it would, I apprehend, only be in very rare cases that your Lordships' House would see fit to disturb a concurrent conclusion of that kind. Even if that consideration were to be disregarded, however, I think it right to say, after a careful examination of the extensive delays which admittedly occurred in this case, that I should have no hesitation in reaching the same conclusion on the matter concerned as was reached in the two courts below.

ii *But* Bremer Vulkan *was binding*

He went on (at page 113) to hold, however, that the mutual obligation concept was part of the ratio decidendi of *Bremer Vulkan* and should be applied:

> . . . The whole thrust of Lord Diplock's speech (on that point) is, to my mind, that, whenever there is a possibility of such delay by either side occurring as would create a risk of a fair or satisfactory trial becoming no longer possible, both parties are under a joint and several obligation to apply to the arbitrator or arbitrators for directions to put an end to such delay. On this interpretation of what Lord Diplock said the question of its being the obligation of the one party or the other to take the initiative does not arise; each party is obliged to take the initiative, with the co-operation of the other if it is forthcoming, without it if it is not.

He was careful to say, however, (at page 113):

> . . . I express no opinion one way or another as to the conclusion which I might have reached if I had been a member of the Committee which decided the *Bremer Vulkan* case. It is sufficient to say that that decision was reached by what Lord Wilberforce described as the best way of resolving doubtful issues known to the law, and that no special or unusual circumstances have been put forward as justifying a departure from it.

iii *Counting heads*

If this issue were to be decided by counting heads, nine of the judges would have held that if the claimant in an arbitration is guilty of such inordinate and inexcusable delay as to make a fair trial impossible, then the court can put a stop to the arbitration. Each one of the nine gave a fully reasoned judgment.

Against these nine there was only one single reasoned judgment. It was by Lord Diplock. It was concurred in by Lord Edmund-Davies and Lord Russell of Killowen who gave no separate reasoning.

iv *It concentrates the mind wonderfully*

I have the greatest respect for all three of them. I am sorry that I criticised them as I did. But I cannot help wishing that each had given a separate judgment. Perhaps I might borrow from Dr Johnson and say: If a Law Lord has to write a judgment of his own, 'it concentrates his mind wonderfully'. You have to think it out for yourself. I have more than once changed my opinion by having to put my reasons into writing.

v *Stare decisis*

Although the House of Lords in *Hannah Blumenthal* (28 October 1982) held themselves bound by *Bremer Vulkan* (22 January 1981) – no doubt in the interest of certainty – yet in *Khawaja v Secretary of State for the Home Department*[1] (10 February 1983) they held themselves not bound by *Zamir v Secretary of State for the Home Department*[2] (17 July 1980) – no doubt in the interest of justice. Which was the better course?

vi *Should there be legislation?*

Hong Kong has legislated so as to restore the Court of Appeal. Should not our Parliament do so also?

---

[1] [1983] 2 WLR 321.
[2] [1980] AC 930.

7 Withdrawal clauses in charterparties

I turn to another big conflict between the Court of Appeal and the House of Lords. It arose out of withdrawal clauses. Most of you will know little about them. They are clauses which are inserted in the time charter of a ship. The owner lets the ship to a charterer for a period of months or years and stipulates that the charterer is to pay him at so much a month. The charterparty contains a clause which enables the shipowner to withdraw the vessel 'failing punctual and regular payment of hire'.

1 A sea of technicalities

i A fascinating game

I described the consequences in *The Laconia (Mardorf Peach & Co Ltd v Attica Sea Carriers Corpn of Liberia)*:[1]

This is the third case recently where shipowners have sought to withdraw a vessel for non-payment of hire. There was *The Georgios C* [1971] 1 QB 488. Then *The Brimnes* [1975] QB 929. Now *The Laconia*. You have only to read the cases to see that the merits have become submerged in a sea of technicalities. The judge made a caustic comment on them. He said: 'They are quite inappropriate to a commercial relationship.' They have deteriorated into a game of wits which is played out between shipowners and charterers, backed up by lawyers and bankers. You take a time charter with hire to be paid through a bank; and the usual clause which enables the shipowner to withdraw the vessel 'in default of payment' or 'failing punctual and regular payment of hire'.

[1] [1976] QB 835, 848–849.

During the charter period the freight market rises. The shipowner is on the look-out for a default. He knows, on the authority of the House of Lords, that the charterer must, at his peril, make payment of hire on the due date. Payment a day or two late – or a minute or two late – will not do. So the shipowner says to himself: 'If only the charterer slips up and is the least little bit late, I shall be able to withdraw the vessel.' Then by some mischance the charterer does slip up. It may be that the hire falls due on the Saturday or Sunday when the banks are closed. The charterer thinks that it will be sufficient if he pays on the Monday. But the shipowner says: 'That won't do. You should have paid last Friday.' He gives notice of withdrawal. Or the charterer's accountants or bankers in London may have got an hour or two late in transmitting the hire to the bank in New York: or vice versa. All owing to the six hours' time difference. The shipowner, who has not suffered in the least bit, at once whips in a notice of withdrawal. The charterer is staggered. He has committed himself, right and left, on the basis that he will have the use of the vessel: but here he is, deprived of the use of it. He seeks to find a way of escape. Sometimes he challenges the time of payment. Sometimes the time of the notice of withdrawal. He says he remedied the breach in sufficient time. He relies upon a waiver or an estoppel. Only to find himself lost in a maze of technicalities, not only of law but also of banking practice. If he cannot escape from the grip of the shipowner, he may turn round on his bankers and say it was their fault.

ii *I try to find a way out*

So the game goes on and on. It may have its fascination for the players, but it is very expensive and very time-consuming, and the outcome is as uncertain as the spin of a coin. I have tried hard to find a way out – to find a solution which would be appropriate to a commercial relationship: but I have found none, except to hope that, in these cases as they arise, the courts will lay down the rules with precision: so that they can be applied quickly and certainly in future cases.

In the present case I think that although the charterers were a day late in paying the instalment, they remedied the breach and the shipowners waived the forfeiture before the notice of withdrawal was given or received. So the shipowners cannot now insist on it. I would allow the appeal, accordingly.

iii *The Lords are very strict*

The House of Lords reversed us. They insisted on a strict interpretation of the withdrawal clause. So they did in other cases. Time after time the Court of Appeal found a way of avoiding the strictness of the withdrawal clause and its technicalities. But time after time the House reversed the Court of Appeal. The cases are: *The Georgios C*;[1] *The Laconia*;[2] *China National Foreign Trade Transportation Corpn v Evlogia Shipping Co SA of Panama*;[3] and *The Chikuma*.[4]

iv *They seek to justify their strictness*

In that last case Lord Bridge of Harwich justified their technical approach in these words:[5]

It has often been pointed out that shipowners and charterers bargain at arm's length. Neither class has such a preponderance of bargaining power as to be in a position to oppress the other. They should be in a position to look after themselves by contracting only on terms which are acceptable to them. Where, as here, they embody in their contracts common form clauses, it is, to my mind, of overriding importance that their meaning and legal effect should be certain and well understood. The ideal at which the courts should aim, in construing such clauses, is to produce a result, such that in any given situation both parties seeking legal advice as to their rights and obligations can expect the same clear and confident answer from their advisers and neither will be tempted to embark on long and expensive litigation in the belief that victory depends on winning the sympathy of the court. This ideal may never be fully attainable, but we shall certainly never even approximate to it unless we strive to follow clear and consistent principles and steadfastly refuse to be blown off course by the supposed merits of individual cases.

v *Uncertain certainty*

But those observations met with a rebuke by Dr Francis Mann.[6] It was headed 'Uncertain certainty'. Dr Mann pointed out that many in the City and in the professions would agree with the Court of Appeal whose decision was just 'common sense'. He then quoted the words of Lord Bridge of Harwich and said (at page 382):

What is the value of such words in a case in which it is plain that both

[1] [1971] 1 QB 488.
[2] [1976] QB 835, CA; revsd. [1977] AC 850, HL.
[3] [1978] 1 WLR 1257, CA; revsd. [1979] 1 WLR 1018, HL.
[4] [1980] 2 Lloyd's Rep 409, CA; revsd. [1981] 1 Lloyd's Rep 371, HL.
[5] [1981] 1 Lloyd's Rep 371, 377.
[6] (1981) 97 LQR 379.

parties would have received a 'clear and confident answer' in opposite senses, that they would not have received 'the same clear and confident answer' even if they had consulted every available commercial lawyer? And does any adviser in this type of case hold the belief 'that victory depends on winning the sympathy of the court'?

2 Can equity give relief?

i *I was once in favour*

In *The Laconia* I wondered whether in order to help the charterers, there could be relief from forfeiture. I referred to it in the *Afovos* case (*Afovos Shipping Co SA v Pagnan and F.lli*) in these words:[1]

When I was drafting my judgment, I wrote a passage saying that I was in favour of granting relief from forfeiture. My two colleagues, however, told me that I had better not include that passage, because the point had not been argued before us. I gave way to their wishes and excluded it from my judgment. So that trifling contribution to law reform is lost to the law reports!

Instead I inserted this timorous passage in *The Laconia* case:[2]

During the course of the argument I wondered whether this was the sort of case in which equity would grant relief from forfeiture. . . . But on reflection I do not think that equity would have intervened in a commercial case of this kind. It would have left the parties to have their rights determined by law. In commercial matters, certainty is of the essence, as well as time and speed; and equity provides none of these.

ii *But it has now been rejected*

Since that time views favouring relief have been expressed by Lord Simon of Glaisdale in *The Laconia*[3] and by Mr Justice Lloyd in the *Afovos*.[4] But the Court of Appeal have rejected it in *The Scaptrade* (*Scandinavian Trading Tanker Co AB v Flota Petrolera Ecuatoriana*).[5] Lord Justice Goff said (at page 308):

. . . We can understand, even sympathise with, the expressed inclination

[1] [1982] 1 WLR 848, 854.
[2] [1976] QB 835, 847.
[3] [1977] AC 850.
[4] [1980] 2 Lloyd's Rep 469, 476–480.
[5] [1983] 1 All ER 301.

of Lord Simon in *The Laconia*, and of Lloyd J in *The Afovos*, to hold that the equitable jurisdiction should be extended to empower the court to grant relief in cases of this kind. . . . When courts have in the past over-stretched established legal principles to achieve what they see to be justice in cases of this kind, the House of Lords has expressed its disapproval in very clear terms. . . .

. . . The policy which favours certainty in commercial transactions is so antipathetic to the form of equitable intervention invoked by the charterers in the present case that we do not think it would be right to extend the jurisdiction to relieve time charterers from the consequences of withdrawal. . . .

As recently as 30 June 1983 the House of Lords upheld this decision. Lord Diplock thought that there were practical reasons of legal policy to support it. But I am sorry about it. I would have liked to have seen equity giving relief against forfeiture.

3 Anti-technicality clauses

The traders so dislike these technicalities of the House of Lords that they are inserting 'anti-technicality clauses' into the time charters. These require the shipowner to give 48 hours' notice to the charterer – during which the charterer can pay the hire – and thus avoid a forfeiture. The Court of Appeal and the House of Lords have construed such a clause favourably to the charterer, see *The Afovos*.[1] So there is no need to rely on equity. The traders have remedied the position themselves.

---

[1] [1982] 1 WLR 848, CA; affd. [1983] 1 WLR 195, HL.

8 *High Trees* up to date

As I told you in *The Discipline of Law*, all students know of the *High Trees* case. I considered the developments up to 1978 at pages 199–223. The Lord Chancellor made a plea that the doctrine needed to be 'systematically explored'.

1 The doctrine has been explored

i *A case about a letter of guarantee*

This exploration has now been done in *Amalgamated Investment and Property Co Ltd v Texas Commerce International Bank Ltd*.[1] There was a site in the centre of Nassau which was ripe for development. The developers (in the name of one of their companies) borrowed $3,250,000 from a bank on mortgage of the site. They also gave a guarantee which the bank mistakenly thought was a guarantee by the *same* company. But on its strict wording it was a guarantee by an *associated* company. Under the influence of that mistake, the bank lent further moneys to the first company. Both parties entered into many further transactions under the same mistake. Afterwards the liquidator of the first company brought an action claiming that it was not bound by the guarantee.

ii *Does it depend on who induced the error?*

It was argued that the bank itself made the error which led to all the trouble: and all that the plaintiff company had done

[1] [1982] QB 84.

254

was to acquiesce in the error. *High Trees* was said to be inapplicable – on the ground that a party could not take advantage of its own error – but this argument was countered by the course of dealing, on which I said (at pages 120–122):

Although subsequent conduct cannot be used for the purpose of interpreting a contract retrospectively, yet it is often convincing evidence of a course of dealing after it. There are many cases to show that a course of dealing may give rise to legal obligations. It may be used to complete a contract which would otherwise be incomplete. . . . It may be used so as to introduce terms and conditions into a contract which would not otherwise be there. . . . If it can be used to introduce terms which were not already there, it must also be available to add to, or vary, terms which are there already, or to interpret them. If parties to a contract, by their course of dealing, put a particular interpretation on the terms of it – on the faith of which each of them – to the knowledge of the other – acts and conducts their mutual affairs – they are bound by that interpretation just as much as if they had written it down as being a variation of the contract. There is no need to inquire whether their particular interpretation is correct or not – or whether they were mistaken or not – or whether they had in mind the original terms or not. Suffice it that they have, by the course of dealing, put their own interpretation on their contract, and cannot be allowed to go back on it.

iii *Conventional basis is sufficient*

To use the phrase of Latham CJ and Dixon J in the Australian High Court in *Grundt v Great Boulder Proprietary Gold Mines Ltd* (1937) 59 CLR 641, 657, 677, the parties by their course of dealing adopted a 'conventional basis' for the governance of the relations between them, and are bound by it. I care not whether this is put as an agreed variation of the contract or as a species of estoppel. They are bound by the 'conventional basis' on which they conducted their affairs. The reason is because it would be altogether unjust to allow either party to insist on the strict interpretation of the original terms of the contract – when it would be inequitable to do so, having regard to dealings which have taken place between the parties. That is the principle upon which we acted in *Crabb v Arun District Council* [1976] Ch 179, 187. It is particularly appropriate here – where the judges differ as to what is the correct interpretation of the terms of the guarantee. The trial judge interpreted it one way. We interpret it in another way. It is only fair and just that the difference should be solved by the course of dealing – by the interpretation which the parties themselves put upon it – and on which they conducted their affairs for years.

So I come to this conclusion: When the parties to a contract are both under a common mistake as to the meaning or effect of it – and thereafter embark on a course of dealing on the footing of that mistake – thereby replacing the original terms of the contract by a conventional basis on which they both conduct their affairs, then the original contract is replaced by the conventional basis. The parties are bound by the conventional basis. Either party can sue or be sued upon it just as if it had been expressly agreed between them.

2 Use as a sword

i *Whatever remedy is appropriate*

It was also argued that the bank was seeking to use estoppel, not as a shield, but as a sword. This argument was countered by reference to the general principle which enables the court to give whatever remedy is appropriate, including a cause of action if need be. I stated the general principle in this way (at page 122):

The doctrine of estoppel is one of the most flexible and useful in the armoury of the law. But it has become overloaded with cases. That is why I have not gone through them all in this judgment. It has evolved during the last 150 years in a sequence of separate developments: proprietary estoppel, estoppel by representation of fact, estoppel by acquiescence, and promissory estoppel. At the same time it has been sought to be limited by a series of maxims: estoppel is only a rule of evidence, estoppel cannot give rise to a cause of action, estoppel cannot do away with the need for consideration, and so forth. All these can now be seen to merge into one general principle shorn of limitations. When the parties to a transaction proceed on the basis of an underlying assumption – either of fact or of law – whether due to misrepresentation or mistake makes no difference – on which they have conducted the dealings between them – neither of them will be allowed to go back on that assumption when it would be unfair or unjust to allow him to do so. If one of them does seek to go back on it, the courts will give the other such remedy as the equity of the case demands.

ii *When the conduct is unconscionable*

That general principle applies to this case. Both the plaintiffs and the bank proceeded for years on the basis of the underlying assumption that the guarantee of the plaintiffs applied to the $3,250,000 advanced by the bank for the Nassau Building. Their dealings in rearranging the portfolio, in releasing properties and moneys, were all conducted on that basis. . . . It would be most unfair and unjust to allow the liquidator to depart from that basis. . . .

I went on to say that the judge summed up his view in this one sentence:

. . . I am satisfied that Mr Foster's (the plaintiffs' director) conduct, though of course completely innocent, so influenced Mr Oldfield's (the bank's director) conduct, as to render it unconscionable on the part of the plaintiffs now to take advantage of the bank's error.

In that sentence – in that one word – 'unconscionable' – the judge was applying the general principle of estoppel which I have stated. I went on to say that I agreed with his analysis of the authorities and with his conclusion. The appeal was dismissed. The House of Lords refused leave to appeal.

9 Interlocutory injunctions up to date

1 A most important jurisdiction

One of the most important jurisdictions of the old Court of Chancery – and now of the High Court – is to grant interlocutory injunctions. When a plaintiff is faced with an actual or threatened injury by a defendant, he is able to come at once to the court and ask for an injunction to stop the defendant from doing or continuing his injurious conduct. This protection is needed immediately – long before the action can be tried. It is of serious import to both sides. If the injunction is granted, it may stop the defendant's business. If it is refused, the plaintiff may suffer irreparable injury.

i *Only by a judge*

The Legislature has recognised the serious nature of this jurisdiction. It cannot be exercised by a master or registrar. It can only be exercised by a judge. The words of the statute, section 37(1) of the Supreme Court Act 1981, are simple and clear. The High Court can grant an injunction

in all cases in which it appears to the court to be just and convenient to do so.

Furthermore, if the judge grants or refuses an interlocutory injunction, either party can appeal at once to the Court of Appeal without the leave of the judge, see section 18(1)(h)(iii) of the Supreme Court Act 1981.

ii *The old principles*

You would think that the principles relating to this jurisdiction would by this time have been well settled. So they were to all practitioners and judges in my time. They were well stated 'by Lord Upjohn in the House of Lords in 1965 in *J T Stratford & Son Ltd v Lindley:*[1]

In these circumstances, the principles which ought to guide your Lordships seem to me clear. An appellant seeking an interlocutory injunction must establish a prima facie case of some breach of duty by the respondent to him. He may even obtain a quia timet injunction in case of a threatened injury, but I need not consider that further because a prima facie case of an actual breach has been established. He must further establish that the respondents are threatening and intending to repeat that breach of duty, but in a case such as this it may readily be inferred and I do so in this case. This being so, an injunction may be granted if it is just and convenient so to do, the remedy being purely discretionary. The balance of convenience in these cases is always of great importance. . . .

iii *They are shattered*

But then in 1975 all our principles were shattered and our experience overthrown by a judgment of the House of Lords in *American Cyanamid Co v Ethicon Ltd.*[2] It was a single judgment by Lord Diplock in which all the others concurred. He said (at page 407):

Your Lordships should in my view take this opportunity of declaring that there is no such rule. The use of such expressions as 'a probability', 'a prima facie case', or 'a strong prima facie case' in the context of the exercise of a discretionary power to grant an interlocutory injunction leads to confusion as to the object sought to be achieved by this form of temporary relief. The court no doubt must be satisfied that the claim is not frivolous or vexatious; in other words, that there is a serious question to be tried.

It is no part of the court's function at this stage of the litigation to try to resolve conflicts of evidence on affidavit as to facts on which the claims of either party may ultimately depend nor to decide difficult questions of law which call for detailed argument and mature considerations. These are matters to be dealt with at the trial. . . .

[1] [1965] AC 269, 338.
[2] [1975] AC 396.

2 Much discussion

i *Often not applicable*

That statement gave rise to much discussion. I ventured in the next year in *Fellowes & Son v Fisher*[1] to point out many cases in which it did not apply. I gave the references in my judgment but do not repeat them here.

These individual cases are numerous and important. They are all cases where it is urgent and imperative to come to a decision. The affidavits may be conflicting. The questions of law may be difficult and call for detailed consideration. Nevertheless, the need for immediate decision is such that the court has to make an estimate of the relative strength of each party's case. If the plaintiff makes out a prima facie case, the court may grant an injunction. If it is a weak case, or is met by a strong defence, the court may refuse an injunction. Sometimes it means that the court virtually decides the case at that stage. At other times it gives the parties such good guidance that the case is settled. At any rate, in 99 cases out of 100, the matter goes no further.

ii *Instances from many fields*

In support of what I have said, I will give instances from many fields of law. Take industrial disputes, where there is a strike, with picketing, blacking, and the like. The plaintiff's business is being greatly injured. They seek an interlocutory injunction. The courts invariably assess the relative strength of each party's case and grant or refuse an injunction accordingly. They give their reasons and that is the end of the matter. . . . All (these cases) were decided on applications for interlocutory injunctions: and never went to trial.

Similarly with breaches of confidence. If the plaintiff has a strong case, an injunction should be granted: for to postpone it would be equivalent to denying it altogether. But, if the defendant has an available defence, it may be refused: . . . (These cases) very recently were all decided on interlocutory applications and never came for trial.

Likewise with covenants in restraint of trade, and the like. Their validity is frequently discussed on interlocutory applications. If the covenant is prima facie valid, an injunction will be granted; but, if not, it will be refused. Once decided, these cases rarely come to trial. . . .

So also with passing-off cases: . . . It is said that 'of the thousand or so passing-off cases there have been in the last decade, all (or virtually all) of them were "decided" on motion.': . . .

[1] [1976] QB 122, 133–134.

To which I may add many commercial cases where the granting of an interlocutory injunction virtually decides the action. . . .

iii *The* White Book *too*

To this I now add the words of the editor of the *White Book* for 1982 (at page 518), commenting on the *American Cyanamid* case:

It does not follow that all the earlier authorities which have proceeded on different principles, must be treated as having been automatically overruled, or have ceased to provide guidance as to whether or not an interlocutory injunction should be granted. . . . It is interesting to note that that case has not been followed by other common law jurisdictions, e.g. Australia . . . or South Africa. . . .

The *American Cyanamid* case has been held not to apply to cases concerning a breach of a restrictive covenant, or (. . .) where the relevant matters are all before the court and are plain and uncontroversial. . . . Similarly it seems *American Cyanamid* does not normally apply to passing-off cases. . . .

iv *A reverse turn*

Finally, in the later case of *NWL Ltd v Woods*[1] Lord Diplock himself seems to have reverted to the old principles:

In assessing whether what is compendiously called the balance of convenience lies in granting or refusing interlocutory injunctions in actions between parties of undoubted solvency the judge is engaged in weighing the respective risks that injustice may result from his deciding one way rather than the other at a stage when the evidence is incomplete. On the one hand there is the risk that if the interlocutory injunction is refused but the plaintiff succeeds in establishing at the trial his legal right for the protection of which the injunction had been sought he may in the meantime have suffered harm and inconvenience for which an award of money can provide no adequate recompense. On the other hand there is the risk that if the interlocutory injunction is granted but the plaintiff fails at the trial, the defendant may in the meantime have suffered harm and inconvenience which is similarly irrecompensable. The nature and degree of harm and inconvenience that are likely to be sustained in these two events by the defendant and the plaintiff respectively in consequence of the grant or the refusal of the injunction are generally sufficiently disproportionate to bring down, by themselves, the balance on one side

[1] [1979] 1 WLR 1294, 1306–1307.

or the other; and this is what I understand to be the thrust of the decision of this House in *American Cyanamid Co v Ethicon Ltd.*

v *It is taken as read*

I think I may say that nowadays all practitioners and judges are so familiar with the *American Cyanamid* case that it is never cited at length. It is taken as read. And the judges grant or refuse interlocutory injunctions in the light of it but they come to just the same result as if the waters had never been troubled.

3 The role of the Court of Appeal

i *The duty to review*

An interlocutory injunction is a much more serious affair than most interlocutory orders. So much so that, as I have said, it can only be granted by a judge and there is an appeal from him without leave to the Court of Appeal. In short, there is a *right* of appeal to the Court of Appeal.

In these circumstances the Court of Appeal has the power and the duty to review the decision of the judge: and, if it thinks that his decision was wrong, even on the materials before him, to reverse his decision and to substitute its own for it. This has always been my understanding of the function of the Court of Appeal which I regularly applied all my time there. But very recently the Lords have upset it all.

ii *The law as laid down by the Lords in 1942*

The law was so laid down by the House of Lords in *Charles Osenton & Co v Johnston*[1] and applied by the full Court of Appeal in *Ward v James.*[2] This is the way in which it was put by Lord Wright in *Charles Osenton & Co v Johnston:*[3]

. . . When the statute gives a right of appeal from an order made by a judge in exercise of his discretion and an appeal is taken, the discretion of

[1] [1942] AC 130.
[2] [1966] 1 QB 273.
[3] [1942] AC 130, 147:

262

the appellate court is substituted for that of the judge, as Brett LJ pointed out in the passage which I have quoted above. . . .

That passage of Brett LJ which he quoted (at page 142) said that:

If we have the jurisdiction to review it seems to me that the legislature places the discretion in this court on an appeal in the place of the discretion of the learned judge, who, this court thinks, has not exercised his discretion rightly. . . .

Lord Wright also quoted and explained the dictum of Lord Atkin in *Evans v Bartlam:*[1]

Appellate jurisdiction is always statutory; there is in the statute no restriction upon the jurisdiction of the Court of Appeal; . . . if it sees that . . . the decision will result in injustice being done it has both the power and the duty to remedy it.

Later on in the same passage Lord Wright explained that instead of '*will* result in injustice being done', Lord Atkin really meant that if there was 'a reasonable danger of injustice'.

iii *But departed from in 1982*

Such being the principle as I have always understood and applied it, I was sorry to see the contrary said by the House of Lords in *Hadmor Productions Ltd v Hamilton*[2] when Lord Diplock, reversing the Court of Appeal (with me presiding), said:

. . . It is I think appropriate to remind your Lordships of the limited function of an appellate court in an appeal of this kind. An interlocutory injunction is a discretionary relief and the discretion whether or not to grant it is vested in the High Court judge by whom the application for it is heard. Upon an appeal from the judge's grant or refusal of an interlocutory injunction the function of an appellate court, whether it be the Court of Appeal or your Lordships' House, is not to exercise an independent discretion of its own. It must defer to the judge's exercise of his discretion and must not interfere with it merely upon the ground that the members of the appellate court would have exercised the discretion differently.

[1] [1937] AC 473, 480.
[2] [1982] 2 WLR 322, 325.

That approach is, I suggest erroneous. It is the same error as befell the majority of the Court of Appeal in *Charles Osenton & Co v Johnston*. The House of Lords there corrected the error. Lord Wright indeed said (at page 147) that the reason given by Mr Justice Singleton (one of the majority in the Court of Appeal) for not acting upon his own view seemed 'to be that it was not a matter for the exercise of his discretion, but for the discretion of the judge. I think that that reason is not sound in law.'

iv *A significant dissent*

It does not appear that *Charles Osenton & Co v Johnston* was considered in *Hadmor Productions Ltd v Hamilton*. The Law Reports show that it was not cited to their Lordships. Nor was it cited in the very recent case of *Garden Cottage Foods Ltd v Milk Marketing Baord*.[1] In it Lord Diplock repeated his observations *ipsissima verba*. Again, in a single judgment (in which three other Lords concurred), the Court of Appeal (with me presiding) was reversed. But there was a significant dissent by Lord Wilberforce, one of the best of judges. He would have granted an injunction so as to restrain the Milk Marketing Board from abusing its dominant position in the Common Market. He said:

Every argument including the balance of convenience would seem to fall in favour of maintaining the status quo until determination of the action, which is the normal purpose for which interlocutory injunctions are granted.

. . . This course of action is in line with what the European Court of Justice thought appropriate . . . I cannot avoid the conclusion that the Court of Appeal's order makes for better justice and I see nothing wrong with it in law.

I hope that in time Lord Wilberforce's view will prevail. It fulfils the statutory precept to grant an injunction 'in all cases in which it appears to the court to be just and convenient to do so'.

[1] [1983] 3 WLR 143.

10 The difference in approach

In considering the conflicts in the courts, I would not overlook the conflict about trade unions and the law. The House of Lords reversed the Court of Appeal in *Heatons'* case, *Express Newspapers v McShane*, *Duport Steels v Sirs* and *Cheall's* case – with political consequences. I have described these in the section on trade unions. These, together with all the other conflicts, show that there has been a different approach. It is this:

The Court of Appeal has sought to mould the law – and to interpret statutes – so as to meet the justice of the case and the needs of the times.

The House of Lords holds that it is not the province of the Court of Appeal to do this or even of their Lordships. They must stick to the letter of the law. Any moulding of the law should be done by Parliament and not by the judges.

11 Exemption clauses up to date

In *The Discipline of Law* I described the position as it was left by the Court of Appeal in *Photo Production Ltd v Securicor Transport Ltd*.[1] That decision was afterwards overruled by the House of Lords: and there has been another *Securicor* case in the House of Lords. These decisions – together with recent statutes – have revolutionised the law as to exemption clauses. We had to consider them in my very last case in the Court of Appeal. It was *George Mitchell (Chesterhall) Ltd v Finney Lock Seeds Ltd*.[2] I mentioned it earlier in this book when I described my last appearance. But now I must tell you of its legal implications.

i *The facts*

This is how I set out the facts in my judgment:

Some farmers, called George Mitchell (Chesterhall) Ltd, ordered 30 lb of cabbage seed. It was supplied. It looked just like cabbage seed. No one could say it was not. The farmers planted it over 63 acres. Six months later there appeared out of the ground a lot of loose green leaves. They looked like cabbage leaves but they never turned in. They had no hearts. They were not 'cabbages' in our common parlance because they had no hearts. The crop was useless for human consumption. Sheep or cattle might eat it if hungry enough. It was commercially useless. The price of the seed was £192. The loss to the farmers was over £61,000. They claimed damages from the seed merchants. The judge awarded them that sum with interest. The total comes to nearly £100,000.

The seed merchants appeal to this court. They say that they supplied

[1] [1978] 1 WLR 856.
[2] [1982] 3 WLR 1036.

the seed on a printed clause by which their liability was limited to the cost of the seed, that is, £192. They rely much on two recent cases in the House of Lords, *Photo Production Ltd v Securicor Transport Ltd* [1980] AC 827 and *Ailsa Craig Fishing Co Ltd v Malvern Fishing Co Ltd and Securicor (Scotland) Ltd* 1982 SLT 377. . . .

The farmers were aware that the sale was subject to some conditions of sale. All seed merchants have conditions of sale. They were on the back of the catalogue. They were also on the back of the invoice each year. So it would seem that the farmers were bound at common law by the terms of them. The inference from the course of dealing would be that the farmers had accepted the conditions as printed – even though they had never read them and did not realise that they contained a limitation on liability. . . .

ii *The natural meaning*

Then I went on to consider the nature of the clause:

The limitation clause here is of long standing in the seed trade. It has been in use for many years. . . .

Taking the clause in its natural plain meaning, I think it is effective to limit the liability of the seed merchants to a return of the money or replacement of the seeds. The explanation they give seems fair enough. They say that it is so as to keep the price low: and that if they were to undertake any greater liability, the price would be much greater.

After all, the seed merchants did supply seeds. True, they were the wrong kind altogether. But they were seeds. On the natural interpretation, I think the condition is sufficient to limit the seed merchants to a refund of the price paid or replacement of the seeds. . . .

It seemed to me that the two *Securicor* cases[1] in the House of Lords had revolutionised our approach to exemption clauses. In order to explain their importance, I traced the history of such clauses. Lord Bridge of Harwich afterwards in the House of Lords described this as a 'fascinating trail' which I had traced in my 'uniquely colourful and graphic style'.

iii *The heyday of freedom of contract*

This is what I said:

None of you nowadays will remember the trouble we had – when I was called to the Bar – with exemption clauses. They were printed in small

[1] [1980] AC 827, 1982 SLT 377.

print on the back of tickets and order forms and invoices. They were contained in catalogues or timetables. They were held to be binding on any person who took them without objection. No one ever did object. He never read them or knew what was in them. No matter how unreasonable they were, he was bound. All this was done in the name of 'freedom of contract'. But the freedom was all on the side of the big concern which had the use of the printing press. No freedom for the little man who took the ticket or order form or invoice. The big concern said, 'Take it or leave it'. The little man had no option but to take it. The big concern could and did exempt itself from liability in its own interest without regard to the little man. It got away with it time after time. When the courts said to the big concern, 'You must put it in clear words', the big concern had no hesitation in doing so. It knew well that the little man would never read the exemption clauses or understand them.

It was a bleak winter for our law of contract. It is illustrated by two cases, *Thompson v London, Midland and Scottish Rly Co* [1930] 1 KB 41 (in which there was exemption from liability, not on the ticket, but only in small print at the back of the timetable, and the company were held not liable) and *L'Estrange v F Graucob Ltd* [1934] 2 KB 394 (in which there was complete exemption in small print at the bottom of the order form, and the company were held not liable).

iv *The secret weapon*

This injustice was remedied to some extent, as I went on to say:

Faced with this abuse of power – by the strong against the weak – by the use of the small print of the conditions – the judges did what they could to put a curb upon it. They still had before them the idol, 'freedom of contract'. They still knelt down and worshipped it, but they concealed under their cloaks a secret weapon. They used it to stab the idol in the back. This weapon was called 'the true construction of the contract'. They used it with great skill and ingenuity. They used it so as to depart from the natural meaning of the words of the exemption clause and to put upon them a strained and unnatural construction. In case after case, they said that the words were not strong enough to give the big concern exemption from liability; or that in the circumstances the big concern was not entitled to rely on the exemption clause. If a ship deviated from the contractual voyage, the owner could not rely on the exemption clause. If a warehouseman stored the goods in the wrong warehouse, he could not pray in aid the limitation clause. If the seller supplied goods different in kind from those contracted for, he could not rely on any exemption from liability. If a shipowner delivered goods to a person without production of the bill of lading, he could not escape responsibility by reference to an exemption clause. In short, whenever the wide words – in their natural meaning – would give rise to an unreasonable result, the judges either rejected them as repugnant to the main purpose of the contract, or else cut them down to size in order to produce a reasonable result. . . .

But when the clause was itself reasonable and gave rise to a reasonable result, the judges upheld it; at any rate, when the clause did not exclude liability entirely but only limited it to a reasonable amount. So where goods were deposited in a cloakroom or sent to a laundry for cleaning, it was quite reasonable for the company to limit their liability to a reasonable amount, having regard to the small charge made for the service. . . .

v *The change in climate*

Then there came a change:

In 1969 there was a change in climate. Out of winter into spring. It came with the Law Commission's Exemptions Clauses In Contracts, First Report: Amendments to the Sale of Goods Act 1893 (Law Com no 24, HC 403) which was implemented in the Supply of Goods (Implied Terms) Act 1973. In 1975 there was a further change. Out of spring into summer. It came with the Law Commission's Exemption Clauses, Second Report (Law Com no 69, HC 605) which was implemented by the Unfair Contract Terms Act 1977. No longer was the big concern able to impose whatever terms and conditions it liked in a printed form – no matter how unreasonable they might be. These reports showed most convincingly that the courts could and should only enforce them if they were fair and reasonable in themselves and it was fair and reasonable to allow the big concern to rely on them. So the idol of 'freedom of contract' was shattered. In cases of personal injury or death, it was not permissible to exclude or restrict liability at all. In consumer contracts any exemption clause was subject to the test of reasonableness. . . .

vi *The effect of the change*

What is the result of all this? To my mind it heralds a revolution in our approach to exemption clauses; not only where they exclude liability altogether and also where they limit liability; not only in the specific categories in the Unfair Contract Terms Act 1977, but in other contracts too. Just as in other fields of law we have done away with the multitude of cases on 'common employment', 'last opportunity', 'invitees' and 'licensees' and so forth, so also in this field we should do away with the multitude of cases on exemption clauses. We should no longer have to go through all kinds of gymnastic contortions to get round them. We should no longer have to harass our students with the study of them. We should set about meeting a new challenge. It is presented by the test of reasonableness.

vii *The two* Securicor *cases*

Then I came to the importance of the two *Securicor* cases:

The revolution is exemplified by the recent two *Securicor* cases ([1980] AC 827 and 1982 SLT 377) in the House of Lords. In each of them the Securicor company provided a patrolman to keep watch on premises so as to see that they were safe from intruders. They charged very little for the service. In the first case it was a factory with a lot of paper in it. The patrolman set light to it and burnt down the factory. In the second case it was a quay at Aberdeen where ships were berthed. The patrolman went off for the celebrations on New Year's Eve. He left the ships unattended. The tide rose. A ship rose with it. Its bow got 'snubbed' under the deck of the quay. It sank. In each case the owners were covered by insurance. The factory owners had their fire insurance. The shipowners had their hull insurance. In each case the Securicor company relied on a limitation clause. Under it they were protected from liability beyond a limit which was quite reasonable and their insurance cover was limited accordingly. The issue in practical terms was: which of the insurers should bear the loss? The question in legal terms in each case was whether Securicor could avail themselves of the limitation clause. In each case the House held that they could. . . .

viii *The Supply of Goods (Implied Terms) Act 1973*

As it turned out, however, there was a statute on the point:

In any case the contract for these cabbage seeds was governed by section 55(4) of the Sale of Goods Act 1893 (as substituted by section 4 of the Supply of Goods (Implied Terms) Act 1973: see now section 55(3) of, and Schedule 1, paragraph 11 to, the Sale of Goods Act 1979). It says:

'In the case of a contract of sale of goods, any term . . . shall . . . not be enforceable to the extent that it is shown that it would not be fair or reasonable to allow reliance on the term.'

That provision is exactly in accordance with the principle which I have advocated above. So the ultimate question, to my mind, in this case is just this: To what extent would it be fair or reasonable to allow the seed merchants to rely on the limitation clause?

ix *Fair and reasonable*

The crucial point was whether it was fair and reasonable.

. . . Our present case is very much on the borderline. There is this to be said in favour of the seed merchants. The price of this cabbage seed was small: £192. The damages claimed are high: £61,000. But there is this to be said on the other side. The clause was not negotiated between persons of equal bargaining power. It was inserted by the seed merchants in their invoices without any negotiation with the farmers. To this I would add that the seed merchants rarely, if ever, invoked the clause. . . .

Next, I would point out that the buyers had no opportunity at all of knowing or discovering that the seed was not cabbage seed: whereas the sellers could and should have known that it was the wrong seed altogether. The buyers were not covered by insurance against the risk. Nor could they insure. But as to the seed merchants, the judge said [1981] 1 Lloyd's Rep 476, 480:

'I am entirely satisfied that it is possible for seedsmen to insure against this risk. . . .'

To that I would add this further point. Such a mistake as this could not have happened without serious negligence on the part of the seed merchants themselves or their Dutch suppliers. So serious that it would not be fair to enable them to escape responsibility for it.

In all the circumstances I am of opinion that it would not be fair or reasonable to allow the seed merchants to rely on the clause to limit their liability.

x *Conclusion*

Although we refused leave to appeal, the House of Lords granted it. Their decision has just been given – on 30 June 1983. They have affirmed the decision of the Court of Appeal. I am gratified to find that they put the same interpretation on the clause as I did and also held that it was not fair and reasonable. So my very last judgment was affirmed by the House of Lords. Lord Diplock paid a tribute to me which I treasure, coming as it does from one who has added so much to our jurisprudence:

I cannot refrain from noting with regret, which is, I am sure, shared by all members of the Appellate Committe of this House, that Lord Denning's judgment in the instant case, which was delivered on 29 September 1982, is probably the last in which your Lordships will have the opportunity of enjoying his eminently readable style of exposition and his stimulating and percipient approach to the continuing development of the common law to which he has himself in his judicial lifetime made so outstanding a contribution.

Epilogue

i *The picture of justice*

Quite recently I have tried to discover more about the conventional picture of justice. She has for centuries been painted blindfold with a sword in one hand and lifted scales in the other. Why is justice painted blind? I have never discovered why. Some sort of explanation is given by Joseph Addison:

Justice discards party, friendship, kindred, and is therefore always represented as blind.

By this I take it that justice is painted blind so as to signify that she is impartial and without prejudice. She favours neither one side nor the other, and bears no ill-will to one or the other.

But in modern times justice is not shown as blind. In the statue on the dome of the Central Criminal Court in London, she is not blindfold. As I said in *Jones v National Coal Board*:[1]

It is all very well to paint justice blind, but she does better without a bandage round her eyes. She should be blind indeed to favour or prejudice, but clear to see which way lies the truth: and the less dust there is about the better.

Why does justice always carry a sword? Again, I have not discovered why. In Roman times, Juvenal (AD 60–130)

---

[1] [1957] 2 QB 55, 64.

thought it inappropriate. He wrote in his *Satires* (iv, 80):

Tractanda putabat inermi justicia (There should be no sword in the hand of justice).

The sword has always been regarded as the symbol of justice. William Dunbar, a poet, writing about 1500 in honour of the city of London, speaks of:[1]

> Thy famous Maire, by pryncely governaunce,
> With sword of justice thee ruleth prudently.

Shakespeare too regarded a sword as an appropriate symbol of justice. He does so when telling the story about Henry Prince of Wales (who afterwards became King Henry V). He was an unruly young man who struck the Lord Chief Justice of the King's Bench and was committed to prison. After the Prince became King, it was thought that he might dispense with the services of the Chief Justice. According to Shakespeare, the Chief Justice challenged the King saying that, if he were dismissed, it would

> . . . trip the course of law, and blunt the sword
> That guards the peace and safety of your person.[2]

Whereupon the King assured the Chief Justice that he would continue in office:

> . . . You did commit me:
> For which I do commit into your hand
> The unstained sword that you have us'd to bear;
> With this remembrance, – That you use the same
> With the like bold, just, and impartial spirit,
> As you have done 'gainst me.

From this, I gather the sword was the symbol of the authority by which justice is done. No judgment of any court, no order of any judge, is of any use unless it can be enforced: and to be enforced it must needs have the authority of the state behind it. The sword of justice is the

[1] *London*, 1.49.
[2] Shakespeare, *King Henry IV*, Act V, sc. 2.

sword of state. It is the symbol of authority which must be upheld.

Why does justice carry a balance in her hand with lifted scales? This is plain. It needs no justification. The balances have always been the symbol of even-handed justice. You remember the awesome judgment in the book of *Daniel*:

Thou art weighed in the balances, and art found wanting.

And if I may quote again from my judgment in *Jones v National Coal Board*:[1]

Let the advocates one after the other put the weights into the scales – the 'nicely calculated less or more' – but the judge at the end decides which way the balance tilts, be it ever so slightly.

ii *The Great Seal*

As I write this in my library, I have beside me the parchment proofs of my judicial authority, now past. I have the Letters Patent for all the offices I have held – a Justice of the High Court, a Lord Justice of Appeal, a Lord of Appeal in Ordinary, the Master of the Rolls. They are large open sheets of parchment with the Great Seal pendant at the bottom. The Great Seal is $6\frac{1}{2}$ inches in diameter, of red sealing wax (now plastic), with the Queen on her horse on one side and on her throne on the other. I have also around many works of fine craftsmanship which have been presented to us on our travels in many countries: such as the large ceremonial bowl of Fiji, the cowboy's horse of Chile (made by the oldest prisoner in the prison at Santiago), the Eskimo of Northwest Canada, the ceramics of Hong Kong, the dolls of Japan, the wood carvings of Ghana, the pewter of Malaysia and the silver of India.

iii *A summons to attend Parliament*

Although I am retired, I am still a peer. There is a general election pending. I have no vote in it. No peer has a vote, because he is already a Member of Parliament in the Upper House. (A query has arisen about the Lords Spiritual, but on

[1] [1957] 2 QB 55, 64.

this I would say nothing.) I do receive a Writ of Summons to the new Parliament. It is embossed with a small reproduction of one side of the Great Seal. Its wording is very old-fashioned but it is an example of English prose at its best. It is all in one sentence.

ELIZABETH THE SECOND by the Grace of God of the United Kingdom of Great Britain and Northern Ireland and of Our other Realms and Territories Queen Head of the Commonwealth Defender of the Faith To Our right trusty and well beloved Counsellor Alfred Thompson Lord Denning (formerly a Lord of Appeal in Ordinary)
Greeting WHEREAS by the advice and assent of Our Council for certain arduous and urgent affairs concerning Us the state and defence of Our United Kingdom and the Church We have ordered a certain Parliament to be holden at Our City of Westminster on the fifteenth day of June next ensuing And there to treat and have conference with the Prelates Great Men and Peers of Our Realm We strictly enjoining command you upon the faith and allegiance by which you are bound to Us that the weightiness of the said affairs and imminent perils considered (waiving all excuses) you be at the said day and place personally present with Us and with the said Prelates Great Men and Peers to treat and give your counsel upon the affairs aforesaid And this as you regard Us and Our honour and the safety and defence of the said Kingdom and Church and dispatch of the said affairs in nowise do you omit WITNESS Ourself at Westminster the thirteenth day of May in the thirty-second year of Our Reign.

OULTON

(Seal)

To ALFRED THOMPSON LORD DENNING (FORMERLY
A LORD OF APPEAL IN ORDINARY)

A Writ of Summons to Parliament

OULTON

By the words 'waiving all excuses', the Writ means that you are to make no excuses. The Queen will not permit of any excuse. You are to attend and 'in nowise do you omit'.

iv *As we are now*

The family (of which I told you in *The Family Story*) is

diminishing. My sister Marjorie died in January 1982 at the age of 91. So only Reg and I are left. Reg is 89 and Eileen, his wife, is 83. I am 84 and Joan is 83. We are all still quite active. We all find our greatest pleasure in the visits of our children and grandchildren. But next to this is our pleasure in the visits of our many friends. As for me, the operation on my right hip was completely successful. I can walk much further and more easily than I did. Joan and I are spending more time at Whitchurch than before. Our garden is our delight. It is kept in perfect order by Charlie. He came to us as a boy of 14. He is now 29. He is helped by Bert who is an old soldier, now 72. He was a sergeant in the Royal Hampshire Regiment. Our good Dolly is now 87 and has just retired, but she often comes to see us.

v *The garden*

To us it is the most beautiful garden in all England. Today is the fourth of June – a glorious day – the first hot day after a rain-filled spring. Let us enjoy it while we can: for, as Shakespeare says, 'Summer's lease hath all too short a date'. The lawn, freshly cut, stretches down to the river. The copper beeches on the island are turning a darker brown. The baby ducklings, just hatched, skim across the water as fast as can be. Beside the grass, the laburnum is breaking into a brilliant yellow. Next to it, the lilac is decked out in rich purple. Across the front wall the clematis is climbing in a profusion of pale pink. Over the garden gate the honeysuckle is trailing its many colours with the sweetest scent. Alongside are the paeonies in their deep red, whilst the cornflowers begin to display their 'excellent blew'. Then take a turn into the kitchen garden. The asparagus and lettuce are here already. The gooseberries are ready for picking. Vegetables and fruits of many kinds – held back till now – will shoot ahead in the warm sun. All the paths are bordered with neat low box, which 'is a marvellous fine ornament'. We often walk along them. You must come some day and see for yourself.

You may note those last two quotations. I have taken them from John Parkinson's *Paradisi in Sole* of which I have told you before. He wrote it in 1629. He asked the Queen (Queen Henrietta-Maria) to accept 'this speaking Garden', praying that she might 'enjoy the heavenly Paradise, after the many yeares fruition of this earthly' one.

vi *So I finish*

As a family we have done our part in our time to make the garden of England what it is – and to keep it what it is – the garden where liberty and justice have grown and flourished more than anywhere else. That is the garden of which I have told you in these five books. So I finish with Kipling:

Oh, Adam was a gardener, and God who made him sees
That half a proper gardener's work is done upon his knees,
So when your work is finished, you can wash your hands and pray
For the Glory of the Garden, that it may not pass away!
And the Glory of the Garden it shall never pass away![1]

[1] *The Glory of the Garden.*

Index

Juge Jean Adrien Forget
Cabinet du Juge
Cornwall, Ontario.